W9-BIP-480

THE STEAMBOATERS

Also by Harry Sinclair Drago

LOST BONANZAS

GREAT AMERICAN CATTLE TRAILS

OUTLAWS ON HORSEBACK

RED RIVER VALLEY

WILD, WOOLLY AND WICKED

WHERE THE LOON CALLS

FOLLOWING THE GRASS

MONTANA ROAD

THE WILD BUNCH

BUCKSKIN EMPIRE

STAGECOACH KINGDOM

RIVER OF GOLD

For Younger Readers

MANY BEAVERS

THE STEAMBOATERS

*From the Early Side-Wheelers
to the Big Packets*

by

HARRY SINCLAIR DRAGO

Illustrated with photographs

VK
23
D75S

992021

DODD, MEAD & COMPANY
NEW YORK

ST. PAUL PUBLIC LIBRARY

Copyright © 1967 by Harry Sinclair Drago

All rights reserved

No part of this book may be reproduced in any form
without permission in writing from the publisher

Library of Congress Catalog Card Number: 67-17647

Printed in the United States of America
by The Cornwall Press, Inc., Cornwall, N. Y.

Introduction

DURING THE NINETEENTH century the inland waterways of the United States were recognized as a great natural resource. Had they been in one of the larger European countries—Russia, for instance—they would not have been allowed to lose their importance as a sound, economical means of transportation; but with the fading of the steamboat era, our rivers lost their usefulness. Freight and passenger traffic left them, and steamboating soon became nonexistent, save for a few excursion boats. It hardly could have happened had we exhibited a little of the pride in our rivers that has been lavished on the Volga, the Rhine and the Danube.

The early French explorers, La Salle, Joliet and others, noted with what awe the Illinois referred to the Mississippi as the Father of Waters. To the Indians the Mississippi and its great tributaries, the Missouri and the Ohio, were one river. Although the validity of this primitive conception of the great river must be questioned, it hardly can be denied that, a century and a half later, it was to become the Mother of the Steamboats.

The steamboat of our inland waterways was not the offspring of the steamship. It was created by former flatboat and keelboat men who, being acquainted with the nature of the rivers it was to navigate, fashioned a craft that could contend with the numerous shallows, sandbars, shifting channels and submerged snags that it would encounter. Realizing that only a very shallow-draft boat would do, they used the wide-beamed keelboat for a model, decked it over and placed boilers and engine on the deck. This was one of the major differences between the steamboat and the steamship, which carried its machinery in the hold.

This was only one of many innovations that originated with Captain Henry Miller Shreve and other experienced rivermen. They owed nothing to Robert Fulton, the acclaimed "inventor" of the steamboat, for the boats the Fulton monopoly built at Pittsburgh for Ohio-Mississippi River trade were only replicas of the deep-draft Fulton steamers plying the Hudson and Long Island Sound. They served their purpose as pioneers, but they were not commercially successful, and it was after their passing that inland river steamboating really began.

I have not attempted to tell the story of Mississippi River steamboating, although I have presented many incidents connected with it, for what happened on the Mississippi largely set the pattern for what occurred wherever steamboating became the recognized and often sole means of transportation.

The early steamers were crude and ugly. But shortly, builders began to produce what was to become the famous Mississippi River style of steamboat architecture. Only thirty years after Nicholas Roosevelt took the first steamer, the *New Orleans,* down the rivers to the city for which it was named, in 1811, boats were coming off the ways whose graceful lines, speed and passenger accommodations were the prelude to the decades of steamboat luxury and elegance that were to follow.

It has often been said, and with little justification, that the railroads opened the West. The great western immigration had been in full swing for years before the first locomotive whistle was heard in the great central valley of the Mississippi. In the years when anything beyond the Alleghenies was still west and thousands of families were spreading out over what was to become the heartland of America, it was the steamboat that helped to get them where they wanted to go. On the little rivers as well as the big, wherever there was navigable water—and they did not ask for much—the steamboats took them. For hundreds of new settlements and growing towns, they were often the only means of communication with the outside world. This was as true on the Rio Grande as it was on the upper Missouri and the rivers of California and the Pacific Northwest.

When a steamboat announced its coming with a long, mellow blast of its whistle, there was something personal about its arrival that was missing when a train of steam cars chuffed up to a depot and, after pausing momentarily to discharge its passengers and express, was off on its way. The steamboat was never in such a hurry. As it lay tied up at the landing, blowing off steam, its big wheels idle, the town would come to life, and there would be a general movement down to the river to see who was coming home and to hear the latest news from "below." If the boat were lying over for the night, one could look forward to a little entertainment that evening, provided by the steamer's singing, dancing, banjo-strumming roustabouts; or if a traveling fire-and-brimstone preacher chanced to be aboard, he could be counted on to conduct an impromptu religious service on the bank.

It was quite different on the big rivers in the days of the fast, fashionable packets, when, as Mark Twain said, one could live better afloat than ashore. They provided everything but safety.

Owners accepted the fact that three years was the average life of a steamboat, no matter how palatial. In that brief time they could, and did, return their cost and pile up a handsome profit. A boat was no sooner lost than its successor was put on the ways. More were lost by striking snags than from any other cause. The tabulated record of the number so destroyed on the Mississippi and Missouri alone totaled more than five hundred, with the Missouri accounting for more than half. What the total was for all Western rivers can only be estimated. Some were lost by fire, collisions and ice, but a far greater number by exploding boilers, collapsing flues and bursting steam pipes.

Explosions of any sort were spectacular and were responsible for the greatest loss of life. Some were traceable to ignorance and carelessness, but the great majority were due to the fool-hardy practice of racing. Any captain who refused to race soon found his boat unpopular, with the patronage going to his rivals. Racing was the great sport of the times, and dangerous as the traveling public knew it to be, it chose to ride the packets that had a reputation for accepting any challenge that was offered.

The steady march westward of the railroads drove the steamboats from the rivers. The Sacramento River steamers were the last to succumb. Government dams, toll bridges and irrigation projects made it certain that they would not be back. So they are all gone—and all we have left are the gasboats with their barges and scows, and they were never a part of the glamorous era when the steamboats ruled the rivers.

If you have ever known the smell of hot oil in the engine room of a steamboat or been lulled to sleep at night by the rhythmic slapping of its buckets hitting the water, you may agree with the thousands of steamboat buffs who feel, as I do, that with the passing of the river steamboat something that was good, and as truly American as the water on which it floated, disappeared from our lives.

We write songs and stories about them which, if they do nothing else, keep our memories of them green. But we can not call them back.

HARRY SINCLAIR DRAGO

Contents

Illustrations

THE STEAMBOATERS

I

Rivers to Tame

"WHEN IT REACHES YOU from somewhere off in the distance, a steamboat whistle is the sweetest music ever heard."

Captain Henry Miller Shreve said it, and no one could have said it better or with more authority, for he had spent forty years of his life on the Western rivers and was the creator of the steamboat just as surely as, perhaps more so than, Robert Fulton was the creator of the steamship. Both vessels were propelled by steam, and that was about all they had in common, for one was not the offshoot of the other.

In the beginning, when the steam whistle (always placed above the pilothouse) had supplanted the gun or bugle with which the early boats had heralded their arrival and departure, it was an unmelodic, hoarse, one-note blast that rent the air. It was not until the days of the grand packets that, along with the many other refinements that had taken place, the steamboat whistle became a mellow, four- and five-note musical chord, starting low, rising high and then dropping back. In those days of the great rivalries, captains strove for individuality, and it was not an empty boast that a boat could be recognized by its whistle long before it was seen.

Such things were far in the future when St. Louis greeted its first steamboat, the slatternly little *Zebulon M. Pike,* a side-wheeler from Louisville, on August 2, 1817. In lieu of bell or steam whistle (the latter was not heard on Western rivers until either 1843 or 1844, and there is some question as to whether that honor belongs to the *St. Charles,* of Pittsburgh, or Captain Abraham Bennett's *Revenue,* of Wheeling), the master of the *Pike* announced his arrival with a series of raucous blasts from an old brass trumpet and tied up to the bank at the foot of Market Street, the little town not yet boasting a wharf or levee.[1]

"The inhabitants of the village gathered on the bank to welcome the novel visitor," commented the Missouri *Gazette.* "Among them was a group of Indians. As the boat approached, the glare from the furnace, and the volume of murky smoke filled the Indians with dismay. They fled to the high ground in the rear of the village, and no assurances of safety could induce them to go near the object of their fears."

The *Zebulon M. Pike,* built at Henderson, Kentucky, was the sixth steamboat to ply Western rivers. Although aided by the muscular power of her crew using their poles on the shoals where the adverse currents were particularly strong, it had taken her six weeks to complete the journey from Louisville to St. Louis. But she was the first boat propelled by steam to turn north at the mouth of the Ohio and conquer the 130 miles of the Mississippi between what was to become Cairo, Illinois, and Mound City. It scarcely could have occurred to those who looked on as she cast her lines ashore and made fast that August afternoon that with her arrival the transformation that was to turn the sleepy little river town into a rich bustling city of 67,000 people in a few years had begun.

For years the Choteaus, the Prattes, Manuel Lisa and the other barons of the fur trade had made St. Louis the fur capital of the nation. By keelboat, batteau, barge and flatboat they had floated their peltries downriver to New Orleans, twelve hundred miles to the south. The produce of a still semiwild frontier, along with honey, tobacco, bear's grease, staves and lead from the mines at Galena, had been moved to market by the same slow, tedious and uncertain means. And costly too, for of the various craft used in this waterborne commerce, only the keel-boats—and not all of them—ever returned upriver; the others, unable to force their way against the current, had to be sold for their lumber, the source from which came the plank sidewalks of New Orleans and the crude houses of Algiers, the rough, raw town across the river from the Crescent City.

Although this work is not principally concerned with the Mississippi proper but with certain of its tributaries and with the rivers of the Far West, steamboating throughout the United States and on the Mississippi are inseparable. Primarily the American steamboat was conceived for use on the great river. That was true in the beginning, when the first crude, ugly, underpowered and poorly engined boats were put in the water, and it remained true throughout the fabulous era of the grand packets. It marked the great difference between the *steamboat* and the unsuccessful Fulton-Livingston adaptation of the *steamship* to Western inland waterways. Even when speed, passenger comfort and the dispensing of such luxury as could not be found ashore were the chief concerns of steamboat owners, the numerous shipyards along the Ohio and its tributaries, all the way from New Albany, Indiana, and the famous Howard yard at Jeffersonville, to the big Ward yard on the Kanawha, continued to build magnificent boats that, despite the gingerbread ornamentation and embellishments they were forced to install, were admirably suited for the navigation of the river they were designed to serve.[2]

To appreciate the role the steamboat played in opening up the great central valley of the United States, from the Canadian border to the warm waters of the Gulf of Mexico, and in the settlement and prosperity that followed in its wake, a brief account of the beginning and flowering of Mississippi River steamboating is necessary.

In 1807, Robert Fulton was already famous as the inventor of the steamboat, an honor that properly should have gone to John Fitch or John Stevens, or at least been shared by them. It was Fulton's successful adaptation of the ideas of others, rather than his own minor inventions, that enabled him to give the world its first practical vessel propelled by steam. Evidence that he was keenly aware of the great financial rewards to be garnered by his steamboats is found in the steps he took to make sure that the profits should come exclusively to himself and his backers, the rich and influential Chancellor Robert Livingston, who had negotiated the Louisiana Purchase for the United States, Nicholas Roosevelt,[3] Governor of New York Daniel D. Tompkins and DeWitt Clinton, among others.

"His [Fulton's] interest in the steam navigation of the western rivers was evidently awakened at an early date," says James Renwick, his biographer, in his *Life of Robert Fulton,* "for Fulton and Livingston, though seeking and obtaining an exclusive grant from the state of New York for the steam navigation of its waters . . . looked to the rapid Mississippi and its branches as the place where their triumph was to be achieved; and the original boat [the *Clermont*], modelled for shallow waters, was announced as intended for the navigation of that river."

That such a sweeping grant of special privilege could have been slipped through the legislature of New York State suggests that politics were much the same then as they are today. The grant was to run for fourteen years, with the way left open for an additional six years. It put an embargo on the steamboats of Connecticut and New Jersey, preventing them from operating on New York waters. Apparently anticipating no great difficulty in getting similar monopolisitc grants from the various states having sovereignty over the Ohio and the lower Mississippi, which Fulton's group foresaw as becoming the heartland of America, they sent Nicholas Roosevelt to Pittsburgh to build a flatboat of some pretentions and float down to New Orleans, gathering such information as he might about the currents and depth of the rivers and the commercial prospects of the country through which they flowed.

In mid-July the Roosevelts (his bride was with him) set out from Pittsburgh on their journey of exploration.[4] On the rear deck of the flatboat there was a cabin, consisting of bedroom, dining room and pantry, up forward a bunkroom for the crew, and on the open deck in between, a fireplace on which the cooking was done. A large rowboat, to be used for making soundings and exploring the tributary streams, completed the equipment. Manned by a pilot, three deckhands, a cook for the crew, the flatboat proceeded comfortably down the green valley of the Ohio.

The Roosevelts were hospitably received at the settlements along the way and reached Natchez without incident. There, for reasons never explained, they left the flatboat and completed their journey by rowboat, a matter of nine days. From New Orleans they returned to New York by sailing vessel as far as Old Point Comfort, the remaining distance being negotiated by stagecoach. Roosevelt's report was so satisfactory that the Fulton group incorporated the Ohio Steamboat Navigation Company and sent him back to Pittsburgh to begin construction of the steamboat for which Fulton had completed the design and specifications.

In a manner that was calculated to infuriate the various governors and legislatures involved, the Fulton group demanded exclusive rights to the steam navigation of the rivers, to which, by reason of the great investment they were making, they claimed they were justly entitled. Officially, they said: "We will build and operate steam vessels on the Ohio and Mississippi and later on their tributaries. In return we demand the sole right to navigate those rivers with steam craft."

They had failed completely to understand the temperament of the populace living west of the Alleghenies. Their imperative demands not only were flatly rejected, but unleashed a wave of bitterness and resentment against the Easterners that found its best expression in the resolutions adopted by the legislatures of Indiana and Kentucky. "Our rivers have always been free," they said, in effect, "and they must remain free. The pioneers and their sons did not wrest this western country from the Indians to have it turned over for the special privilege of any group of Eastern capitalists." This was always a popular rallying cry: the exploitation of the West by the East.

Of the nine states on which the Fulton interests made their demands—Pennsylvania, Ohio, Indiana, Kentucky, Missouri,

Arkansas, Tennessee, Mississippi and Louisiana—only the last-named capitulated. At the time, Louisiana was emerging from its territorial status into statehood. One of Governor W. C. C. Claiborne's intimates was Edward Livingston, the Chancellor's brother, a prominent and politically influential New Orleans lawyer. Undoubtedly he was in great measure responsible for the favorable action that was taken. Although Fulton and his backers had been rebuffed by eight of the nine states, they could be well satisfied, for Louisiana was the key to the situation, since, legally, they could prevent all shipping, other than their own, from reaching its destination at New Orleans.

On a blustery St. Patrick's Day, March 17, 1811, having been properly christened *New Orleans* by Roosevelt's young wife, the first vessel powered by steam to appear on Western waters slid down the ways from the yard at the foot of Boyd's Bluff, on the Monongahela River, across from Pittsburgh. It was said, and believably so, that she cost $38,000—no niggardly sum in that day. To obtain the necessary timbers for her keel, ribs and beams, gangs of men had been sent into the forests on the upper Monongahela to cut and then raft the logs downstream to the Suck's Run yard at Boyd's Bluff, which was well known for the keelboats, barges and flatboats built there.

To augment the local workmen available, fifty assorted ship-wrights, mechanics and machinists had been brought out from New York City. Also from the East, her low-pressure Watt and Bolton engine, boiler and hardware had been laboriously freighted over the mountains by ox teams. Built to the plans and specifications of her creator, Robert Fulton, she was, according to all existing accounts, a handsome craft as she rested on the Monongahela that St. Patrick's Day. To make the gala complete, Fulton himself was on hand, having journeyed out from New York by stagecoach.

The *Orleans*—in popular usage she was seldom referred to as the *New Orleans*—had masts for sails fore and aft, which, when the wind was favorable, were expected to increase her speed. She was 116 feet long overall, with a beam of 20 feet. Powered by a wheel at the stern, with her machinery below decks and a draft of five feet, she was more steamship than steamboat, which the fate that awaited her was to prove.

Roosevelt engaged Captain Andrew Sack, who was acquainted with the Ohio and Mississippi, as pilot. Signing on other officers and a crew for what was considered "the perilous voyage to New Orleans" consumed time. Also, the "appointments" for the passenger cabins were late in arriving. With one thing and another, including trial runs on the Monongahela, it was September before the *Orleans* weighed anchor and pointed her helm down the two thousand miles of turbulent, uncharted waters for the home port whose name she bore.

The crowd that lined the bank watched her leave with mingled emotions. When she disappeared behind the first headlands, on the right bank of the Ohio, the cheering ended and the dire prediction that Pittsburgh would never see her again was made by many. She might, with luck, the more optimistic allowed, reach New Orleans, but she would never be able to make her way upstream against the powerful current of the Mississippi and the Ohio.

Mrs. Roosevelt, soon to give birth to her first child, and her brother, J. H. B. Latrobe, were the boat's only passengers.[5] The ladies in the crowd, concerned only for the former's safety, dabbed their eyes with their handkerchiefs and condemned her "headstrong" husband for imperiling her life in this fashion, exposing her to the dangers of fire, explosions and wreck. Their fears proved to be groundless; the *New Orleans* reached Louisville on the first of October (the baby was born there) and, running the Falls of the Ohio, arrived at New Orleans on January 12, 1812.

Amid great excitement the whole city turned out to give her an ecstatic greeting. "Steam power has conquered the mighty Mississippi," the Louisiana *Gazette* trumpeted. "The future prosperity and growth of this city is now assured. With fast, economical transportation bringing the commerce of the great Upper Valley to New Orleans, we can look forward to the day when this city will be the greatest ocean-river port in the United States." The *Democrat* was also extravagantly optimistic, visualizing the day when a multitude of steamboats would be plowing up and down the Father of Waters with their riches. Unrestrained as these predictions were, time was to see them surpassed.

While the Roosevelts were being hosted by the elite, cargo for her return voyage was taken aboard the *New Orleans*. When all was in readiness, she set off. All went well as far as Natchez. Soon thereafter it was apparent that she could not proceed any farther; she was sitting so deep in the water that her tired engine could not drive her against the current. But all was not lost. For the rest of her days she engaged in the rich Natchez–New Orleans cotton trade at tremendous profit to her owners.[6]

To say only that the *New Orleans* was the first boat to steam down the Ohio and Mississippi and let it go at that would be to ignore the fact that with her appearance began the controversy that was to affect steamboating on our Western rivers for many years. She was a Fulton "monopoly" boat, the first of five that were built, in this order: the *New Orleans, Vesuvius, Aetna, Buffalo* and a second *New Orleans,* each having some improvement in structural design and motive power over its predecessors. With these boats as a beginning, it was the ruthless, imperialistic intention of the Fulton group to choke off all competition, and with the law on their side they were in position to attach any boat rash enough to attempt to reach New Orleans.

The prospect of becoming entangled in expensive litigation was a threat that held back steamboat navigation for years. But the Fulton forces received a rude awakening just when they seemed to be in complete command, for they had reckoned without Captain Henry Shreve, a man of modest means but a dauntless fighter for justice, who refused to be awed by the monopolists. In open defiance, he steamed into New Orleans and put up bail for his boat even before it was attached. It was the beginning of years of legal skirmishing, so punctuated with appeals and reversals that neither side could claim victory. By 1815 the Fulton boats were confining themselves to running between Natchez and New Orleans in the cotton trade, past experience having demonstrated that they were poorly designed for navigating the upper river, despite the fact that both the *Vesuvius* and *Aetna* had made several round trips from New Orleans to Louisville. The *Vesuvius* had been hung up on sandbars several times, once for five months.

Both Fulton and Livingston died that year. Undoubtedly it was a combination of these happenings that weakened the militant position of the so-called steamboat monopoly. The sale of two of its remaining boats virtually ended its attempts to enforce its privileges; and after 1816, long before the U.S. Supreme Court ruled that all such grants were unconstitutional and invalid (1824), the freedom of steam navigation had been established.

The West had found not only a new hero in the person of Henry Shreve, an ex-flatboat captain, but its greatest benefactor. His contributions to river navigation by steam power were many, not only on the Mississippi but wherever paddle wheels turned on the inland waters of America. Steamboats carried the first great tide of emigration westward long before the railroads conquered the Allegheny barrier and pushed their rails across the valleys and flatlands to the plains and prairies of the Far West; they turned sleepy little river towns into thriving cities and brought a measure of culture, romance and prosperity to regions where the blanket Indian was not yet a novelty.

Shreve was a riverman, first and last, and almost singlehandedly he worked out the structural and mechanical innovations without which the steamboat would have been relatively useless. What he created must have been good, for other builders, down through the era of the grand packets, continued to incorporate his ideas in their boats, until there were no more steamboats to be built, and the barges, and scrubby towboats that pushed and pulled them, had the big rivers to themselves.

Ask anyone about Mark Twain and he'll know the name and be able to tell you something about the man. Not one in a hundred has ever heard of Henry Miller Shreve.

II

Steamboat 'Round the Bend

TODAY ONLY FLEETS of battered coal and petroleum barges going about their plebian tasks serve to remind Pittsburgh of the time when, situated at the confluence of the Monongahela and the Allegheny rivers, it was the prosperous and undisputed head of navigation between the lush Ohio Valley and New Orleans. That was true for years before the first steamboat appeared on Western waters, and it retained its preeminence as a great river port even after it was forced to share its trade with Cincinnati (old Losantiville), Louisville and St. Louis.

By raft, flatboat and keelboat, a surprisingly great amount of produce from the farms, mills, mines and forests of the North was transported down the Ohio. The extent of this commerce can be judged by the following figures in Hezikiah Niles' *Weekly Register* listing the tonnage passing the Falls of the Ohio for the period between October 5, 1810, and May 5, 1811:

Flour, barrels	206,855
Bacon, pounds	1,008,026
Whisky, barrels	15,797
Pork, barrels	22,602
Corn, barrels	79,695
Merchandise (general)	592,640

Lumber, feet 2,325,210
Lard, pounds 775,000
Hemp, cwt. 1,050,492
Fowls 2,012,224
Country Linen, pounds 13,066
Tobacco, hogsheads 3,891

Other figures are given, and including salt from the furnaces
on the Kanawha and miscellaneous items, they total another
200,000 tons. And it was all moved by barge, flatboat and keelboat.

Although the keelboat has often been described in detail,
many misconceptions regarding its size and practicality continue to exist. It is believed by many to have been a frail, shallow-draft vessel, manned by a crew of two or three, and of very
limited carrying capacity. Captain E. W. Gould, in his authoritative *History of River Navigation,* describes it thus: "The
keel-boat was of a long, slender and elegant form, and generally
carried from 15 to 20 tons . . . and crew of eight to ten men. Its
advantage lay in its small draught of water and in the lightness
of its construction. Its propelling power was by oar, sail, setting
poles [and] the cordelle, and when the water was high and the
boats ran on the margin of the river, 'bushwhacking,' or pulling
upstream by the bushes."

When it was necessary to resort to cordelling, a mast thirty
feet high was raised in the center of the boat, with a heavy line,
usually a thousand feet long, attached at the tip. All hands, except the captain and the *bosseman* (boatswain's mate), went
ashore to proceed along the bank, dragging the line. To prevent
the boat from seesawing, the long line was connected to the bow
by means of a bridle (or auxiliary rope) fastened to a loop in the
bow, through which the cordelle passed. The *bosseman* took his
position there to watch for snags and used his pole to keep the
boat off the bank. The *patron* (captain) handled the rudder.
Under average conditions, fifteen to seventeen miles a day was
the rate of advance.

Many keelboats were built in Kentucky, but none were as famous as those that originated at Brownsville, fifty miles up the

Monongahela from Pittsburgh, where lumber was cheap and plentiful. Rivermen knew from long experience that the keelboat was admirably suited for coping with the hazards of the big rivers, and when it came time for them to build steamboats, they copied the lines of the keelboat in their hulls. To that beehive of boatbuilding at Brownsville, Colonel Israel Shreve, a veteran of the Revolution, brought his wife and family of six small children in 1785, and began farming. Next to the youngest in the family was a boy named Henry Miller Shreve. Ten years later, he was haunting the boatyards along the Monongahela. The swaggering rivermen, with their well-filled purses and tales of adventure in faraway places, were heady wine for a youngster in his teens, and he was not twenty when he joined a keelboat crew bound for New Orleans.

Aside from the financial success that the following six years brought to young Shreve, both as master of his own keelboats and as flatboat captain, they provided him with an intimate, firsthand knowledge of the hazards and vagaries of the Ohio and Mississippi that he could have acquired in no other way. He is generally credited with being the first flatboat owner to transport lead from the Illinois mines to New Orleans, where it was readily salable for transshipment to Baltimore and Philadelphia. He was only twenty-eight when he returned to Brownsville, married, and associated himself with Daniel French, the inventor, and Daniel Smith.

French had patented a marine engine with oscillating cylinders, a radical departure from the English Watt and Bolton engine installed in the Fulton boats. From Shreve's interest in French's invention, it must be assumed that as early as this (1810) he already envisioned the day when the steamboat would supersede all other forms of river transportation. A few months later, accompanied by Daniel French, he went down the Monongahela to inspect the *New Orleans* as she stood on the stocks below Boyd's Bluff. Although he admired the workmanship of her builders, he was not impressed by her lines: she was a deepwater boat, and even without cargo would sit so low that she would not be able to pass over many of the countless shallows and sandbars of the Mississippi.

He inspected her again as she lay at the wharf boat having her machinery installed. He shook his head as he saw her boiler and engine being placed in the hold. All this ran contrary to what he believed a steamboat should be. Time was to prove he was right.

With the financial backing of Daniel Smith, Shreve acting in an advisory capacity, French built the little *Comet,* only twenty-five tons, in 1813. She made her way safely to New Orleans but lacked the power for the return voyage. Her engine was taken out and sold to a planter to power his cotton gin. The following year, French built the *Enterprise,* forty-five tons. She made two trips from Pittsburgh to Louisville and on December 1 took on a cargo of ordinance stores at Pittsburgh. Under the command of Captain Shreve, she left for New Orleans, then under attack by the British, and arrived there fourteen days later. She was attached by Edward Livingston, on behalf of the Fulton group, but Shreve having posted bail, she could not be held. The situation was further complicated when General Jackson commandeered her for military duty.[1]

With the siege of New Orleans lifted, and the case against the *Enterprise* still pending, Captain Shreve steamed north on May 6 and reached Shippingport (Louisville) on May 30, or in twenty-five days, being the first steamboat that ever arrived at that port from New Orleans. After being feted as the conqueror of the Mississippi, Shreve went on to Pittsburgh, where the command of the *Enterprise* was turned over to Dennis Worley, who lost her in Rock Harbor, at Shippingport, several months later.

Shreve had come up the river with one idea in mind: to build his own boat, after his own ideas and with a high-pressure engine based on French's patent, but with some improvements of his own. Instead of French's oscillating cylinders, he designed oscillating pitmans (connecting rods) that permitted the cylinders to remain stationary. He wanted two engines, one for each wheel, to double the boat's maneuverability. And they were to be horizontal engines—another radical change. The cutoff valve, which would utilize the expansive force of the steam and make a saving of one third in fuel, was another Shreve innovation. That saving was going to be necessary, for he meant to have a battery of boilers—four in all—and he would place them on the guards, two on each side of his boat.

These were radical ideas, unheard of before his time. They must have had merit, for steamboat builders down through the years were to follow them in practically all of the two thousand and more boats that were to ply Western rivers.[2]

Having secured the financial backing he needed in Wheeling, West Virginia (Virginia, at that time), he went there to build his boat and hired George White, a competent river mechanic, to do the work under his exacting direction. Before the first stick had been laid, he had named her the *Washington,* in honor of his father's wartime commander.

Wheeling was an old river town, its future prosperity assured by the completion of the National Road from Washington City to the Ohio River, of which it was to be the western terminus. As the hull began to take shape on the ways, the spectators who came down the bank to see how the work was progressing were of the opinion that what young Shreve was building was nothing more than an overgrown keelboat. And they were right; let the Fultons build deep, round hulls and set their machinery deep in them; what he wanted was a flat, shallow hull that would skim over the water rather than plow through it.

The consternation of the skeptics grew as they saw the hull being completely decked over, and they were convinced that Shreve was surely daft when he placed his boilers and engines on the planked-over deck. He further amazed them by installing a trusslike arrangement of heavy timbers, rising at an angle fore and aft and running longitudinally eight feet above the deck for two thirds the length of the *Washington* (she was 148 feet long). It was to be known ever afterward as the *hogging* frame. It seemed to be a device to overcome any limberness the boat might have. That was not the purpose for which Shreve orig-inated it; he wanted to control, not eliminate, all limberness, since he saw the advantage of some flexibility at bow and stern in getting a boat over shallow water.[3]

The hogging was also to serve as the main support of an up-per deck for passenger staterooms. When Shreve confided in

Daniel French, who built her engines under his supervision, that the *Washington* was to be a double-decker, the latter tried to dissuade him, warning Shreve that he was going too far with his radical ideas; that the boat would be topheavy. The *Washington* and her multitudinous offspring were to prove French wrong.

Her tall, twin stacks, with their ornamental crowns, were stepped in place after she slipped down the ways into the river. Weeks passed as she got her final touches and her furnishings (appointments was the popular word for them in those days). Shreve took on a crew of former keelboat and barge men, brawny fellows who could be depended on if an emergency arose. He took her up the Ohio to Pittsburgh and back on her trial runs. She behaved beautifully, and after taking on cargo and passengers, she set off down the Ohio for Louisville and New Orleans on June 4, 1816. To paraphrase the words of Herbert and Edward Quick in their *Mississippi Steamboatin'*, she was so ugly she was beautiful.

Beyond question Henry Miller Shreve gave us the American steamboat of our Western rivers as we know it today. Into the *Washington* he put his own original ideas of what a steamboat should be. He borrowed nothing from Robert Fulton. Fulton's boats were side-wheelers; so was the *Washington*, but her wheels were stepped much farther back, Shreve's theory being that so placed the paddles would have greater thrust when they hit the water and that as the revolution was completed they would emerge with a feathering action and a minimum of braking.[4]

Touching at Shippingport (Louisville) the *Washington*, after taking on passengers and cargo, made a record run to New Orleans. The lawsuit against the *Enterprise* was still unsettled, and the *Washington* was impounded by the Fulton group. Shreve countered by getting a court order holding them liable for any damages he might suffer while he was being denied the use of his boat. Sentiment had turned against the monopolists; New Orleans was as determined as the North to have the Mississippi made free. Edward Livingston, seeing the battle going against him, offered Shreve an equal share in the company if he (Shreve) would arrange to lose the suits pending against him. The latter's adamant refusal to enter into such an arrangement seems to have ended the matter. The suit against the *Washington* was dropped, and Shreve was soon on his way up the river.

The *Washington* made two round trips from Louisville to New Orleans in 1817, the second one in forty-one days, completing the second leg of the last trip in twenty-five days. These trips dispelled any further doubt about the ability of steamboats to navigate the great rivers of the Mississippi Valley and most of their tributaries. Fast, reliable, economical transportation would bring even the remotest towns and settlements closer together and provide a market for the products of farms, factories, mills and mines. It was equally obvious that with the steamboat and the great National Road to Wheeling, the tide of emigration streaming west (anywhere beyond the Alleghenies was considered west) would be increased tenfold.

Of course, that glittering prospect was fulfilled many times over. The credit for making it possible must go to one man— Henry Miller Shreve; he not only gave the West the steamboat, but by his courageous stand broke the chain with which the Fulton-Livingston interests had tried to shackle its rivers. In later years other honors were to come to him as U.S. Superintendent of Western River Improvements during the administrations of Presidents Adams, Jackson and Van Buren and as the inventor of the snag boat. In two years, 1830 and 1831, he cleared three hundred miles of the Mississippi south from Trinity (Cairo), Illinois, of thousands of snags and, in the words of the Cincinnati *Spy,* "made it as harmless as a mill-pond." [5] Similar success attended his years of breaking up the Great Raft that had closed Red River to navigation for a hundred and fifty miles. The thriving city of Shreveport, Louisiana, bears his name. Of that, more later.

Gould reprints from Sharf's *History of St. Louis* a list of the first sixty steamboats running on Ohio-Mississippi waters and says: "Capt. H. M. Shreve seems to have been about the only one who figured in the different boats named." This is not surprising, for Shreve was either the owner or part owner of many different steamboats. But the *Washington,* his first boat, remained his favorite. He did not have her long. On June 9, 1819, bound from St. Louis to Pittsburgh, she was moving up the Ohio at full speed and was within several miles of Marietta when one of her starboard boilers let go. The explosion shattered her. Enveloped in a cloud of scalding steam, she drifted helplessly toward the Kentucky shore and sank in deep water. Captain Shreve was among the injured, having been pitched from the pilothouse into the river, which may very well have saved his life. Eight others were not so fortunate.

The loss of the *Washington* was the forerunner of a staggering number of similar accidents that were to follow. The most reliable accounting of the number of boats lost by fire, explosion and related causes during the first thirty years of steamboating on the Ohio, Mississippi and Missouri was published in *DeBow's Review* of 1848. It lists the boats so lost at 233; passengers, officers and crewmen killed at 1,015; persons injured, 1,805. It is hardly necessary to remark that traveling by steamboat had its element of danger. But so was traveling by rail a hazard, and is today by plane and motorcar. The advantages the steamboat offered far outweighed any fear of it that the public may have entertained. What better proof of this is needed than that by 1834, 230 boats were transporting goods and people on the two big rivers, and eight years later the number had grown to 450, their boilers and engines coming from the foundries and machine shops at Brownsville, Cincinnati and Louisville.

Boatbuilding became a prosperous business. Up and down the Ohio there was a proliferation of so-called shipyards, many of them owned and operated by men who knew nothing about the craft of the shipwright and, of necessity, employed workmen who were equally inexperienced. The competition of such experts as the Howards at Jeffersonville, the Walkers at Elizabethtown, Pennsylvania, and a dozen other builders hardly less famous, soon put the others out of business. Beginning with "Uncle Jim" Howard, which is going back to the 1820's, four generations of Howards, doing business at the same stand, are credited with building 50 percent of all Ohio-Mississippi steamboats, the total from all yards numbering well above three thousand.

The Howards built the third and last of the *J. M. White*'s, the most luxurious of the river packets. With her, luxury afloat really came of age. Her staterooms were equipped with private baths and washstands. Passengers slept in brass double beds. All of which was a far cry from what Captain Shreve called his "staterooms" on the *Washington,* which were only divided sections of the cabin, the after sections reserved for ladies, with the gentlemen placed up forward. Although the Howards built the third *White,* they followed the design of the old (second *White*), who had shown her heels to all other steamboats of her day. She had made Billy King, of Elizabethtown, her creator, the most famous steamboat designer of his time. A follower of Shreve, he had gone the old master one better and moved the *White*'s paddle wheels even farther back than Shreve had in his numerous boats.

It was the universal custom of Western newspapers to overwork the adjectives when mentioning steamboats, referring to them as elegant, magnificent, luxurious, long before they could boast of anything even faintly resembling those terms. That the accommodations some were offering, as late as 1843, were miserable is found in the following letter written by Audubon, the naturalist, to James Hall, one of his inlaws:

And such a steamer as we have come in from Louisville here!— the very filthiest of all filthy rat-traps I ever travelled in; and the fare worse, certainly much worse, and so scanty withal that our worthy commander could not have given us another meal had we been detained a night longer . . . on board the *Gallant*—a pretty name, too, but alas! her name, like mine, is only a shadow, for as she struck a sawyer one night we all ran like mad to make ready to leap overboard; but as God would have it, our lives and the *Gallant* were spared—she from sinking, and we from swimming amid rolling and crashing ice. The ladies screamed, and the babies squalled, the dogs yelled, the steam roared, the captain (who, by the way, is a very gallant man) swore—not like an angel, but like the very devil—and all was confusion and uproar. Luckily we had had our *supper,* as the thing was called aboard the *Gallant,* and every man appeared to feel resolute, if not resolved to die.

I would have given much at that moment for a picture of the whole. Our *compagnons de voyage,* about one hundred and fifty, were composed of Buckeyes, Wolverines, Suckers, Hoosiers, and gamblers, with drunkards of each and every denomination, their ladies and babies of the same nature, and specially the dirtiest of the dirty. We had to dip the water for washing from the river in tin basins, soap ourselves all from the same cake, and wipe the one hundred and fifty with the same solitary one towel rolling over a pin, until it would have been difficult to say, even with your keen eyes, whether it was manufactured of hemp, tow, flax, or cotton. My bed had two sheets, of course, measuring seven-eighths of a yard wide; my pillow was filled with corn-shucks . . . our stateroom was evidently better fitted for the smoking of hams than the smoking of Christians. When it rained outside, it rained also within, and on one particular morning, when the snow melted on the upper deck or roof, it was a lively scene to see each person seeking for a spot free from the many spouts overhead.[6]

Perhaps some of Audubon's aggravation was due to the fact that he was sixty-three, not in the best of health, and that he and his party of five (all naturalists, bound for the wilds of the Upper Missouri) had left Baltimore in a snowstorm that accompanied them all the way west to St. Louis. It was the middle of March. The annual spring breakup had just taken place, and masses of ice were drifting down the rivers. The great man was not always so critical of steamboating. Although Charles Dickens, the famous English novelist, and Mrs. Trollope, his fellow countrywoman, had expressed their low opinion of steamboats, other visitors from abroad saw them in a quite different light. In 1850, the widely traveled French journalist Bertrand Dureau said in Paris: "Today steamboats are the salvation of the valley of the Mississippi. They are the most essential agents of its business and social life, and if it were possible to imagine them wiped out for a time, the rising civilization of those extensive regions would disappear with them."

The third *White* cost $200,000. The cost of such other giants as the *Grand Republic* and the *Ed Richardson* must have been nearly as great. The *Ed Richardson* was not as fast as the *White*, but she won the reputation of "setting the best table on the river." One sat down to a ten-course dinner, with a choice of six roasts, six entrées, fish, game, boiled meats, an assortment of cold dishes, a bewildering array of vegetables and half a hundred desserts. Her bill for fruit and nuts alone ran to five hundred dollars a week.

Steamboating was still a young business but already it was reaching its peak. The little Louisville and Portland Canal, which hugged the Kentucky shore for two miles, was proof enough of how navigation had advanced in recent years. When completed in 1830, making it possible to bypass the Falls of the Ohio, the canal was hailed as the greatest of all river improvements; but by 1850 the steamers were so big that they could not use it. And they were becoming so numerous that competition was forcing owners to pool their boats in so-called packet companies, such as the Anchor Line, Memphis Packet Company, the Chalmette Line, the New Orleans Packet Company and a hundred others. Competition also began pulling down freight rates and passenger fares. For fifty dollars one could go first class from St. Louis to New Orleans. Deck passage, which meant supplying one's own blanket and food, fell to as low as eight dollars.

The big boats vied with one another in the quality of the music they provided—sometimes a small brass band, but always an orchestra for dancing in the main ballroom. Each sought to outdo its rivals in the ornateness of its barroom, usually let out as a concession to a popular, white-coated purveyor of alcoholic beverages, who often netted himself as much as a thousand dollars a round trip.

The catastrophes multiplied as racing became more prevalent, reaching its climax in 1870 in the famous duel of the *Natchez* and the *Robert E. Lee*. The traveling public shrugged off the accidents and gave their patronage to those captains who they knew would race at the slightest provocation.

Just when the South got its second name of Dixie, no one can say, but it was back in the days of the keelboatmen, who brought it up the Mississippi. In those years, before national banking laws were enacted, every bank issued its own notes. Whether good or worthless, they were viewed with suspicion a few hundred miles from the point where they were issued. The Banque des Citoyens at New Orleans was the exception; its paper was good anywhere. Its ten-dollar note had the French word DIX printed on its face in large letters. When the keelboatmen were homeward bound, they preferred the Dix to any other form of currency. Any man with four or more of them was said to have a bunch of "Dixies." They began to refer to New Orleans as "Dixie land," which soon came to include all of the South. When Dan Emmett, the minstrel, wrote *Dixie* as a walk-around for himself, the South seized on it at once; and in the War between the States, it became the Confederacy's battle song.

The war threatened to mark the end of steamboating as a business. Both the North and the South seized what boats they could get their hands on and turned them into rams, gunboats and troop carriers. Of the number forced into military service, fully two thirds were destroyed. When it became apparent that the Union had won control of the Mississippi, boats remaining in the hands of the Confederacy scurried into the bayous and up Red River to avoid capture, dismantling their stacks and covering their upperworks with brush. There, in the trap of their own making, most of them rotted and never returned to service.

Two years after the end of hostilities Northern shipyards began putting new boats into the water. They were deluged with orders. At the great Howard yard, the work often went on by torchlight. It soon became apparent that, instead of fading into oblivion, what was to become the golden era of the packets was beginning. It was a phenomenon that was to continue until the advancing railroads ruined them with competition they could not meet.

Passengers on the big packets came from all walks of life— men of high position, traveling with their wives, families and servants; wealthy cotton planters from Mississippi and Louisiana; lawyers, politicians, businessmen, cotton factors. And along with them professional gamblers, gunmen and prostitutes—beautiful Creoles recruited from the bagnios of New Orleans who knew how to conduct themselves with decorum. Money was plentiful; on some boats a gentleman's every need could be supplied, whatever it chanced to be.

III

Up Where the Big River Begins

St. Louis was founded by the French, and culturally it remained French under Spanish and American rule until the steamboats opened the vast and still almost virgin regions between the Appalachians and the Rocky Mountains to immigration and commerce. Wherever the steamboat could make its way, new settlements sprang into existence; those already established cast off their frontier status and grew miraculously into industrial towns of ever-increasing importance.

It was not only on the mainstem of the Ohio and Mississippi that the magic touch of steamboating became apparent; wherever there was a navigable river—the Kanawha, Muskingum, Licking, Wabash, Illinois, Cumberland, Minnesota and Tennessee—the area awakened with new life. And, of course, that was true of the great Missouri, winding northward from its confluence with the Mississippi, eighteen miles above St. Louis, to the mountains of Montana, 3,100 miles away.

The Wild Missouri, with its multiple barriers to steamboat navigation, was the last to respond. And with good reason, for as late as 1817, when the *Zebulon M. Pike* fought its way up the Mississippi to St. Louis, the only white men who could claim any knowledge of the Big Muddy north of Fort Leavenworth were the trappers and fur traders. Fort Leavenworth was garrisoned by troops. Beyond it and the little town of the same name that became established in its protective shadow (not until June, 1854) there were no settlements. The so-called forts were merely strongholds of the American Fur Company and the Rocky Mountain Fur Company.

Further east on the rich farm and timber lands of the Upper Mississippi and its principal tributary, the Minnesota River, pioneer civilization had become firmly established. Millions of feet of yellow pine timber were being rafted downstream to St. Louis, Natchez and New Orleans. Great quantities of rough-dressed lumber were going in the same direction by flatboat. Fur-bearing animals, it was realized, would soon be trapped out, but the boastful prediction was made that the prosperity of that northern country would continue forever—or to the day when the forests of yellow pine were exhausted, an unlikely prospect on May 10, 1823, when Captain Crawford brought the little stern-wheeler *Virginia* up the seven hundred miles of the un-charted Upper Mississippi and across dangerous Lake Pepin to the Falls of St. Anthony, the first steamboat to get that far, but not the first to try it, the before-mentioned *Zebulon M. Pike* having made the effort and been forced to turn back earlier that year.

The *Virginia* dropped back from the Falls and was made fast at a collection of log cabins and rough pine board buildings that bore the fitting name of Pig's Eye, a short distance from Fort Snelling, a military post of little consequence then but destined to become important in the great Indian uprising preceding the Civil War, and thereafter. As she lay tied up at the bank, the *Virginia* was 729 miles north of St. Louis. She had run the long Des Moines Rapids at Keokuk and the Upper or Rock Island Rapids. Aside from the mines at Galena and the settlements at Keokuk, Rock Island, Prairie du Chien and La Crosse, most of those miles were wilderness miles. And yet, two years later, the estimated value of the hides, furs, lumber and farm products brought down from the upper rivers totaled more than a quarter of a million dollars.

Incredibly, old records show that seven steamboats were trading regularly as far north as La Crosse, and four or five were going all the way to the mills at the Falls, the head of navigation. Two boats were serving the Illinois River towns on a semiweekly basis, going up as far as La Salle, water permitting. Later, the business was taken over by the Naples Packet Company, employing four steamers. Great as these changes were, they were no match for what the following decade was to bring.

America was on the move westward; the Erie Canal had been opened in 1825, providing New Englanders with an easy means of reaching the Great Lakes and spreading out into the great Central Valley. From their rocky farms and factories they came by the thousand, and along with them a stream of German and Scandinavian emigrants who were being dumped on the wharves of New York, Boston and other cities of the Eastern Seaboard. What are today's great states of Wisconsin and Minnesota were fortunate in getting more than their share of these thrifty, industrious, foreign-born newcomers.

Pig's Eye, in line with its suddenly aroused aspirations, cast aside its baptismal cognomen and renamed itself St. Paul. As a town it was beginning to amount to something. In 1841 it became an organized town, and five years later was named the territorial capital of Minnesota. That year there were over three hundred steamboat arrivals at St. Paul, a big share of them from the Minnesota River. Some idea of the amount of money that was spent to operate them can be gained from the fact that the average monthly cost of maintaining a steamboat of 120 tons was roughly $1,800, divided as follows: 36 percent for wages of officers and crew; 18 percent for provisions; 12 percent for incidentals and insurance; and the rest for 25 cords of wood per day, at $2.50 per cord. In return, its earnings from freight and passenger fares often amounted to twice as much. Steamboating in the North not only was a very profitable business but gave employment to several thousand men other than those on the payrolls. The woodyards alone kept hundreds of "woodhawks" busy cutting fuel for the ravenous boilers. The livelihood of additional hundreds of Metis (French-Canadians of

mixed blood), who drove the trains of Red River carts, depended on the steamboats to provide them with the goods they
hauled.[1]

When flour ground from Minnesota wheat became an important commodity, St. Paul did not hesitate to vote money for
exploring the feasibility of establishing steamboat service between the Minnesota River and the Red River of the North in
order to capture a Canadian market.

Red River, flowing north, formed the boundary between Dakota Territory and Minnesota. Crossing into Manitoba, it
reached Fort Garry (today's Winnipeg) and Lake Winnipeg.
Two small steamboats owned by the Hudson Bay Company
found the Red navigable the greater part of the year. It could
be reached from St. Paul by following the roundabout Minnesota to Big Stone Lake and Lake Traverse, the so-called Boundary Lakes, just widenings of the river, and then going down the
Bois de Sioux, a shallow tributary of the Red which flowed
north out of Lake Traverse. The trip could be made only in
high water; at other times there was the danger that a sudden
drop would leave a boat stranded. But for the greater part of
the year freight had to be transported over the connecting portage.

The little *Fanny Harris,* of Galena, drawing only nineteen
inches, made the crossing successfully, but other steamboats that
tried it ran into costly and embarrassing difficulties. Young Captain John B. Davis, in command of the *Freighter,* a stern-
wheeler of thirty-eight tons, lost the channel as he crossed Big
Stone Lake in high water. Determined not to be stopped, he
headed his boat in the direction of Red River and took off
across the flooded prairie. Ten miles from Big Stone Lake he
ran the *Freighter* so hard aground that he wrecked her. Another
famous trip across the prairies occurred in the early spring of
1861, when the old *Fanny Harris,* under government charter,
went up the Minnesota from Fort Snelling to Fort Ridgely,
about a hundred and fifty miles by air but twice that distance
by the twisting, looping river, to bring out the Buena Vista battery of light artillery, earmarked for combat duty on the eastern
front.

Although the river was over its banks in many places, because of melting snows, the *Fanny Harris* reached Fort Ridgely. Her troubles began when she turned around to make her way down-river in the raging current. Brevet Major John C. Pemberton (later general) was in command of the battery. In forceful language he impressed on the captain of the *Fanny Harris* that time was of the essence. But after having been slammed right and left against the trees that lined the channel, with extensive damage to the boat's superstructure, the captain of the *Fanny Harris* refused to run by night. Repairs were made as she lay tied up that evening. The following day, as she neared Belle Plain, miles of flooded fields could be seen beyond the intervening fringe of trees. The sight of all that placid water was too much for the master of the *Fanny Harris.* Calling for more steam, he pointed her bow at the trees and tried to ram his way through. One of her stacks was knocked down and the other broken off a few feet above deck; trees were pushed over and limbs snapped; one ripped through the pilothouse. After a few moments of uncertainty the *Fanny Harris* wrenched her way through the barrier. Two days later she ran out her landing stages and discharged the battery on the green at Fort Snelling.

In 1859, J. C. and H. C. Burbank, St. Paul's leading overland freighting outfit, built a small (and grotesque) steamboat named the *Anson Northrup,* in honor of her captain, who had transported her machinery across Minnesota. Her principal, if not only, purpose was to propel rafts and flatboats up and down the Red River. Doubtless it was with some satisfaction that the Burbank brothers inserted the following advertisement in the St. Paul and Winnipeg newspapers, following the attempt to establish an all-water route to Red River and the north: "Owning the steamer *Anson Northrup* (re-named *Pioneer*) and a line of over one hundred transport wagons, which we shall run in connection with the boat, we can furnish the settlements with anything they desire to import upon better terms than is possible for any other house."

They were a breed apart, those steamboatmen of the north, and they had little in common with their brethren of the Lower Mississippi. They didn't go in much for elegance and luxury or for personal adornment. To them the steamboat was a work-horse rather than a convenience. They were not steamboat builders; the records disclose that practically all of the boats plying the Upper Mississippi and the Minnesota River were laid down in the yards along the Ohio. The competition on Northern waters was so keen and fares sometimes fell so low that they gave rise to the saying: "It's cheaper to live aboard a steamboat than to stay at home."

The French explorers and Jesuit missionaries had been the first white men to see that country—Marquette, Hennepin, Joliet, Nicollet, to name a few. French bushrangers and fur traders had followed. They had done very little to advance the country, but they are not forgotten; their names grace a thousand towns, rivers and lakes. The fur trade was still important in the Upper Mississippi region in 1822, when Joseph Renville sold his Columbia Fur Company posts to the American Fur Company, and it remained so for another half-dozen years. It dwindled rapidly after the American withdrew and focused its attention on its Missouri River business.

The government had been removing the Indian tribes piece-meal—principally the Santee and Sisseton Sioux—from Wisconsin and Minnesota for years and, piling one injustice on another, setting the stage for the Great Sioux Uprising of 1862. In the panic that followed, the mass evacuation of the Winnebago Indians to a new reservation near Chamberlain (South Dakota) was ordered, although it does not appear that they were active participants in the uprising.[2]

After the removal of the Winnebagos, in 1863, the taking and selling of furs became a relatively unimportant factor in the economy of the country.

It was not unusual for the Ohio River to be frozen over for weeks at a time during the course of a hard winter. Only on rare occasions, however, were steamboats icebound at St. Louis. But they were in dire straights if they were caught tied up at the unprotected St. Louis levee when the annual breakup to the north occurred and the river was filled with swirling masses of ice. Winter presented no problem several hundred miles south of Cairo. On the Upper Mississippi and its tributaries it was a different story. Save for a sudden and unexpected freeze-up, the boats had ample warning of the approach of winter to leave for the South. Many did; others sought the safest berth available and remained there to await the coming of spring. Even after the Emancipation Proclamation had made them free men, the Negroes who had come north on the steamboats as deckhands, firemen and stewards had no desire to return to the scenes of their former bondage. By one means or another most of them remained where they were. There are Negroes living in Wisconsin and Minnesota today whose ancestors worked their way up the Mississippi as members of a steamboat crew.

Of all the hundreds of steamboat captains who commanded craft on our Western rivers, only two rose to the rank of commodore, an honorary title bestowed on William P. Davidson, of St. Paul, by his fellow rivermen, and on W. J. Kountz, of Allegheny, Pennsylvania, by the United States government. In his old age, as a banker in Allegheny, Kountz never failed to remind any interviewer that his life on the rivers had begun when he was only ten. In truth, he had gone down the Ohio to Cincinnati as a passenger in a keelboat owned by his brother Hiram. Perhaps this was (as he chose to regard it) the beginning of his long and successful career on the water. He must have learned fast, for when he was eighteen he was appointed captain of the keelboat *Townsman*. The following year he went to New Orleans as linesman on one of Zachary Reno's coal barges. Switching to steamboats, he served in one subordinate position after another—linesman, cub pilot, clerk and finally pilot and then captain.

Captain Kountz's first command was the grubby little *Gallant* that had conveyed James Audubon and his party from Louisville to St. Louis. She was almost as old as her skipper. But it was a beginning. Bigger and better berths were in store for him. A perusal of the directory of steamboats plying the Ohio and Mississippi from 1843 to 1878 reveals him as pilot, master, owner or part owner of sixty-nine boats, a number never even remotely equaled by any other person.

The "Kountz Line" and the "Kountz Boats" were known to everyone. When his *City of Memphis,* a noble three-decker, was launched in 1857, she was the largest and finest boat built up to that time. She gave her cabin passengers the novelty of a daily newspaper printed aboard. Every morning they found a copy on their breakfast plate containing the bill of fare and what purported to be the news of the past twenty-four hours, edited and printed by the boat's chief clerk and his staff.[3]

At the outbreak of the Civil War, Captain Kountz was commissioned a commodore and placed in charge of river transportation. In that capacity he purchased all the steamboats to be converted into gunboats or used as troop transports. Unlike so many others, he served without compensation, which must stand as a monument to the character of the man.

Captain Kountz's years on the Ohio practically spanned the lifetime of steamboating. He could go back to the days when, it seemed, every ambitious man who had a little credit or could scrape together a few thousand dollars was building a contraption that came under the heading of "steamboat." With a small Brownsville engine and a paddle wheel at the stern, they were ready for business. They were not built to compete with the so-called packets, of which the miserable *Gallant* was one: the best they could hope to do was to scratch a living on such relatively unimportant rivers as the Allegheny, Guyandotte, Little Kanawha and Scioto.

When steamboats built below the Falls of the Ohio became so big that they couldn't make their way through the canal, Captain Kountz introduced the "short boat," designed for the special purpose of running down the Ohio to Louisville and through the Louisville-Portland Canal to Portland or Shippingport, several miles below, where freight and passengers could be transferred. The "short boats" were, as the name implies, short, an average 125 feet overall, and slow. But they were well suited for the work they had to do. Instead of turning back at Shippingport, some of the more venturesome went all the way down to New Orleans.

Marine architecture had undergone great changes since Captain Shreve came out with the first two-decker. A third deck had been added, and atop that, quarters for the officers of the boat, which, because it was an "addition" to the superstructure, was referred to with some flippancy as "the texas"—the thought behind it being that it was an addition to the boat much as the state of Texas was an addition to the Union. The name stuck and took its place in the language of the rivers. The pilothouse was moved to a new position atop the texas. Although it put the pilot high in the air, it gave him an unobstructed view up and down the river. The towering superstructure, thirty-five feet or more above the water, had one great disadvantage; a buffeting crosswind often made it impossible to hold a boat on her course. Many were blown upon known shoals and sandbars.

The three-deckers were handsome, and they quickly became the vogue. The great superstructure was all wood, every inch of it, and this increased the danger of fire. Up until 1848, exploding boilers had been the chief cause of steamboat disasters. Thereafter, losses by fire soon outnumbered destruction by explosion and all other hazards. It is part of the legendry of steamboating, especially steamboat racing, that the boilers were always fed with fat pine, resin or even lard. As a matter of fact, a great many, perhaps the majority, of steamboats on the Lower Mississippi had been using bituminous Pittsburgh coal for years. When the greatest of all steamboat catastrophes occurred, that of the *Sultana,* she was burning coal.

Equipped with modern (for that day) tubular boilers—one of which it was afterward alleged had been found defective when inspected at Vicksburg, three days previous—she had 2,200 mustered-out troops and liberated military prisoners aboard, on their way home, and in addition, 200 civilians, among them several bridal couples, when in the dead of night, a few miles north of Memphis on April 27, 1865, her whole battery of boilers exploded. "For weeks afterwards," to quote the reliable Garnett Askew, "the Mississippi below Memphis was strewn along its shore with stark, mangled bodies, lodged in the crotches of trees, caught horribly in the undergrowth of willows and cotton-

woods." According to the best figures available, 1,647 persons
perished.[4]

Far less tragic as to numbers but perhaps more spectacular
was the sinking of the palatial packet *Mississippi,* bound north
from New Orleans, on February 28, 1870. She was leaving
Natchez when she struck a snag and began to settle at once. As
she went down, her cabin parted from the hull and drifted off,
lights burning and some of her one hundred or more passengers
still sound asleep in their staterooms. The strange craft hung
together and was still afloat when it neared the mouth of Red
River in the graying dawn, where a towboat rescued its passengers. Ninety persons were saved; only the few who had leaped
into the water in their terror were lost. Testifying at the inquiry, Captain Sylvester Doss said: "I met the cabin of the
Mississippi on February 29th, at the mouth of Red River while
on my way up at the wheel of the towboat, *Tom Rees, II.* After
the passengers were rescued the cabin landed on the head of
Tunica towhead." Asked what his first thought was when he
saw a boat without a hull being swept along by the current, he
shook his head. "I knew I'd never seen nothing like that before."

Then, as now, the public's concern about steamboat disasters was largely confined to the tragedy of the dead and the
maimed; little thought was given to the staggering financial
losses of the owners. Many owners were able to survive only
because, barring accidents, the business in which they were engaged was so incredibly profitable. In the early days of steamboating, that is, up to the early 1840's, when the cost of a
steamboat seldom amounted to more than $50,000, it was often
demonstrated that she could pay for herself in one good season,
especially if engaged in the lucrative cotton trade, and leave
something over. As the boats increased in size and became palatial, this was no longer true. The *Grand Republic,* a giant of
887 tons burden, was reputed to have cost $300,000.

Ironically, the years preceding the outbreak of hostilities between the states were both the most active the steamboat business ever enjoyed and also the years of its heaviest losses: 299
steamboats were either destroyed or damaged in 1861–1862,

and of that number, 120 were a total loss. The Kountz Line lost two, both by fire. Sharf's *History* lists a great number of boats wrecked or destroyed by various causes on the Upper Mississippi and the Minnesota River.

Captain William P. Davidson's name does not appear in Sharf's book, but he had already begun the long career that was to establish him as the leading steamboat magnate of the upper rivers. Because of the constantly changing ownership of steamboats and the bewildering frequency with which even the old established lines—such as the St. Louis and Keokuk Packet Company, the Quincy Packets, Northern Line Packets and Captain Davidson's Northwest Union Packet Company, as well as half a dozen opposition lines—merged or were absorbed by competing lines, it was not always possible to say how many boats he owned or what lines he was seeking to control. In 1868 the two big competitors, Commodore Davidson's Northwest Union and the Keokuk Northern, merged, leaving only Joseph Reynolds' independent Diamond Jo Line, which was to become famous and survive all the others, as stubborn opposition.

Although the two merged lines, called the Keokuk-Northern Line Packet Company, did a tremendous business, it was so heavily overcapitalized that it never paid a dividend on its stock. After years of litigation, it was forced to reorganize in 1881. Davidson had engineered it, and when the smoke cleared away, he was in complete control of the old company. Its corporate name was changed for the last time, and under his skillful management the St. Louis and St. Paul Packet Company became a fixture.

Throughout the golden age of steamboating it was the boats themselves, not their owners, that won wide acclaim, even fame; the owners remained comparatively unknown to the public at large. The reverse was true on the Upper Mississippi and the Minnesota. Perhaps this was because St. Paul attracted a rare breed of men, individualists who had their own ideas of what was fitting. Davidson was one, and there were many like him. A Methodist but never markedly religious, he was "converted" in the winter of 1870–1871, while wintering with his family in

St. Louis. Thereafter, he became an ardent worker in temperance and religious reforms. He not only banned the sale of whisky on his boats but forbade gambling, dancing and all forms of diversion not sanctioned by the Methodist Church.

These edicts were bitterly resented by the men and women who traveled on his boats. It was bad for business, but he refused to relent. His business rival, Orrin Smith, a hidebound, God-fearing Methodist, when president of the Minnesota Packet Company, had refused to permit his boats to run between midnight Saturday and midnight Sunday and compelled the idle crew of his boats to attend services on board. When no minister was available, Orrin Smith himself sometimes delivered the sermon. Commodore Davidson didn't go that far, but on pain of dismissal, his captains were ordered to maintain proper Sabbath Day decorum aboard their boats.

Undoubtedly there were some infractions, for top-rated captains were too scarce a commodity to be dealt with so cavalierly. Most of them were as strong-willed as the commodore. Bill Laughton, master of the *Alexander Mitchell,* the company's finest boat, was one. He had a number of young people aboard who had been up to Mankato attending the fair when he steamed downriver one Sunday evening in September. They had a musician or two in the group, and they begged Captain Laughton to let them dance. Although it meant going against orders, he saw no harm in a little innocent diversion and told them to go ahead.

By midnight the dancers were safely in bed and apparently had escaped the wrath of heaven for their frivolity. Two hours later, however, a tornado tore down the river. The *Alexander Mitchell* lost both of her stacks, the roof of her pilothouse, and a piece of her hurricane deck. When the commodore surveyed the damages, he didn't fire Laughton, but he was stern with him. "Captain, you see what comes of dancing. Let this be a lesson to you."

IV

The Railroads Take Over

In the decade preceding the digging of the Erie Canal and the years following its successful completion, it was the widely held opinion that a great system of interlocking canals was the answer to the country's growing transportation problem. If canal travel was slow, it was also safe, clean and cheap. So confident was the public that canals were a sound investment that promoters had no difficulty in raising money for their construction. The number multiplied rapidly; they blossomed everywhere—Pennsylvania, New York, Connecticut, Massachusetts, Ohio and Indiana.

Some were profitable; others were dismal failures; some were begun and never finished. The introduction of steamboating on our Western rivers caused the canal enthusiasts no concern; the canalboat and the steamboat were bedfellows, both being waterborne; each would supply the other with new business. This proved to be true on the two canals running down from Lake Erie to the Ohio River. But as long as New Orleans remained the prime market for the produce and commodities of the great Central Valley, the steamboats got the long haul and, consequently, the better of the canal-river mutual assistance arrangement.

This is important because it very likely explains the fatuous thinking of steamboatmen a few years later, when their adversary was the railroad. While the canal interests had raised no outcry against the steamboat, it was a different story when the primitive railroads emerged from the experimental stage and began to challenge the canal companies for a share of the rich transportation business. Realizing that they had come face to face with their greatest enemy, they began a campaign of vilification against the railroads such as the country has seldom witnessed. Colored lithographs, depicting the slaughtering of women and children by the steam trains, appeared everywhere. In newspaper advertisements the railroads were assailed as the work of the devil; the clergy was enlisted to declaim from the pulpit that trains must not be permitted to run on the Sabbath; politicians, with a personal ax to grind, raised their voices against the steam cars.

It was all to no avail; the railroads had come to stay. They multiplied, spread out and put their iron fingers into the flatlands of the Middle West, where railroad building was comparatively inexpensive. The canals could not compete with them, and one after another were abandoned.

Under other corporate names than they bear today, three railroads—the Chicago and Northwestern, the Chicago and Rock Island, and the Great Western—reached the Mississippi at La Crosse, Prairie du Chien and Rock Island. Farther south the Mississippi and Ohio (a disguise for the Baltimore and Ohio) was driving hard for St. Louis. Why steamboatmen should have assumed that, having reached the Mississippi, the railroads would stop there defies explanation. But even such astute men as Commodore Davidson were of that opinion. He was in great haste to get control of the railroad business at La Crosse.

Having reached the great river, the railroads put out branch lines north and south, tapping country that heretofore had depended solely on the steamboats for their transportation needs. This ran contrary to the widely held opinion that the railroads were to be feeders for the steamboats. It soon became painfully clear that it was to be the other way around, that steamboats were to be relegated to being feeders for the rail lines.

In 1853, with no semblance of legality other than a charter granted by the state of Illinois, the Chicago and Rock Island Railroad began construction of a drawbridge at the Rock Island Rapids to span the Mississippi. Of it Captain Gould says: "It . . . was the most dangerous obstruction to navigation ever constructed, on account of its being located over a chain of rocks, producing boils and cross-currents which were difficult to keep a boat in. Many lives were lost in passing through the draw, and under the bridge, and many rafts were broken up. One fine steamboat, the *Effie Afton,* was sunk and many lives lost. An effort was made by the river interest to have the bridge removed as an illegal structure and dangerous to navigation. But such was the persistency of the proprietors that they defeated every effort in the several courts to which it was carried, and after fighting the bridge for more than ten years with the money and influence of the Merchants' Exchange of St. Louis, as well as that of many citizens along the river, and the best legal talent that could be employed, the bridge remained until removed by act of Congress in 1872, when by a sort of compromise the government built another bridge higher up the river at the head of the island, and removed the old one." [1]

Captain Gould neglects to say that among the counsel employed by the bridge company was a tall, lanky young lawyer by the name of Abraham Lincoln. He adds, however: "After the expenditure of more than $20,000 in litigation, of which the boatmen contributed very liberally, and to no purpose, they concluded it was not worth time or money to attempt to defeat a railroad in building bridges wherever they desired. Hence, whenever a road reached the bank of the river, they met with but little opposition in building any kind of bridge they fancied. The result is, there are already (1889) sixteen bridges on the Upper Mississippi, scarcely any one of which has been built with any regard to the navigation of the river, except the government bridge at Rock Island." [2]

It is unlikely that any opposition the steamboats could have mustered would have delayed for long the swift advance of the railroads throughout the Mississippi Valley. We may smile today at the boasted train speed of thirty miles an hour, which all roads claimed and seldom met, but it was so much faster than the finest steamboats that the latter could not hope to compete. The Civil War years postponed, but in no way averted, the inevitable ascendancy of one and the virtual demise of the other.

The Illinois Central Railroad, building down the length of that state, reached Cairo, at the mouth of the Ohio, in 1858. It was heavily burdened with debt, but it had the backing of the state and its land grant of better than two and a half million acres (the first ever granted to an American railroad) to keep it vigorous. "No railroad was ever more a child of the state than the Illinois Central," observed Stewart Holbrook, "and certainly no railroad ever did more for its parent . . . nor with such speed. In six years the Central turned great open spaces into a busy and, on the whole, prosperous commonwealth, perhaps the most striking metamorphosis accomplished by a railroad anywhere." [3]

Largely on the initiative of Captain Kountz, the best of all rail-boat accommodations was reached with the Illinois Central and the Mississippi and Ohio Railroad for the forwarding of freight and passengers to points in the Deep South, and the acceptance in turn of the freight and passengers brought north by the boats. Operating as the Railroad Line, ten of the best steamboats on the river enjoyed the privileges of this exclusive and immensely profitable arrangement. For the first time in steamboat history a schedule was maintained, the boats working in rotation. If for any reason one of the ten partners elected to sell his "place in the line" to an outsider for a given day, he was free to do so. Some idea of the lush business the Railroad Line was doing can be found in the prices paid for a "day in the line," which often amounted to a thousand dollars.

The war years brought an abrupt halt to this bonanza. The Railroad Line attempted to function in postbellum days, but the railroads were soon on the march again and closing the gap between the North and the South.

Undoubtedly it was the rich pickings enjoyed by the steamboats of the Railroad Line in the prewar years that led to the formation, in 1866, of the mighty Mississippi and Atlantic

Steamship Company, with a capital stock of $2,240,000, representing the appraised value of the twenty-five steamboats, the finest on the Ohio and Mississippi rivers, which it numbered among its assets. It was said, and it was very likely true, that it was the richest organization of its kind in the world. It issued its own tickets, which were accepted by all railroads and steamships plying between New Orleans and New York. That its ultimate intention was to monopolize steamboating on our Western rivers can hardly be doubted. In the first year of its existence it did a tremendous amount of business; it had agencies everywhere to speed passengers and freight on their way; its boats ran on schedule, and its captains, who had exchanged their boats for company stock, vied with one another in providing the traveling public with luxurious fare and accommodations without any regard for expense, since the company was paying the bills.

The directors of the corporation were practical steamboatmen, but without any knowledge of high finance or the management of an operation of that size. They made many mistakes, and coupled with the misfortune of losing three of their boats by fire while lying at the St. Louis wharf, and of others sinking, with consequent damage suits resulting from loss of life, the Mississippi and Atlantic Steamship Company was soon in financial trouble. The stockholders were assessed, but it was only a temporary stopgap. Its stock, which had been selling at par, became a drug on the market. In financial trouble, it sold its assets to pay its creditors; its stockholders got nothing. Captain Gould, who was its second president, says one man lost $450,000, but he does not identify him.

After several reorganizations the stable Anchor Line—St. Louis to New Orleans—emerged from the wreckage. But the railroads were to catch up even with the famous Anchor Line. Captain Gould says plaintively: "It hardly seems possible to those who once knew of the large number of regular freight and passenger boats employed in this trade that one boat per week would at this date (1889) be sufficient to accommodate that trade. But those who have witnessed the result of railroad competition need not be surprised at even this . . . from Pittsburgh

to Cincinnati, from Louisville to New Orleans, from St. Louis
to the Missouri River, in less than thirty years, the number of
regular boats has been reduced from sixty to none at all." [4]

The Government had been spending vast sums (they were
regarded as vast in those days) on the improvement of navigation on the Mississippi. A canal ten miles in length had been
dug around the Des Moines Rapids at Keokuk, and a safe channel blasted through the rocky Rock Island Rapids. And up in
St. Paul, men had begun to notice the youngster who had arrived there in 1856, at the age of eighteen, whose name was Jim
Hill, and who was to become the biggest "improvement," the
region of the Upper Mississippi was ever to receive. He was to
be many things to many different people; hated, reviled as the
Curse of the Northern Plains, the Evil Eye of all homesteaders;
and honored as the Wilderness Breaker, the matchless genius,
the Empire Builder of the Northwest.

In his lifetime Jim Hill—James Jerome Hill—was all of those
things and many more. His appearance in his youth has to be
left to the imagination. In his ripe middle-age he was a short,
stocky, shaggy-haired man, all shoulders and chest, who could
see more with his one eye than most men could with two. He
was from Ontario. His Canadian parents had wanted him to become a doctor, but the accidental discharge of an arrow had
cost him the sight of an eye. With a career in medicine closed to
him, he left home to do what he had always really wanted to do,
head west and make his way to the Orient. He was not to get to
the Orient until more than half a lifetime later, but when he
did, he was to view it from the deck of his own ocean liner.
Perhaps that was as it should have been, for he had begun his
rise to fortune as a steamboatman—one of the few if not the
only one to quit the water to become a builder of railroads.

Hill's first job in St. Paul was as a clerk in the office of the
Northwestern Packet Company. By applying himself to his
work, advancement came, and the following year he was given
the responsibility of fixing passenger and freight rates on the
company's boats. It put him in a position to observe the steadily
increasing number of immigrants coming into the country and

taking up land. Settling on or near one of the rivers, they formed their own little communities. The idea that the boats could do a profitable business supplying them with groceries and farm implements is said to have originated with young Hill. The packet company was induced to try it, and it soon became an important adjunct to its other business.

When the war came along, Hill tried to enlist and was rejected. It did not stop him from helping to organize the First Minnesota Volunteers. One effect of the war was the sudden demand for Minnesota wheat. When more and more flouring mills came into production, he set up in business for himself as a forwarding and transportation agent for the Northwestern Packet Company, the Milwaukee and Prairie du Chien Railway, and the Illinois Central. In 1866, he built his own warehouse and, in addition to the other lines, became agent for the St. Paul and Pacific, a decrepit little railroad, connecting St. Paul with the future Minneapolis, bogged down in debt, that somehow managed to keep a train or two rolling over its rusting rails. Presently, he contracted to supply the St. Paul and Pacific with fuel for its wood-burning locomotives.

Characteristic of the farsightedness he was to display throughout his life, Jim Hill, when he was only twenty-eight, set about securing options on the locally available sources of coal. When he had them tucked away, he persuaded the St. Paul and Pacific to convert from wood to coal. The experiment was so successful that Hill soon found himself in the coal business. Teaming up with Chauncey W. Griggs, another go-getter like himself, who was doing well in wholesale groceries, he established a fuel, freighting and merchandising concern under the name of Hill, Griggs and Company. Taking top billing for himself was typical of him; it was not his intention to run second to anyone.

With Jim's driving force behind it, Hill, Griggs and Company soon had a monopoly of the fuel business, wood and coal, of St. Paul and the far northern reaches of the Upper Mississippi and its tributaries. By steamboat, horseback and canoe, he traveled back and forth across Minnesota, cataloging its resources. No one knew the country better than he, and what he

learned he kept to himself against the day when he could ex-
ploit it to his own advantage. He journeyed to Pembina, the
only important American settlement on Red River, south of
Fort Garry (Winnipeg), the western headquarters of the powerful Ancient and Honourable Hudson's Bay Company, which
was fighting to maintain its stranglehold on the fur business of
that vast northern region stretching from the Great Lakes in the
east to the western Rocky Mountains.

As he watched the Red River of the North, a big, muddy
stream sweeping along ever northward, it did not take him long
to realize its practically untouched commercial possibilities. The
only steamboats plying the Red were the inadequate *Pioneer*
and the Hudson's Bay Company's boat, which in keeping with
company policy was forbidden to carry the freight of the numerous independent traders. That a line of boats serving the independents would do well was hardly open to question. But it
would require money, far more than he possessed.

The shaky little haywire St. Paul and Pacific, miring itself
ever deeper into debt, was of almost equal interest to him. Properly managed and extended to Pembina and north into Manitoba, with its untold miles of rich, black prairie soil, just waiting for the plow, it had possibilities that fired his imagination.
That he could ever hope to grab control of the road, and re-
vitalize and whip it into shape to reap what he was sure was its
potential worth, must have seemed to him at that time no more
than an interesting dream.

But things not of his doing were about to change the course
of his life. In 1869, the Hudson's Bay Company transferred its
territorial rights to the Dominion national government.[5] This
aroused the ire of French-Canadians everywhere and particularly of the Metis, the half-breed French-Indian population of
Rupert's Land (Manitoba), who feared that they were to become the pawn of the English-Scotch-Irish majority in Ontario
and the Maritime Provinces. Under the leadership of Louis
Riel, they rebelled, captured Fort Garry and at the International Boundary turned back the recently appointed Dominion
governor. In December, they set up a provincial government of

their own and named Riel president. The Red River Expedition, a force of fourteen hundred men, with artillery, was dispatched to the scene at once. Riel and his lieutenants fled at its approach and sought sanctuary in the United States.[6]

To ameliorate the situation the Dominion granted Manitoba full provincial status, renamed the former Red River settlement Winnipeg and designated it the provincial capital. It appeared to end the difficulties arising out of the Riel Rebellion, but in the United States, particularly in St. Paul, rumors grew that the Fenian Brotherhood was preparing to launch another invasion of Canada, presumably from Pembina, Dakota Territory, and join forces with Riel's followers. As a consequence, two companies of U.S. infantry were sent to Pembina in 1870 and ordered to erect a fort there, adjacent to the International Boundary. The Canadians and the United States had long maintained customs houses there; and a few miles to the north, the Hudson's Bay Company had a trading post. It was an agreeable arrangement, men and goods passing back and forth across the imaginary line with little or no formality.

William B. O'Donoghue, a fire-eating Irishman, and one of Riel's former lieutenants, was the self-proclaimed leader of the proposed insurrection, saying publicly that when his plans were perfected he would invade Canada at the head of several thousand men for the purpose of overthrowing the government of Manitoba and having the province annexed to the United States. How the small garrison at Fort Pembina (fifty-three enlisted men and three officers) was to turn back an invasion in such force, War Department records do not disclose. But time dragged, and with the coming of winter, always long and severe on the Northern Plains, it seemed that any attempt at invasion would have to be held in abeyance for months.[7]

Why, in dead winter, 1870, Jim Hill crossed Minnesota to the little settlement of Georgetown and went down frozen Red River a hundred and forty miles to Pembina on horseback, and on north from there by dog team, his destination Winnipeg, is a minor mystery. It was on this trip, by what appears to be accident, that he met Donald A. Smith, governor of the mighty

Hudson's Bay Company, for the first time. They met on the open, snow-covered plains, far from any human habitation. Smith was on his way to Ottawa, by way of St. Paul and the United States; Hill was bound, we are asked to believe, for Winnipeg. That meeting, and it was destined to be a memorable one—Hill always referred to it as the most important meeting of his life—has been painted by several famous artists— Smith, in his sled, surrounded by an escort of Northwest Mounted Police, and Hill, a solitary figure, swathed in furs, in his sled.

Donald A. Smith was the most important man in Western Canada; Jim Hill was still more or less a nobody. There is no telling what they found to talk about, what promises, if any, were made. But Donald Smith must have been impressed with the shaggy-haired, iron-jawed younger man with the rocky forehead. Certainly it was the beginning of an association—friendship would not be too strong a word—that was to last for the rest of their lives.

Hill must have brought something back with him, for presently Norman Kittson, the Hudson's Bay Company's purchasing and forwarding agent in St. Paul, became his confidant and advisor. When Hill informed Kittson that he planned to put a line of steamboats on Red River as soon as he could raise the money to finance the operation, the latter surprised him by offering to put up the capital and suggesting that they form a partnership. This was done, and the Red River Transportation Company came into existence. Its first boat, the *Selkirk,* a stern-wheeler, 133 feet overall, was the first steamboat of any consequence to ply Red River. An old line-cut pictures the rather handsome two-decker arriving at Winnipeg crowded to the rails with the first colony of Mennonite immigrants to reach Manitoba.

The *International,* the Hudson's Bay Company's old boat, boasting some improvements, continued to serve the company's own traders and posts. Several of the latter were located on the upper reaches of Red River, deep in U.S. territory and permitted to transact business by government license. In favorable stages of water the *International* got up as far as *Moorhead* (opposite Fargo).

Whether it was due to an arrangement made by Kittson, or some understanding Hill had with Governor Smith, there was never any conflict between the Red River Transportation Company and the Hudson's Bay Company. As Hill has said:

> I took over the representation of the outside parties—the outside traders and the different Church Societies and persons other than the Hudson's Bay Company. . . . I received their furs and skins and sold them for them; received their merchandise or anything they wished to buy; acted for them as their factor and agent.

The fact remains, however, that Hudson's Bay Company was his biggest customer. A great share of the assorted merchandise and material that his steamers and flatboats carried downriver to Winnipeg was consigned to Hudson's Bay. The Chicago, Milwaukee and St. Paul Railroad and Mississippi River steamboats were dumping tons of goods and hundreds of immigrants at St. Paul to be sent on to Winnipeg and other points in Manitoba. To handle this load, which had to be moved across the state to Red River, Hill put long trains of Red River carts and heavy ox-drawn freighters on the stage road that ran from St. Paul to St. George and provided passage for immigrants at a fraction of the regular stagecoach fare.

But this prosperity, bountiful though it was, was to be eclipsed tenfold when construction of Canada's great transcontinental railroad, the Canadian Pacific, moved westward out of Ontario and the railhead began marching across Manitoba. For weeks, the construction crews had been moving farther and farther away from their Canadian base of supplies at Fort William, at the head of Lake Superior. The only solution to that problem was to get the necessary steel and iron from Duluth, Minnesota, via St. Paul and Red River. Hill got the contracts. An accurate idea of their monetary value can be gained from Contract No. 18, dated May 22, 1875, with the Red River Transportation Company, amounting to $227,133.41, covering the "Carriage of rails, fish plates, bolts, etc. from Duluth to Winni-

peg, Man., or any point on the Red River between Pembina and
Winnipeg, at the rate of $15, per ton, U.S. currency, and in the
event of the Channel of the Red River being improved, same
rate, viz. $15. per ton, from Duluth to the point of crossing of
the Canadian Pacific Railway north of Stone Fort."

In the panic of 1873 that swept over the United States, the
St. Paul and Pacific Railroad was forced into bankruptcy. So
were many other railroads, including Jay Cooke's Northern
Pacific. In 1878, a syndicate composed of Hill, Donald A. Smith,
R. B. Angus and George Stephen, head of the Bank of Mon-
treal, and reputed to be the wealthiest man in Canada, bought
the St. Paul and Pacific for what Hill often said was "a fifth of
its value." A state land grant went with the franchise. It would
be better than gold in the bank; he would cut it up into quar-
ter-sections and sell them at a pittance to prospective settlers,
bringing families halfway across the continent at his expense if
necessary to get them to take up land along his railroad.

Hill was by now a rich man, but he needed millions, many
millions, for what he had in mind. The St. Paul and Pacific became the St. Paul, Minneapolis and Manitoba; but he had no
intention of stopping when it had been rehabilitated and its
rails reached Pembina. As early as 1879, he gave St. Paul the
best laugh it had had in some time by publicly declaring that
the St. Paul, Minneapolis and Manitoba was going all the way
through to Puget Sound. This grandiose idea was promptly
dubbed Hill's Folly. Without a government subsidy or federal
land grant, how could any railroad hope to build across two
thousand wilderness miles, cross the Rocky Mountains and the
Cascade Range? Jim Hill was to show them how.

When the St. Paul, Minneapolis and Manitoba reached Pembina, the Canadian Pacific built a branch line down from Winnipeg to meet it. It at once became a very busy line.

With his rear protected against the rival Northern Pacific
Railroad, Hill began the long march across Dakota and Montana. And he was out where the dirt was flying or ahead with
his surveyors. Neither heat nor snow, nor twenty-below-zero
temperatures, swollen rivers nor insect hordes could stop him.

The building of the Canadian Pacific was the saga of many men; the building of the Great Northern, which the Hill road became in 1890, was his alone. If ever one man can be said to have carried a railroad on his back to its final success, that man was he; in 1893 Great Northern rails reached the shores of the Pacific at Everett, Washington.[8]

Another financial panic was sweeping the country. The Northern Pacific went into receivership again. When the smoke cleared, the Northern Pacific was a Hill line. He also got control of the Chicago, Burlington and Quincy with its network of main lines and branches in the Mississippi Valley. Stateside, his railroad empire was complete when, despite all the powerful Southern Pacific could do to stop him, he put his rails into California. Eventually his trains were to reach San Francisco over the tracks of the Western Pacific. But there was another world to conquer—the Orient that had fired his imagination when a young man. From the preposterous castle he had built for himself in St. Paul, he dispatched several hundred agents to Japan and China to learn what those countries could buy from us and what we could buy from them.

It opened a whole new world of foreign trade—American cotton to Japan, American flour to China, and a thousand other things. Back came tea, silk, rubber and strange goods in endless variety. The Seattle waterfront became a very busy scene, yellow-funneled Hill liners rubbing shoulders with the sleek steamships of the Nippon Yusen Kaisha.

It was said of Jim Hill that there was nothing as loathsome to him as an empty Great Northern freight car. He didn't see many, for the long trains out of the Northwest carried a fabulous quantity of lumber to Iowa and the Midwest, and brought back machinery, sugar, flour and cotton. He went to his grave in 1916—he was seventy-eight—mourned by a few and unmourned by the many who blamed him for the recurring droughts, crop failures and the locust plagues. Steamboats, on which he had founded his fame and fortune, were gone from the Red, the Minnesota and Upper Mississippi. More than any other man, he was responsible for their disappearance.

V

The Wild Arkansas

WHEN THE DENVER and Rio Grande Railroad built a hanging
trestle to get its trains through the Royal Gorge of the Arkansas, in Colorado, the feat was hailed as one of the engineering
marvels of the times. Of the probably millions of passengers
who have experienced the thrill of traveling through that steep,
rocky canyon, the wild, furious river rushing along a few feet
below the car window, the great majority would find it difficult
to believe that the meandering, muddy stream flowing lazily
into the Mississippi, 1,450 miles away (which makes it the
fourth longest river in the United States), was the once "wild"
Arkansas they had observed in Colorado.

The character of the Arkansas, once it breaks out of the
Rockies and begins flowing through eastern Colorado and
across the Kansas plains, has changed so drastically in the past
century that it is asking almost too much to believe that less
than eighty years ago a shallow-draft steamboat was navigating
it as far up as Arkansas City, Kansas. Irrigation projects have
diverted so much of its natural flow that for ten months a year
it is a sluggish, meandering stream by the time it reaches Dodge
City, Great Bend, Wichita and the other famous old cowtowns.
To anyone familiar with its wide bottoms, sandbars and its

timid, uncertain channel, it must have seemed incredible that it could ever again show its teeth, but only in 1965, after weeks of rain in the mountains to the west, it went over its banks, flooded the low-lying bottoms and seriously threatened to put south Dodge City under water.

To understand the vagaries of this, the least known of America's big rivers, it will help if it is divided into an upper and a lower river, the division to occur where its name changes from *Ar-kansas,* which it is called in Colorado and Kansas, to *Arkansaw* in Oklahoma and the state of Arkansas.[1] That would be about where it flows through Arkansas City, Kansas. It should be realized also that its drainage basin is considerably larger than that of the Upper Mississippi.

If the Mississippi is excepted, no American river has wrought greater havoc than the periodic floodings of the Arkansas. These have destroyed thousands of acres of good cotton and corn land, swept away towns and taken the lives of an unknown number of people. The hills that largely confine the river to its course until it passes Little Rock have spared the upper country from its ravages, but once past Little Rock it is a different story. The river enters a flat, alluvial plain, with nothing to keep it from spreading out, often to a width of ten miles or more, putting everything in its path underwater and making a vast lake of the so-called delta country (trans-Mississippi Arkansas) and leaving it a region of sloughs, cypress swamps and miasmic jungle.

In his *Life on the Mississippi,* famous but often erratic Sam Clemens (rivermen seldom referred to him as Mark Twain), tells a fantastic tale of the total destruction of the sizable town of Napoleon, Arkansas, nestling at the confluence of the hungry Arkansas and Mississippi rivers. Napoleon was the prosperous county seat of Desha County. The federal government had thought well enough of it to erect there a four-story brick Marine Hospital. "The Arkansas River burst through it, tore it all to rags and emptied it into the Mississippi," Clemens quotes a steamboat captain as telling him. "Just a fifteen minute job, or such a matter. Didn't leave hide nor hair, shred nor shingle of it."

We expect some exaggeration from the remarkable Mark, but he goes the "whole hog" here. True enough, there wasn't "hide nor hair" left of Napoleon when the Arkansas got through with it, but its disappearance was not the result of any one flood or several floods; in fact, eating away the ground on which it stood was a slow, inexorable advance that began in 1864 and engulfed building after building until, in 1872, there truly was neither "shred nor shingle" of it left.

Since then, Little Rock, the state capital, has suffered on several occasions, and Pine Bluff, fifty miles downriver and the state's second largest city, has been overwhelmed on numerous occasions. But under the provisions of the U.S. Flood Control Act of 1938, reservoirs and check dams have been built on White River and other tributaries of the lower Arkansas, which have materially reduced the frequency and violence of the periodic floods of the past.

However wild the Arkansas has been on numerous occasions, it was on this river that Arkansas Post was established, the first permanent white settlement in the present state, sixty miles above its mouth. This was established by Henri de Tonty, Lasalle's able lieutenant, in 1686, and named by him Post Aux Arcansas, after the friendly Indians living there. It became the main, in fact only, thoroughfare to the West until the railroads began crisscrossing the state.[2] In a land without roads, transportation had to be by water—canoe, pirogue, keelboat and flatboat—prior to 1822, when the first steamboat, the *Robert Thompson*, ascended the river as far as Fort Smith, where the Poteau River, coming in from the south, flows into the Arkansas.

This followed by two years the first appearance of a steamboat on the Arkansas, Captain Byrne having ventured as far as Arkansas Post on March 31, 1820, with the little stern-wheeler *Comet*. On March 17, 1822, the diminutive *Eagle* reached the firmly established settlement a hundred and some miles farther upriver that had discarded its French name of Petit Roche for its English equivalent, Little Rock.

Although the *Comet* and the *Eagle* were propelled by steam, they were no better than converted keelboats. The *Robert Thompson* was of a different class. She was an authentic side-wheeler, all the way from Steubenville, Ohio. Her cargo consisted of three hundred tons of military supplies for Fort Smith. Before the year was over, she made three round trips from the Ohio to the Arkansas.

Although Fort Smith was only five years old at the time, it was our most important military post in what had been French Louisiana. The settlement that had grown up adjacent to it had as yet no commercial importance; the rich frontier trade in furs and peltries was located another 135 meandering miles upstream at the Three Forks, which marked the confluence of the Arkansas, Verdigris and Grand (called the Neosho, in Kansas) rivers. Looking for a return cargo, the *Robert Thompson* made it all the way to the Three Forks the following year. It may be said to have marked the opening of sporadic steamboat traffic between that region and the New Orleans market. Over the years the Three Forks trade grew in importance. Furs and peltries were the backbone of it, but there were other items in such volume that they were almost as important. Whatever the Indians had to barter they brought down the rivers to the Forks in their hollowed-out cottonwood pirogues, whole fleets of which often arrived at Webbers Shoals (the Falls of the Arkansas a hundred yards above the mouth of the Verdigris) in the course of a day.

Arkansas had only recently been detached from Missouri Territory and become organized as a territory in its own right, in 1819, with legal jurisdiction over the vast region beyond its western border vaguely known as "Indian territory," in which the Three Forks was located. If it was a wild land without any semblance of law, the same could be said of most of Arkansas.

In the early spring of 1824, the War Department, in one of its surprise moves, dispatched the steamboat *Florence,* a side-wheeler of sixty tons, to the Three Forks, with material for building Fort Gibson, on the Grand River, six miles from the Three Forks Landing. Aboard the *Florence* were Colonel Matthew Arbuckle, the designated commandant, and one hundred enlisted men, part of the force that was to garrison the new fort; the balance of the command had been forced to leave their boat at Fort Smith, owing to a breakdown of its engine, and were marching overland to their destination. They arrived two weeks later.

Fort Gibson was not built to offer protection to the traders and frontier merchants congregated at the Three Forks. They were in no need of protection; their relations with the Osages and the mountain Cherokees, who had voluntarily migrated to old Miller County, Arkansas, and the Three Forks country, were friendly. But the public (east of the Mississippi) had to be given an explanation, and it was told that Fort Gibson would complete the chain of frontier posts stretching down from Fort Leavenworth, Kansas, through Fort Scott and Fort Smith to old Fort Towson on Red River, with a consequent improvement in communications and travel between them.

But one wonders if the real reason was not to be found in the fact that the federal government was already resolved not to be thwarted in its long-deferred plans to remove the so-called Five Civilized Tribes (the Cherokees, Choctaws, Chickasaws, Creeks and Seminoles) from their homelands in Tennessee, the Carolinas, Georgia, Alabama and Mississippi, to what is now Oklahoma, known then simply as Indian territory—without a capital T—despite the violent opposition of the North. A military post in the Three Forks region would be in a strategic position to deal with the recalcitrant "civilized" tribes and the dispossessed Osage nation as well.

Both before and for years after the *Robert Thompson* inaugurated steam navigation to the Three Forks, New Orleans was the only market for the furs, hides, wild honey, bear grease and other homely products of that wild frontier. By pirogue, keelboat and flatboat they had been moving down the Arkansas for years. The extent of that trade can be judged by the fact that the leading traders, August Pierre Chouteau, Nathaniel Pryor, Hugh Glenn and others, had their own boatbuilding yards along the deep water at the mouth of the Verdigris.

Few regions—an area of less than fifty square miles—are as

rich in history as the Three Forks. Cutting through it ran the
famous Osage Trace, the most important Indian highway west
of the Mississippi. Running across Missouri from St. Louis to
the Grand (Neosho), it followed that river south to the Three
Forks and on down through today's Oklahoma to the Red River
and Texas. Over it, long before the white man made his appearance, Osage war parties had ridden to battle or on their horse-
stealing forays into Texas. Annually they came down to the salt
springs at La Saline, where August Chouteau had established
his great trading post, to make salt and trade, bringing their
women and children with them.

When Texas cattlemen began to trail their herds of Longhorns to northern markets—this was a quarter of a century before Joseph McCoy opened his Kansas market at Abilene—the
Osage Trace was to lose its old identity and become famous as
the Texas Road.[3] Texas had no sooner won its independence
than the Texas Road became the route of the speeding mail
coaches to the Southwest, and on their heels came thousands of
emigrant families from the Midwest, bent on taking up free
land in the new republic. In 1845, Lieutenant J. W. Abert, on
his way north from Fort Gibson to St. Louis wrote: "In the past
several days we have passed hundreds of wagons burdened to
bursting with household impedimenta and children, and many
of them trailing a cow or two behind. The men are lean,
bearded fellows. Most of them are from Kentucky, and have
only a vague idea of where they are going to settle. But they're
all bound for Texas." [4]

In its early days, being on the outermost fringe of civilization, the men who foregathered at the Three Forks were, as
could be expected, trappers, hunters, traders and adventurers
of one sort or another. But there were exceptions. The little
redhaired man who came up the Arkansas by keelboat in 1819
was one. He was not looking for riches that could be measured
in gold. He was Thomas Nuttall, the traveled English naturalist
who was both botanist and ornithologist. The furs and skins
brought into the frontier trading posts had given the scientific
world a fairly comprehensive idea of the fauna of the Western

Plains, but little or nothing was known about its avifauna and flora. Nuttall's inner excitement as he tarried at the Three Forks, knowing that he was to be the first man of a scientific turn of mind to explore the virgin wilderness beyond, can be imagined. He knew he would be exposing himself to the gravest sort of danger, but the thought of the veritable Pandora's Box of rare treasures that he would be able to open must have made any fear of personal danger of very little importance.

When he began to outfit himself and let it be known that he proposed to go alone to the headwaters of the Arkansas, gathering specimens of flowers, grasses and bird life, rough men, who thought to befriend him, tried to dissuade him. But to no avail.

Nuttall was shy and withdrawn and somewhat eccentric. He stammered, and he was very sensitive about it, even in his later years when he had largely overcome the impediment and was curator of the botanical gardens at Harvard University. Miraculously, he escaped attack by the warring Pawnees, who were making life miserable for their old enemies, the Osage nation, which was torn with tribal dissensions. He was unfortunate enough to lose many of the specimens he had collected by the accidental overturning of a dugout.

Such incidents were of small consequence to the indomitable little man; if work had to be done a second time, he had the energy and perseverance to do it. When he went up the Arkansas he was already an experienced wilderness traveler. It was not to be the last of his Western explorations—in all, he logged over five thousand miles on his wilderness roamings.

His experiences and scientific achievements aroused the lasting enthusiasm of John Kirk Townsend, the well-known ornithologist of the Academy of Natural Sciences, of Philadelphia, and established a bond between them. Nuttall was not an easy man to know or even to get along with, but the younger Townsend seems to have understood him better than most, and some years later induced him to join him in accompanying Captain Nathaniel Wyeth's expedition to the Columbia River and the Oregon country.

Nuttall had predicted, as Meriwether Lewis had before him

in a letter to President Jefferson, and as General James B. Wilkinson had in 1806, that the "transportation advantages so apparent at the confluence of the Arkansas, Grand and Verdigris, were such as to leave no doubt that, coupled with the irresistible tide of Western emigration, it was only a matter of time that a thriving town would be established there that would dominate the commercial life of the region." [4]

Washington Irving, the first giant of American literature, was similarly impressed when he visited the Three Forks in 1832. The river steamboat was a proved success by then, and his prediction took that into account—the first to do so. At least a dozen steamboats were plying the Arkansas. In the New Orleans newspapers, as early as 1829, the steamboat owners were advertising sailings from that city to the "Creek Agency," which was the Three Forks. Irving could not have foreseen, nor anyone else, at that time, 1832, that railroads would be invading this country while it was still the frontier (forty years hence, to be exact), and that transportation by water would fade into insignificance.

Many tales have been told about the luxury in which Colonel Auguste Pierre Chouteau indulged himself at Grand Saline, his trading post on the Neosho River, forty miles north of Fort Gibson. His father, Jean Pierre Chouteau, and his father's brothers had amassed great wealth in the fur trade, and his son was well qualified to add new luster to the family name. He was both fair and just with the Indians, and stern when occasion demanded. It was a combination of virtues that the redmen understood and respected. His wife was a comely Osage woman, about whom travelers have spoken highly, which further guaranteed him the loyalty of the Osage nation. With Negro slaves to serve him and Indian hunters to provide his table with wild turkey, venison and other gustatory delights of the forest, he lived the life of a wilderness potentate.

Trading with both St. Louis and New Orleans enabled him to supply himself with the finest wines, liquors and other luxuries. He must have imported them in quantity, for he was famous for the lavish hospitality he dispensed. No one found it more enjoyable than the officers at Fort Gibson. For them it made frontier duty bearable. But while Colonel Chouteau entertained and relaxed at Grand Saline, his business was largely conducted at his trading post on the east bank of the Verdigris, across that river from the Osage subagency where his half-brother Paul Liguest was the Indian agent. He couldn't have selected a more favorable spot on which to locate the headquarters of his trading enterprises; the steamboat landing was at his door, and could be easily reached by his bushrangers and the *bourgeois* (agents) from his distant posts.

Certainly Chouteau was the first, or one of the first, to know that changes were about to take place in the region of the Three Forks and its hinterlands that would seriously threaten the future of his frontier empire. The hour of decision had come for the government to resort to arms in its efforts to remove all Five Civilized Tribes to the unpopulated lands west of the Mississippi. The Creeks, betrayed by their principal chief, had consented to go, but the great majority of the Cherokee nation refused to be bribed or intimidated. President Jackson signed the order for their removal and dispatched General Winfield Scott with three thousand troops to bring them to terms, "using such force as may be necessary."

In white Georgia the order was hailed with delight; in the North it was called "the darkest blot ever put on the escutcheon of the United States." What followed—the betrayal and subjugation of the Cherokees, ending in their "Trail of Tears"—is too well known to need repeating here.[5]

In 1827, Chouteau sold all his buildings on the east bank of the Verdigris to the U.S. government and retired to Grand Saline. His old trading post became Creek Agency, and the following February, the steamboat *Facility*, owned and commanded by Captain Phillip Pennywit, arrived at the Three Forks with 780 Creeks, several hundred of whom were packed in the two keelboats the *Facility* had in tow. It was the first contingent of the 20,000 who were to follow.

The exiles were bewildered and starving—the government had made no arrangements to feed them. But they had arrived safely, which was not the fate that awaited many others.[6] Under the direction of David Brearly, the U.S. agent, and his assistants, they spread out over the tremendous reservation, west of the Three Forks, to which they had been assigned, and established their tribal capital and named it Okmulgee for the capital they had left behind and would not see again.

If the coming of that first party of Creeks has its niche in the history of Indian Territory, so does Captain Pennywit, the master of the *Facility,* who brought them to the Three Forks. He was to bring thousands of Indian émigrés up the river. But quite aside from that, his foresight and progressiveness were to lift haphazard Arkansas River steamboating to the level of an organized, scheduled business.

When the *Facility* left the Forks on her first downriver trip, her manifest included, in addition to the usual furs and hides, "2 casks of bacon, 4 tubs of beeswax and 350 barrels of pecans." She arrived at New Orleans nine days later and was back with cargo for Fort Gibson in less than thirty days. A round trip every thirty days from Fort Gibson to New Orleans was the goal Captain Pennywit was striving for. When he followed the *Facility* with the *Waverley,* a new and faster boat, he had no difficulty in maintaining it.[7]

Downriver, the red soil of Arkansas was producing an ever-growing crop of cotton. It meant prosperity for the planters and the steamboats. When he tied up at the Little Rock landing, Pennywit found the bales piled high, waiting to be carried off to New Orleans. Naturally such bounty attracted competition. In April, 1827, three steamers, the *Velocipede, Scioto* and *Catawba,* arrived at Fort Gibson in one day. Arkansas River steamboating was surely picking up.

VI

Rebel River

ALTHOUGH YEARS WERE TO PASS before the enforced migration
of the Creek nation was complete, they were settled on their
new lands when the embittered and war-weary Seminoles began
arriving in Indian Territory (given a capital T by now) and
were placed on their designated reservation to the west of the
Creeks. Of the Five Tribes only the Creeks and the Seminoles
came by way of the Arkansas River; the Cherokees arrived by
land, marching the last several hundred miles over the Osage
Trace or Texas Road; the Choctaws and Chickasaws were
brought up Red River, on which their reservations fronted, by
steamboats.

Steamboating on the Arkansas had increased to the point that
the Little Rock *Gazette* was moved to remark: "The sight of a
steamboat gliding majestically through the waters of the Arkansas can no longer be considered a novelty. Fully eighteen
steamboats are regularly ascending to the Three Forks. Their
average speed is eight miles per hour, and one can travel to
Fort Smith or Fort Gibson in safety and without any inconve-
nience as regards meals and sleeping accommodations."

This was painting the lily somewhat, as the following letter
from a disgruntled subscriber, lately a passenger on the steamboat *Swallow*, testifies:

She is typical of a numerous class on this river [the Arkansas] and no better than a scow with a pointed stem. Flatbottomed and drawing only a few inches of water, she still managed to ground several times and it became necessary to set the poles [those steamboat "crutches" or "shears" which all steamboats carry] and when they were firmly embedded in the river bottom and tackle fastened to the bow, all hands fell to at the windlass and we literally lifted her over the shoals. Cord wood, freight, crew and passengers were all crowded together on one deck. The public should be warned of what to expect before embarking on one of your elegant steamboats.

In 1830, Sam Houston, the erstwhile governor of Tennessee, who had hurriedly resigned his position and fled the state to escape the calumnies growing out of his marital difficulties, arrived by keelboat at the Three Forks, bringing with him an estimated forty tons of assorted merchandise with which to stock the trading post it was his intention to establish.

Evidently he was aware that the band of Cherokees with whom, as a young man, he had lived off and on for two years in the wilds of eastern Tennessee would be on hand to welcome him. He settled among these old friends, midway between the Verdigris and Fort Gibson, and with Cherokee labor built the log house that he named Wigwam Neosho. There he lived for more than two years with his new Cherokee wife, Diana Rogers, called by the Indians Tiana. Will Rogers was her nephew, three generations removed.[1]

The fact that Houston's funds were limited leaves little doubt that he made a serious attempt to support himself on the profits of his trading business. There is no evidence, however, at any time, up to 1832 when he left on his Texas adventure, that his trade had ever been extensive enough to provide him with a living. By his own admission, he was often his own best customer, as far as potables went. But even when he was in his cups, he claims to have made a virtue of never selling whisky to the Indians. In his autobiography, written many years later, he says:

During the entire period I resided in that region [two years], I was unceasing in my efforts to prevent the introduction of

ardent spirits among the Indians; and though, for a year, I had
a trading establishment between the Grand River and the Verdigris, I never introduced or trafficked in those destructive drinks.
This, too, was at a period when I was far from being a practically
temperate man myself. But, whatever might be my own occasional
indulgences during my visits to Fort Gibson and other white settlements, I had too much humanity and love for the Red man,
ever to contribute to their crimes or their misfortunes by introduc-
ing or trafficking in those damnable poisons.[2]

Whether he conducted himself with the nobility he claims,
or was just making another of the flowery rhetorical statements
for which he was famous, must be measured against the following letter to Colonel Matthew Arbuckle, the commandant at
Fort Gibson, dated July 21, 1830:

I have the honor to inform you of the arrival of my Boat with
an assortment of goods which I will proceed to open and make
sale of soon as convenient.

I ordered to this point for my own use and the convenience of
my establishment, five barrels of whisky (four of Monongahela
and one of corn), one barrel of cognac brandy, one of gin, one of
rum, and one of wine. . . . The whisky excepting one barrel will
be stored with the [post] sutler, Gen'l Jno. Nicks, subject to your
orders . . . and not to be used without your knowledge or consent
nor shall one drop of whisky be sold to either soldier or Indian.
I entertain too much respect for the wishes of the Government—
too much friendship for the Indians and too much respect for
myself.[3]

In this one shipment he acknowledges receiving nine barrels
of intoxicating spirits. Presumably in two years there were other
shipments. If he was foresworn against selling liquor to the
Indians or soldiers, he could dispose of his potables only to
white hunters and trappers, very few of whom were trading with
him.

His letters are testimony that his fortunes were at a low ebb
and that he had little hope of improving them. Andrew Jackson was his great friend, and it had been widely predicted that
he would be Jackson's successor in the White House. That was

all behind him now. In his despondency he began drinking heavily. In fact, he was drunk so much of the time that he lost face even with the Cherokees for whom he had tried to do so much. Behind his back they laughed at him and called him Big Drunk.[4]

How he could have expected any favors from Washington after exposing the dishonesty of Indian agents who were paying their charges their annuities in scrip instead of gold, as had been guaranteed them, and then purchasing the paper at a discount of 25 percent, is difficult to imagine. Nevertheless, he put in a bid to supply the Indians with their rations. It backfired on him and involved both John Eaton, the Secretary of War, and himself in charges of fraud.

Houston was still at Wigwam Neosho, in October 1832, when Washington Irving arrived at Three Forks, in the party accompanying Henry L. Ellsworth, newly appointed U.S. Commissioner to treat with the Western Indians. Houston and Irving met, but Irving mentions him only once in his vivid and zesty *A Tour of the Prairies,* a brief description: "Gov. Houston, tall, large, well-formed, fascinating man—given to grandiloquence. A large and military mode of expressing himself." [5]

Possibly traveling in the party of an official of a government with whom Houston was in disfavor may account for their not becoming better acquainted. Or it could have been that the famous visitor found the man so besotted that it was a kindness to ignore him. However that may have been, it was only a few weeks later that Houston left for Texas to win fame and everlasting glory, having given Wigwam Neosho and what lands he owned to Tiana.

It was the Indians who captured Irving's attention. He wrote:

> The Osages are the finest looking Indians I have ever seen in the West. They have not yielded sufficiently, as yet, to the influence of civilization to lay by their simple Indian garb, or to lose the habits of the hunter and the warrior; and their poverty prevents their indulging in much luxury of apparel.
>
> In contrast to these was a gaily dressed party of Creeks. There is something, at the first glance, quite oriental in the appearance

of this tribe. They dress in calico hunting shirts of various brilliant colors, decorated with bright fringes, and belted with broad girdles, embroidered with beads; they have leggings of dressed deer skins, or of green or scarlet cloth, with embroidered knee bands and tassels; their moccasins are fancifully wrought and ornamented; and they wear gaudy handkerchiefs tastefully bound round their heads.[6]

Irving had the same eye for color and detail that characterize the Indian paintings of George Catlin. It is erroneously believed by some that when he visited Fort Gibson he became acquainted with Captain Benjamin Louis Eulalie de Bonneville, the well-known Western explorer and fur trader, whose biographer he became in his *Adventures of Captain Bonneville*. It is true that Bonneville was stationed at Fort Gibson when several rich and politically powerful friends of John Jacob Astor secured for him a two-year leave of absence from the army. But he had left Gibson approximately a year prior to Irving's arrival, and it was not until 1834 that they met for the first time in New York City.[7]

Other notables were stationed at Fort Gibson in the years before the Civil War, among them Lieutenant Jefferson Davis and General (later President) Zachary Taylor.

By 1838 the task of settling the Five Civilized Tribes on their vast reservations in what we know today as Oklahoma was largely completed. Placing over one hundred thousand semi-civilized Indians on their allotted lands was only the beginning of the government's treaty obligations to the redman; they had to be supplied with rations, the basic implements of husbandry, which included some livestock, and their cash annuities, the last being quite apart from the sums paid into the various tribal treasuries. Since all supplies for the Cherokees, Creeks and Seminoles had to be transported up the Arkansas, the steamboat business enjoyed an unparalleled prosperity. Anything that would float was pressed into service.

Small steamers from the Yazoo and the Bayou country came up to get in on a good thing. The newcomers and the natives were all thin-shelled, fragile craft of a hundred tons or less. Accidents were frequent, but if a snag ripped through a boat's hull, she usually was raised, hastily repaired and returned to duty—sometimes hiding under the alias of a new name if lives had been lost. The casualness with which accidents were treated may be gathered from this item in the Arkansas *Gazette* of June 30, 1835:

> The steamboat Tom Bowling which recently had a hole stove in her bottom by running on a rock at Webbers Shoals, and was brought to this place to be repaired, sank at our landing last night and is now lying completely under water to her hurricane deck. It is presumed that she will be raised at once.

An advertisement in the same issue of the *Gazette* is further evidence of the complacency with which steamboat accidents were accepted by the traveling public. The *Eveline* had blown a boiler, killing three people:

> S.S. EVELINE, B. Irwin, Master.
> The steamboat *Eveline* having undergone thorough repairs cannot be surpassed by any boat on the river, for speed or the convenience of passengers or safety of freight.
>
> > Henry & Cunningham, Agents,
> > Van Buren, Ark.

In addition to the boats engaged in the local trade, there were several larger steamers running on the lower river that could hold their own with the best Mississippi River boats of comparable size. In Little Rock and Pine Bluff one could book passage for such distant points as St. Louis, Louisville and Cincinnati. Passengers for New Orleans sailed with Captain Pennywit. Pennywit had become the unofficial press-agent of Arkansas. For years he had been spreading word of the equable climate of central Arkansas and the health-giving wonders of the baths at Hot Springs. It was he who launched the state in the tourist business by bringing forty ladies and gentlemen up from New Orleans to spend the summer at Hot Springs.

Coincident with the coming of the Five Tribes, the fur business had declined—not so much because of the influx of the thousands of Indians, but because the interest of the big St.

Louis fur companies had shifted to the beaver country of Wyoming and the Rocky Mountains. As the fur business waned,
traffic up and down the Texas Road began to reach its peak, and
the pulse of the Three Forks–Fort Gibson region quickened to
new life and importance. As the 1840's drew to a close, the
number of Texas Longhorns crossing the Arkansas at the Three
Forks rose to an annual figure of forty thousand or more. The
riverbanks, cut down by their hoofs, still show where they
passed. Trail driving had become an organized business. Thirty
years later it was to result in the greatest mass movement of
cattle the world has ever known, when no fewer than four million Longhorns (a conservative estimate) carved deep in the
prairie sod those most famous of all cattle trails, the Chisholm
and the Western Trail.

Right of way on the Texas Road was in daily dispute between
the northbound herds and the long trains of wagons headed for
Texas. Stories are told of wagons being lined up for a mile or
more as they waited to be ferried across the Arkansas. Turnouts
on the road were frequent, and in places they became a mile
wide.

Ever since the coming of the Five Tribes the military duty
of the Fort Gibson command had been so anomalous as to leave
it practically impotent. In a land where there was no law other
than tribal law, the command was charged with keeping peace
between the tribes, and at the same time expressly forbidden to
interfere in any matter involving only Indians. Among the
Cherokees, murders were committed almost daily as the result
of the bitter intratribal feud between the so-called Treaty Party
and the Nontreaty Party (one side accusing the other of being
responsible for the removal to the West). Since it was a matter
in which only Indians were concerned, the army could do nothing about it.

One morning in early December, 1855, traffic on the Texas
Road was forced to draw aside as the newly commissioned U.S.
2nd Cavalry from Jefferson Barracks, south of St. Louis, came
pounding down from Tahlequah, the Cherokee tribal capital,
on its way to Texas, where it was to take part in the campaign

to subdue the wild Plains Indians, principally the Comanches and Kiowas. With its ten companies numbering 750 men, 800 horses and its commissary and supply wagons drawn by 650 mules, making in all a line several miles in length, it must have been an imposing spectacle.[8]

Before long the hostilities that were to disrupt the nation began casting their shadow before them. The character of the families moving southward over the Texas Road began to change; they no longer were from Illinois, Kentucky and Ohio; they were Southern sympathizers fleeing Missouri, where the Border War between proslavery and nonslavery guerrillas was beginning to ravage the western counties of that state.

When the Great War finally came, Arkansas was one of the last of the Southern states to secede from the Union. On May 6, 1861, it formally cast its lot with the Confederacy. Prior to secession, Governor Elias Rector sent two steamboats loaded with militia and cannon up the Arkansas, under command of Colonel Solon Borland, to demand the surrender of Fort Smith to the state of Arkansas. In some manner U.S. Captain S. D. Sturgis, post commander, learned the purpose of the expedition in time to transfer his troops and all movable material across the line into Indian Territory.

Even among Civil War buffs, the Battle of Pea Ridge, in the extreme northwestern corner of the state, is regarded as the only major engagement fought on Arkansas soil. It was acclaimed a "glorious victory" by both sides, and it still is, depending where your sympathies lie. The Union command numbered between 10,000 and 11,000 men, supported by 40 fieldpieces; General Van Dorn, the Confederate, had a combined force of 16,000 infantry and cavalry, which included General Albert Pike's Indian brigade of approximately 2,500. The casualty figures show that the losses on both sides were about even. However, after the Battle of Pea Ridge, Van Dorn retired to the east and moved his army across the Mississippi River, leaving the state at the mercy of the Union forces.

There were engagements that were little better than skirmishes throughout the summer, and it was not until December 7,

1861, that the second of three major battles fought within the boundaries of the state took place at Prairie Grove, in Washington County. Thomas C. Hindman, a Helena lawyer, had raised and trained a well-equipped army of 10,000 men. When the battle was joined, General Hindman found himself facing General Francis J. Herron and his Iowa militiamen. Hindman was giving them a trouncing when Union General James G. Blunt and 7,000 Kansas volunteers joined the fray and turned the tide against the Confederates. They retired south across the Arkansas and devoted themselves to keeping the river open for the steamboats that were supplying the Rebel armies east of the Mississippi with food and grain. This they were able to do until Union gunboats blockaded the mouth of the river.

In the meantime, Union troops had captured and fortified the town of Helena, on the Mississippi. In the hope of relieving the pressure General Grant was putting on Vicksburg and opening a new supply line to the Rebel armies, General Sterling Price, in command of what Confederate forces remained in Arkansas, ordered General Theophilus Holmes, a West Pointer, to attack Helena. The fortifications proved too strong for him. It was the third and last major engagement in Arkansas.

It was a double defeat for the Arkansans, for on that day, July 4, 1863, Vicksburg fell. Grant immediately ordered General Frederick Steele to move his forces to Helena and organize an attack on Little Rock, the Rebel capital. It was September 7 before General Steele marched down from Helena to the Arkansas. He was harassed most of the way by rifle fire. Ahead of him he had General Price waiting with at least 8,000 troops. He had every reason to believe that General Price would resist him at all costs, but when he reached Little Rock, Price and his army were gone. Burning fiercely at the wharf were eight steamboats to which the torch had been applied. Also burned at Arkansas Post were the steamers *Rose Douglas, Little Rock, Chester Ashley, Daniel B. Miller, Violet, Cedar Rapids* and the *St. Francis* on White River. A week before Little Rock was captured, Fort Smith fell without a struggle. As far as Arkansas was concerned, the war was over.

Across the line in Indian Territory the fighting continued, most of it confined to the Texas Road. The country had been laid waste and thousands of Indians were facing near-starvation. On July 16, 1863, the combined Confederate forces of General Douglas Cooper (Choctaws, Chickasaws and Texans) and the Indian Brigade of Colonel Stand Watie (later commissioned a general by the CSA and the last to surrender) had been dealt a crushing blow at Honey Springs, fifteen miles south of Muskogee.[9] But the war dragged on, and it was not until June 23, 1865, when Stand Watie rode into old Fort Towson and surrendered his command, that peace of a sort returned to the Texas Road and the Three Forks.

In less than forty years it had witnessed the disappearance of the fur trade that had given it its first importance, the coming of the Five Tribes, the passing herds of Longhorns, the great migration to Texas, the excitement of the thousands of gold seekers rushing to California and the prosperous days of Arkansas River steamboating. All these were gone and would not come again. Save for the notoriety it was to gain as the refuge of desperate outlaws, many of whom had their careers of crime cut short by Judge Isaac Parker, the famous "Hanging Judge" at Fort Smith, its future history was to be of only local interest.

Of all the seceding Southern states, Arkansas was the poorest financially and its population the smallest. At war's end it was prostrate. Of its able-bodied men, fewer than three thousand had died on their native soil, but many times that number had lost their lives on the blood-soaked battlefields of Mississippi and Tennessee. Arkansas had stripped itself of food—hogs, beef cattle, corn and other grains—to help feed the armies of the Confederacy. The Arkansas, the lifeline of the state, once so busy, showed no sign of life; no plume of smoke rose to the skies to mark the passing of a steamboat. Months passed before several steamers that had lain in the mud at the bottom of the river for a year and a half were raised, repaired and put into service.

Just when the state showed signs of pulling itself together, it was slapped down a second time by Reconstruction and the imposed carpetbag government. But the Arkansans were a tough-minded people, and five years after the surrender at Appomattox, they were clawing their way back to prosperity. There was money in the state treasury again, and new steamboats that rated comparison with the finest to be found anywhere on the Western waters were plying the old Rebel River.

For such steamers as the *Pat Cleburne,* built at Cincinnati, named for the Irish-born Arkansas general, the *Albert Pike* and the *James Howard* (the latter from the famous Howard yard at Jeffersonville, Indiana), Little Rock was the head of navigation; the *Gem, Thirty-fifth Parallel,* the *Arkansas* and other small fry still ran to Fort Smith, which was no longer a military post. The cry was for more and more cotton, and Arkansas found itself sending more than 150,000 bales downriver annually.

The high postwar price of cotton was bringing a flood of Yankee dollars into Arkansas. With this unexpected prosperity, steamboat travel became the most exciting adventure of the times. In St. Louis the gentlemen put up at the new and luxurious Planters Hotel and matched wits with Northern speculators; from New Orleans the ladies brought back the latest in French fashions—or so they believed.

But the days of steamboat glory on the Arkansas were short-lived. In a dozen different directions little independent, poorly financed railroads (later to be absorbed into the Cotton Belt–Missouri Pacific System) were laying tracks and reaching out for the river business. As they merged and were able to offer better and faster service, the old, old story was repeated: the steamboats lost their popularity and trade and were forced to find a living elsewhere. To all intents, it marked the end of Arkansas River steamboating.

Somehow, in June, 1878, the *Aunt Sally,* no larger than an inland-water tug, made her way up to Arkansas City, Kansas, where no boat driven by steam power had ever been seen. Local merchants, in the mistaken belief that the town could be established as an inland shipping point, built the small steamer *Kansas Miller* (later renamed the *Cherokee*). After numerous groundings the experiment was abandoned, and the *Cherokee* became a local excursion boat, operating when the stage of the river permitted.

Without any regard for sentiment the railroads gave Arkansas River steamboating the final *coup de grace* when the Little Rock, Memphis and Texas road purchased the disemboweled hull of the once-famous *Robert E. Lee* and towed it up to Little Rock for its wharf boat. The fine old boat endured that ignominy for several years before it caught fire and became a total loss. The once great *Natchez,* its formidable rival of other days, suffered even greater shame, ending its days, before it too was destroyed by fire, as a storage hulk for a refuse oil plant at Vicksburg, Mississippi.

The patron saints of steamboating must have turned away in tears.

VII

Red River of the South

MANY STEAMBOAT BUFFS have in their collections of old photographs a picture of the *R. T. Bryarly* as she was pulling away from the landing at Shreveport, Louisiana, in early September, 1859, so heavily laden with baled cotton that only her texas, pilothouse and stacks are visible. Recent rains somewhere on the upper river had the Red standing higher than usual for that time of year. It enabled her to clear the rapids at Alexandria without difficulty, and two days later she was discharging cargo at New Orleans.

The *Bryarly* could lay no claim to luxury, nor could the hundred and more steamboats with whom she was running in competition. They were just river workhorses, engaged in moving a tremendous tonnage of cotton, molasses and other sugarcane products, sulphur and assorted farm produce out of one of the richest valleys in America to the outside world, which meant almost inevitably the New Orleans market. What they brought back was as varied as the needs of such towns as Alexandria, Natchitoches (pronounced Nak-a-tosh, unless you want to be identified as an outsider), Shreveport, a dozen smaller towns and innumerable plantation landings.

Some idea of the volume of Red River steamboating can be

gained by examining the New Orleans wharf records for the 1859–1860 season ending on October 31, admittedly the banner year of steamboating: arriving from Red River, 488, while arrivals from St. Louis numbered only 472.

These figures become even more remarkable when it is remembered that practically all of the approximately seven hundred miles of navigable water on Red River is found within the state of Louisiana—that is, from its confluence with the Mississippi north to Fort Towson Landing, in Oklahoma. Several times in periods of high water, boats risked going up the river the additional few miles to Preston, on the Texas side. Towson, however, was generally accepted as the head of Red River navigation.[1]

A glance at a map will reveal the Prairie Dog Town Fork of Red River, which has been established by law as its main channel, flowing out of Palo Duro Canyon, the deep crack in the Llano Estacado or Staked Plains that stretch away in New Mexico. From its source it strikes across the breadth of the Texas Panhandle in a generally southeast direction until it reaches Cache Creek, and from there, still persuing the same general course, it forms the boundary between Oklahoma and Texas. Fifty miles east of old Towson Landing it enters Arkansas, and in another fifty miles, when it reaches Fulton, it changes direction sharply and strikes south through the lush green central valley of Louisiana.

If the Arkansas must be regarded as two rivers in one, with the upper and lower rivers having little in common, the same is doubly true of the Red River of the South—a name, by the way, that is almost never used by the people who live on or near it. To them it is just Red River or, more familiarly, the Big Red. Although it had long enjoyed historical importance, having been used in our treaty with Spain in 1819 to mark the boundary between their possessions and ours, and again to the same purpose in our treaty with the United Mexican States in 1828, and a third time in a boundary treaty with the Republic of Texas in 1838, it was a river of mystery, unknown, unmapped west of Fort Towson, until the expedition commanded by Captain Randolph B. Marcy traced it to its source in 1852.

Previously, in 1849, Marcy, as the commander of the military escort accompanying a party of several hundred gold seekers on their way to California, had staked out what came to be known as the "California Road" between Fort Smith and Santa Fe, New Mexico. So, in exploring the upper course of Red River, he was seeing much of that country, inhabited only by roving bands of Comanche and Kiowa Indians, for the second time. In his report to Congress, he calls it "that sterile land, deserted even by the wandering Indians at certain times of the year, not adaptable for agriculture."

Time was to prove him grossly mistaken, but as an economic factor the river itself was to have little to do with bringing about the changes that were to come. Cattlemen were to take the water they needed for rangeland out of the ground with wells and windmills; oil and gas would come out of the ground—and the railroads would be standing by to carry the rich pickings away. No one needed a river, not one as unpredictable and unserviceable as the upper Red was for hundreds of miles.

Above Towson Landing it contributed nothing to the country through which it flowed—other than to devastate it periodically when it was on a "big rise." Every Longhorn and Mustang that was driven north out of Texas had to cross it somewhere. Rock Bluff, Red River Station, Doan's Store, they were the famous crossings. When the last herd had passed, only a great stillness remained; no towns or cities had been called into existence by the bawling herds. But if the Red was of little importance to Texas and Oklahoma, it was vital to the prosperity and growth of Louisiana.

Doaksville is not to be found on any modern map. It has disappeared along with Pecan Point, Frog Creek, Dexter, Horseshoe Bend, Hurricane Bluff and many other old Red River landmarks, and yet Doaksville was for some years the capital of the Choctaw nation. Located within a mile of Fort Towson, its post office address was for some time Fort Towson. It was founded by Josiah Doaks, a white trader who had lived with the Choctaws in Mississippi and migrated with them to Indian Territory. The extent of the business he was doing can be judged by the fact that in the spring of 1843, the little *Fort Towson,* a stern-wheeler of 100 tons, 106 feet long, with $10,000 worth of merchandise aboard, consigned to Doaks, was "arrested by low water and the cargo stored at Bryarly's Landing on the Texas side of the river."

Not all of the goods he was receiving were sold over the counter at Doaksville, for by pack train he was conducting an enormously profitable business with the Chickasaws and the wild Plains Indians farther west. The chief of this operation was a French-Canadian named Joseph R. Berthelet. Berthelet did so well for himself that he presently opened a trading post of his own at Doaksville. He hired as his clerk a young half-blood Choctaw named Robert Jones. It was the beginning of an association that was to endure and make both wealthy.

Young Jones was the son of a prominent Choctaw family. His father, a member of the Tribal Council, a high honor, had sent him to the Choctaw Academy, the best Indian school in the country, in Scott County, Kentucky. Robert Jones was destined to become its most famous graduate and the richest Indian of his time.

Branching out from the trading business, he bought three hundred acres of good bottomland and planted it in cotton. It did so well that three years later he owned five plantations aggregating almost four thousand acres. Down in Louisiana, he acquired a sugar plantation and mill. At Scullyville, the capital of the Northern Choctaw District, he opened a general store. His principal interest there was that it gave him a point on the nearby Arkansas from which he could ship his cotton down that river whenever high or low water prevented Red River steamers from reaching Towson Landing.

To some extent all of the Five Tribes were slaveholders, especially the Choctaws and Chickasaws.[2] At the peak of his operations Robert Jones is reputed to have owned five hundred slaves, which very likely is not an exaggeration, considering the vast acreage he had under cultivation.

Rose Hill, overlooking Red River, was his favorite plantation. To it he brought his second wife, Susan Colbert, the niece
of Ben Colbert, the remarkable Chickasaw who had become
wealthy and famous as the proprietor of Colbert's Ferry. For
her Jones pulled down the twelve-room house he had built for
his first wife and replaced it with a mansion that was as luxurious as *Mal Maison,* the fabled home of Greenwood Leflore, the
Choctaw chieftain, in Mississippi.[3] With its extensive gardens,
roses, redbuds and magnolias, its furnishings imported from
France, it was the showplace of the region, which Robert Jones
certainly intended it to be, for his hardheadedness had given
way to illusions of grandeur.

The mansion at Rose Hill, deserted and falling to ruin, was
destroyed by fire in 1912, long after its owner's death in 1872.
But a large part of Rose Hill, including its private cemetery,
has been designated a State Memorial Park, and obliging at-
tendants point out to visitors the spot where Jones lies.

In the years immediately preceding the outbreak of hostilities between the states an item in the *Doaksville Intelligencer*
states that Jones, with Berthelet and Isaiah Wells, of Doaksville, as co-owners, built the steamboats *Choctaw* and *Woods-
man* "according to Jones' specifications." What those specifications were, where the boats were built, who commanded them
and where they ran do not appear; neither do their names appear in Gould nor in N. Philip Norman's comprehensive log
of Red River steamboats. This does not necessarily mean that
they were not bulit. They could have been sold and renamed by
their new owners, which was often done.

The outcome of the war could not have been of greater concern to anyone even remotely connected with Red River than
Robert Jones. Victory for the North would mean the collapse
of his empire and the loss of his fortune. He hurried to Richmond to offer the Confederacy the support of the great majority
of the Five Civilized Tribes and to plead for arms and ammunition and recognition of the rights of the Indians. Behind him
he left an able lieutenant in Stand Watie to do the actual fighting. Few men were in a better position to contribute heavily to

the treasury of the Confederate States. In return he got all he asked for and more. Not only was he given the rank of colonel and made a delegate to the Confederate Congress, but he was able to return home with the promise that the Five Tribes would be given full citizenship and that an Indian State would be created at war's end.

Returning to Richmond, he remained there and saw the hopes of the South fade into bitter defeat after its initial successes. For him it was a personal catastrophe. With his fortunes shattered beyond repair, he settled down at Rose Hill to live out his life in obscurity.

Soon after Red River enters Louisiana the country through which it flows begins to change. The wide, sunbaked and scantily clad vistas of the Texas plains and the barren hills and scrub timber of Oklahoma give way to a lush, almost subtropic world of greenery, long and short leaf pine and a variety of hardwoods on the uplands, and tupelo, water oak, magnolias and hackberry in the swamps and lowlands. Proceed far enough south and the cypress, the crape myrtles and an occasional oleander greet the eye.

It is pleasant country. In spring, the slopes and bottoms are gay with yellow jasmine, dogwood and wild azalea. In the pine woods, when the warm days arrive, phlox of many hues, asters, foxglove, deergrass, carpet the ground. The air is melodious with the singing of hooded warblers, marsh wrens, tanagers and white-eyed vireos, punctuated with the cheeping of snipe and the scolding of the pileated woodpecker. Red River Valley is the central flyway of the migratory geese and ducks. They are either bound for their winter home on the bays and marshes of the Gulf Coast in the fall or lining out for the lakes and fens of Canada in the spring. From their great height as they cleave the sky in military formations, they look down on Red River, but with the exception of the brilliantly accoutered wood duck they do not stop.

A steamboat rounds a bend and drifts into a plantation landing, perhaps bringing someone up the river who has been down to the "city," and that could mean either Baton Rouge or New

Orleans. Or perhaps it is stopping just to deliver a barrel of flour. Commotion follows as children, black and white, run down from the direction of the big, columned house set back from the river front. Its errand accomplished, the steamboat salutes the world with a blast of its whistle and moves on. Life was easy, leisurely, in those days. Of course, that was long before oil was discovered in the Caddo Lake region and Louisiana suffered the pangs of progress.

Red River steamboating began with Captain Henry Miller Shreve; and although it did not end with him, no name is so closely woven into its history as his. When he brought the *Enterprise* down from Pittsburgh to New Orleans, in December, 1814, General Andrew Jackson impressed the boat into military service. Accordingly, in the spring of 1815, Captain Shreve piloted the *Enterprise* up Red River as far as the rapids at Alexandria on two occasions to move troops, making her the first steamboat to ply that river. She was followed by the *Newport* in 1819. A year later the *Yankee, Beaver, Alexandria, Governor Shelby, Neptune* and *Arkansas* were running between New Orleans, Baton Rouge and Alexandria. When the stage of the river permitted, they reached Natchitoches.

Shreve had accomplished so much with his snag boats since being appointed superintendent of improvements on the Ohio and Mississippi in 1828, that the river from Cairo to New Orleans and twenty miles of the Arkansas had been cleared of snags. In December, 1831, he was ordered to proceed to the mouth of Red River with his snag boats, two tenders and a hundred and fifty laborers (slaves leased out on contract to the government), to remove some of the difficulties steamboats had to contend with at the confluence of the two rivers.

The trouble was all of the Red's making. In its last forty miles it gave every indication of not knowing where it wanted to go. Beyond question there was a time when it and the Atchafalaya were one; but "it has always shown a marked affinity for the Mississippi. Whenever the latter has shifted eastward, as it has on several occasions, the Red has followed it, using the Great River's abandoned channels in unashamed servility. Once it breaks through the Avoyelles Hills, the course it takes defies reason. . . . After reaching the mouth of Black River, it uses an abandoned channel between Moncla and Acme, but keeping in character, it flows in the opposite direction." [4]

As it turns away from Bay Ronde Bayou, it takes a still older abandoned crevasse and gets around Red River Bay to Bayou Natchitoches. "From there to the head of the Atchafalaya, it flows almost straight south, and eight miles beyond their junction it flows through still another old crevasse to its final rendezvous with the Mississippi, two thousand one hundred miles from where Randolph Marcy located its source." (This is Captain Marcy's figure, which allows for its multitudinous bends and meanderings.)

The distance around the bend of the Mississippi, where the Big Red empties itself, is eighteen miles. It is a thin neck of land. By cutting through it at is narrowest point, Shreve believed he could lower the level of the Mississippi eight to ten inches and speed the discharge of the Red and thereby confine the latter to its channel. On January 14, he began making his cut, a channel seventeen feet wide and twenty-two feet deep. The excavation was made by the original snag boat, the *Heliopolis,* using steam scrapers. The water was let in on January 28, fourteen days later. In two days the current widened the channel to thirty feet, and the steamboat *Belvidere* passed through the cut with ease.

The Shreve Cutoff shortened the distance to New Orleans by fourteen to fifteen miles. But it worsened rather than improved the situation. Before long it was the main channel of the river, the scouring action of the silt-laden Mississippi voraciously cutting away the crumbling banks. Instead of increasing the discharge of the Red, the reverse happened, owing, Shreve discovered, to greater drainage into the Atchafalaya. Log booms were built to check the flow in that direction. This helped, but it was only a temporary improvement, for with its increased current the Atchafalaya soon washed out the barrier and continued to divert a large volume of water from the Mississippi.

Captain Gould, a great admirer of Shreve, comments caustically in this instance on what he calls "this ill-advised attempt at river improvement." He says:

> Captain Shreve, who was one of the earliest river experts, followed his good work in the way of snag removal by a very unfortunate act. At that time, the general idea of river improvments was to shorten the river—smooth out the wrinkles, as it were. With this in mind, he inaugurated his grand scheme by what is now known as Shreve's Cut-off. . . . The evil effect of this act is felt to the present day. The State of Louisiana endeavored to offset it soon afterward by making a second cut-off across Raccourci Point. While these cut-offs did not affect the Mississippi itself seriously, they ruined the entrance to the Red, Ouachita and Atchafalaya rivers, and have caused the expenditure since of hundreds of thousands of dollars.

The problem at its mouth and the rapids (or falls) at Alexandria were hindrances, but the real barrier to Red River navigation was the Great Raft, the snakelike, water-logged monstrosity, growing every time the river was in flood. It is well described as a floating but stationary island of tightly woven flotsam and debris that for unknown centuries had been growing on the offscourings of a thousand miles of the upper river. It was covered with a junglelike growth of vines, weeds and brush. Living trees, cottonwoods, half a foot in diameter, gnarled red cedars and an occasional shiny-barked blackjack had made it their permanent home. U.S. Engineers estimated its overall length at a 130 miles in 1831. When it was finally eliminated in 1871, forty years later, with the aid of nitroglycerine, it had grown twenty-six miles.

When it was ravaged by storms, it often broke up briefly, but its parts, as though responding to some magnetic attraction, quickly closed ranks. By impeding the flow of the river, it caused the water to spread out and form the numerous bayous that line its course. To get around it, a steamboat had to leave the channel and run the ever-present risk of being snagged. Dangerous as it was, some captains tried it. Some boats got through to Fulton or Towson Landing and returned safely; others left their bones to whiten on some wilderness mudbank.

The task of breaking up the Great Raft was given to Shreve. On April 11, 1833, he reached Loggy Bayou, the foot of the Raft, with his little flotilla, consisting of the snag boat *Eradicator* and the tenders *Pearl* and *Laurel*. Captain Moorehead joined him several weeks later with the *Heliopolis*.

Had such modern explosives as dynamite or nitroglycerine, even giant powder, been on the market, Shreve's task might not have appeared so formidable; black powder was the most powerful explosive available, and it quickly proved to be ineffective. He tried using the snag boats as battering rams. They made so little progress that he abandoned the experiment. Being a man of great ingenuity, he turned the snag boats into floating sawmills. Logs were snaked out of the mass, brought aboard. When cut into lengths that his Negro laborers could handle, they were tossed overboard and herded like sheep by the *Pearl* and the *Laurel,* the two tenders, into the first convenient bayou.

When the operation had become systematized, the work proceeded so well that by the end of the year the river had been cleared as far as Bennett and Cane's Bluff, a distance of eighty miles.

VIII

Steamboats in the Bayou Country

FREEING OLD NATCHITOCHES and Natchitoches Parish from the strangling grasp of the Great Raft produced a remarkable upsurge of trade almost at once, resulting in New Orleans receiving from Red River in 1834 a total of 42,500 bales of cotton, with the steamboats *Beaver, Planter, Lioness, Bravo* and *Caspian* competing for this lucrative business.[1]

The beneficial results of clearing the river having been demonstrated, it was expected that Captain Shreve would push ahead without delay. That was not to be, for when he established his base camp at Bennett and Cane's Bluff, the funds voted for removing the Great Raft had been exhausted. Months were to be lost before Congress authorized an additional grant.

That was to be the recurring story of the battle to remove the Great Raft. It was a living thing, growing all the time, and the work should have been pressed forward unremittingly. But in the six years Shreve spent fighting it, he was stopped repeatedly by the tardiness of the government to grant money with which to continue.

At Bennett and Cane's Bluff, Shreve, in association with Dr. William Bennett, James Cane, Bushrod Jenkins and several others, bought 640 acres of land centering about the bluff and organized the Shreve Town Company. A town was platted, streets laid out. In 1839 the settlement was incorporated as Shreveport. It was strategically located on the main east-west road to Texas, and with Red River now open to the south, it began to prosper at once. It was new country; land was cheap. Planters from downstate were quick to realize that there was no better cotton land anywhere than in the red hills of Bienville and Claiborne parishes.

By 1840 no fewer than thirty-six steamboats were in the Shreveport trade. The frontier had disappeared and cotton was king. Along the river in Bossier Parish and Red River Parish the number of plantation landings multiplied. There was a personal relationship between even the wealthiest cotton planter and the steamboat captain who owned his own boat that did not exist when he was dealing with the master of a "company" boat, which came later. If the mistress of a plantation wanted a ribbon matched or a piece of lace from the Maison Blanche, in New Orleans, Captain Mike Welsh, of the *Creole,* or Captain Ben Crooks, of the *Hunter,* would gladly run her errands.

River steamboats, even in their rosiest days, when the only competition they faced was among themselves, could, if they looked hard enough, see a cloud on the horizon, often no larger than the proverbial "man's hand," which all too often resolved itself into a railroad, their mortal enemy. In fact, until the discovery of oil in Caddo Lake in 1906 and the opening of the great East Texas Field, which was to bring six different railroads hurrying into Shreveport, Red River steamboating remained an important means of transportation.

On June 4, 1838, five years and a month or so after he had begun attacking the Great Raft, and despite numerous delays, Shreve succeeded in hacking a channel through its entire length, which he was the first to acknowledge was not the same as removing it; he knew his channel would close up unless kept under constant surveillance. In his official report, he says: "On March 1, 1838, the first boat was able to forge her way through the upper section of the raft, and up to the 29th, five merchant steamboats passed up through the raft. On May 1, the navigation through the extent of the raft was considered safe. There were two boats lost near the head of the raft—the *Black Hawk* and *Revenue.* The amount expended in opening the raft has been $311,000."

He gives no details as to how the two boats were lost; presumably it was by snagging. But the river was now open all the way to Carolina Bluffs and Towson Landing. He resigned from government service in 1841 after devoting fifteen years of his life to bettering the lot of all steamboatmen, and purchased a farm near St. Louis, where he died in 1854. It was not until 1871 that the U.S. Engineers blasted the last of the Great Raft out of existence. It came too late to have great commercial importance. The rail lines were converging on Shreveport. The steamboats, of which there were too many for the amount of business they could still attract, were fighting among themselves, slashing rates; many of the owners who had made fortunes in the bumper postwar years, when every boat that went down Red River was loaded to the Plimsoll mark with stored cotton, refused to believe that those days were gone forever.

The Kouns brothers, of whom there were six—George, the head of the clan, and Captains Ben, Isaac, John, Lou and Mart —attempted to bring order out of chaos by organizing the New Orleans and Red River Transportation Company. They were experienced steamboatmen, and they had the boats. Comprising the line were *Col. A. P. Kouns, R. T. Bryarly, La Belle, Texas, Lorts 3, Belle Rowland, O. H. Durfeev, W. J. Behan* and the *Ashland.* They were topped only by the *Julia Randolph,* a beautiful boat and the fastest on Red River.[2]

The Kouns brothers made a valiant and sustained effort to make the Red River business profitable. But it wasn't possible. An advertisement appearing in the *New Orleans Picayune,* on July 17, 1882, stated: "The *Ashland,* leaving today for Red River ports, will be the last boat sent out by the New Orleans and Red River Transportation Company prior to its dissolution next Tuesday at midnight."

In the years immediately following the war, money was the great need of the bankrupt South. All it had to sell was cotton.

Without slave labor to produce it and plantation life disrupted, the prospects were not bright. But money began to appear. The only explanation is that cotton was coming out of hiding. Union troops had found and burned untold tons, but obviously they had not found it all. Estimates of the quantity received at New Orleans from Red River Valley in the sixteen months following the war run as high as 250,000 bales—a figure which undoubtedly permits of some trimming, but certainly great enough to confirm Commodore Porter's charge that "the principal object of the Red River expedition (commanded by General Nathaniel Banks, supported by Porter's flotilla of gunboats) was to allow northern speculators to take out cotton under the protection of the army."

Beyond doubt the speculators were aware that a vast quantity of cotton was being held in the Red River parishes. The war had sent the price sky high. With the Union in control of the Mississippi and New Orleans, the way was now open to ship it to the English mills that were clamoring for it.

It does not appear that any important military advantage could be expected from sending General Banks with his 25,000 men and Porter's 2,000 naval personnel up Red River Valley. When Banks had captured Baton Rouge and Alexandria, with scarcely a shot being fired, the capital of Louisiana had been moved to Shreveport, where it was being defended by the only Confederate force left in the State, numbering some 12,000 effectives, commanded by General E. Kirby Smith and General Richard (Dick) Taylor.

The stage of water being favorable, Commodore Porter worked his gunboats over the rapids at Alexandria and steamed up the river to the vicinity of Natchitoches, where they were stopped by grounding. In the meantime, General Banks was marching up west of the Red in the direction of the little town of Mansfield, the seat of De Soto Parish. There, on April 8, at Sabine Crossroads, the only real battle of the campaign was fought. Though holding a two-to-one advantage, the invaders were soundly defeated. They fell back to Pleasant Hill, twenty miles to the south, where another engagement occurred, with neither side being able to claim victory.

Banks then began retreating to Baton Rouge, burning houses, slave cabins and laying the countryside waste. When he reached Alexandria, he put it to the torch. In the business section of the town only one building was left standing. With the army evacuating the valley, Commodore Porter was faced with the necessity of floating his boats or blowing them up to avoid their falling into the enemy's hands. With time of the essence, the decision was made to construct a temporary dam at a convenient distance below the rapids and pray that in a few days it would raise the level of the river sufficiently for him to get his flotilla out of the trap into which it had wandered.[3]

We are told that "cotton gins, sugar houses, and other structures were demolished to provide materials; and rails, cross ties, bridge timbers and rolling stock of the Red River Railroad were dismantled and dumped into the river." [4]

The stratagem was successful. When the Yankee gunboats had been floated over the rocky shoals, the dam was destroyed and the flotilla steamed back to Baton Rouge.

The argument has been made by apologists for the Red River invasion that it was undertaken to capture or destroy the concentration of Confederate rams and armored boats that had found refuge at or above Shreveport when the North won control of the Mississippi. Southern partisans said it was just a reprisal for the humiliation the Confederate ram *Webb* had inflicted when it steamed out of the mouth of Red River and passed New Orleans flying the Stars and Stripes only to pull down the Union colors when it was opposite the point at Algiers and run up the Stars and Bars. Fifty miles down the river she had encountered the *Hartford,* Commodore Farragut's flagship, the *Webb* then being scuttled by her crew before she could be boarded.

The foregoing is sheer speculation, but speculation has a wide range when the purposes of the Banks-Porter Expedition are being considered. The fact that the boats that had scurried up Red River when New Orleans fell and were at Shreveport in 1863—the rams *Webb, Trenton,* and *General Beauregard;* the transports *Eries No. 4,6,7; Doubloon, Countess, General Quitman* and half a dozen other small packets—were not there in 1864 (which must have been known to Federal Intelligence) does not tend to clarify the situation.

It is doubtful, if the boats *had* been there and the water permitted, that Commodore Porter's gunboats could have dug them out of the bayous, for they were commanded by men who knew every secret waterway on the river. Once a boat had been run deep into a bayou, taken down her stacks and covered her superstructure with camouflaging trees and brush, she was reasonably safe.

What is even more difficult to understand, if capturing the remnants of the Confederate Navy was of the first consideration: why didn't Commodore Porter bottle them up for the duration of the war by sinking one of his gunboats and blocking the channel, which would have amounted to the same thing. Nothing, it seems, could have been easier.

But no matter what may have been the purpose underlying the Red River campaign, no one profited from it.

For years, except in high water, steamboats had discharged their cargo to lessen their draft before running the barrier to navigation at Alexandria, variously referred to as the "falls," "shoals" or "rapids," and had it transported around the obstruction by wagon. This hauling had developed into such a lucrative business that a tramway around the rapids was projected in 1852, only to be nipped in the bud when Congress voted money two years later to deepen the channel. Some work was done, but the war had come and gone before the project was carried to a successful conclusion.

The Emancipation Proclamation had put an end to slavery and given the enfranchised Negro a number of "rights," in which he was not greatly interested, since they did not provide him with what he needed most—a living. Thousands of them knew how to chop cotton or cut timber in the pine forests, and little else. Inevitably they were forced to go back to doing what they had done before the war, even though under changed conditions. They now worked for wages, and however small they were, it gave them some money to spend, which white and black scalawags had little difficulty in getting away from them.

The ex-slaves were even more gullible than the ignorant white shantyboaters and were easily taken in by the wiles of the professors of astrology, healers, dentists and doctors who worked the lesser rivers from their towboats. They bought quantities of charms, "electric bracelets" and concoctions that were guaranteed to cure all the ills human flesh was heir to.

A boat would tie up at a public landing, put on some semblance of a show (usually a banjo player or two and a buck-and-wing dancer) to attract a crowd. The "doctor" or "professor" would then appear, and after a lengthy oratorical outburst, one of his shills would step forward to get business going by buying the first bottle. However small the "take" might be, it was almost all profit.

Red River began to see more and more of this gentry as the effects of the war began to wear off and a measure of prosperity returned. The grubby little "medicine" boats were not related to the big, glamorous showboats, with their calliopes, brass bands and professional actors.

The Dan Rice Circus toured the Mississippi and Red River, among other tributaries, for many years. Minstrel shows, very popular in the seventies and eighties, traveled from town to town by steamboat. It was not unusual to find rival companies bidding for patronage in Brewer's Hall and the Grand Opera House at Shreveport. Of all the minstrel troupes, none became quite as famous as McIntyre and Heath, which originated in Louisiana and played all over the United States.

Such well-known showboats as the *Cotton Blossom, River Maid* and the *Water Queen* presented dramas (invariably melodramas of the East Lynne and St. Elmo genre) or a musical vaudeville. As a guarantee to the public of the high morality of the performers, married couples and single women were quartered in staterooms on the showboat; bachelors and otherwise unattached males slept on the towboat which accompanied it.

Admissions were low, and audiences were too hungry for entertainment to be critical. After the railroads made it possible for famous touring stars from the East to follow their New Orleans engagement by a week of one-night stands at Baton Rouge, Alexandria, Monroe and Shreveport, the showboats lost their vogue. Only the cheapest survived, growing shabbier with each passing year. Very often they were just scows that had been decked over with a central cabin, one end of which had a raised stage, the rest of it being the "theatre" with its rows of wooden benches. A "gas" boat, a grimy tug powered with a gasoline engine, dragged it from one river settlement to the next. All hands, with exception of the engineer of the gasboat, took part in the performance.[5]

All showboats were firetraps. Miraculously, holocausts almost never occurred. The only one that burned on Red River was *French's Sensation* as she was tied up at Elmwood Plantation. She was completely destroyed, but no one was injured.

A map of Louisiana, again, will show a pinprick in Natchitoches Parish marked Chopin. It is the site of the little settlement located on the old Chopin Plantation. For decades a historical controversy has swirled about the Chopin Plantation giving it a notoriety, deserved or undeserved, depending on which side of the question one is aligned. One either can believe, as thousands do, that Chopin Plantation was the Red River setting Harriet Beecher Stowe used for her famous but less than great novel *Uncle Tom's Cabin* or can agree with the dissenters who, basing their case on the fact that Mrs. Stowe was never in Louisiana, would dismiss the whole matter as just one of those long-standing legends that will not die. This latter conclusion ignores several pertinent facts that would seem to make it untenable.

Granting that Mrs. Stowe's only firsthand observations of plantation life were gained on her visits across the Ohio River into Kentucky, during the eight years that she and her husband were living in Cincinnati, it is also true that her brother, Henry Beecher, lived for some time in New Orleans, where he was collection clerk for a large mercantile firm, the nature of his

job taking him into the various parishes, including Natchitoches. While on Red River he could hardly have failed to visit
Lammy Chopin, a fellow New Englander, who had purchased
from Robert McAlpin, its original owner, what came to be
known as Chopin Plantation.

McAlpin himself was from New England, a native of Massachusetts. Both Chopin and he were widely respected men.
Whether Henry Beecher became acquainted with him has to be
left to conjecture, but Mrs. Stowe in her *A Key to Uncle Tom's
Cabin,* published after her novel had become a worldwide success, acknowledges that it was on information supplied by her
brother, on his return to Cincinnati, that she drew heavily for
her Red River color and background material. In order to picture slavery at its inhuman worst, she needed a plantation
owner who was a sadistic brute. Using her novelist's privilege,
she apparently fashioned out of either Chopin or McAlpin her
historic villain, Simon Legree.

In 1893, over the strong objections of both pro and con parties to the argument, who recognized it as crass fakery, a cabin
in the former slave quarters of Chopin Plantation was dismantled and taken to Chicago, where it was exhibited at the
World's Fair as the "home" of Uncle Tom.

Of course, by then, the sight of an old paddle-wheeler making
its way up Red River, bravely trailing its twin plumes of smoke,
had become almost a rarity. In a business faced with ever dimin-
ishing returns, no new boats arrived to replace the old. It wasn't
only Red River steamboating that was suffering. Captain Gould
comments regretfully:

> Of this trade, that of the *Arkansas, White, Tennessee,* and
> *Cumberland* may be said to be entirely gone. Today no vessels
> run up Bayou Vermilion or Gross Tete. . . . The Red River trade
> is less than one-fourth what it was then [1875]. The Texas and
> Pacific strikes the Red at Shreveport, Alexandria and other points
> and diverts a large traffic from it. The recently completed Vicks-
> burg, Shreveport and Pacific carries a large amount of cotton
> across the country to Vicksburg, to be thence distributed by rail-

road. The Red River is seldom navigated above Shreveport, and whereas in those days vessels ran through to Jefferson, Texas [by way of Caddo Lake], and even to White Oak Shoals, this is rare and almost unknown today.

An era had come and gone.

IX

Stern-Wheelers on the Rio Grande

THERE WAS A LIMITED AMOUNT of steamboating on several of the coastal rivers of Texas, but on the 253 navigable miles of the lower Rio Grande it shaped the course of history, made a little handful of men unspeakably rich and played a leading role in convincing Mexico that it was the Rio Grande, not the Nueces River, that was the boundary between the two republics.

It was across the uncertain Rio Grande, with its sandbars and shifting channel, a treacherous torrent when in flood and a trickle in periods of extended drought, that three wars were fought, all within thirty years. Ten years after the Texan War for Independence, the United States declared war on Mexico; it was followed fifteen years later by the great War between the States, with Texas taking its stand with the Confederacy.

Whether during war or between wars, the approximately 175 miles of grassland lying south of the Nueces River, a blank space on the map designated as the Wild Horse Desert, was a region of unequaled lawlessness, not to be found elsewhere within the confines of the United States. Except for a few small settlements on the north and south banks of the Rio Grande and raiding bands of Lipan and Comanche Indians, its only inhabitants were bandits, outlaws, cattle and horse thieves and the renegade offscourings of the frontier, both Texan and Mexican. In the interior, along the creeks, the smoke-blackened ruins of deserted ranchos, the owners of which had considered themselves fortunate to escape with their lives, met the eye, grim reminders of attempts that had been made at settlement.

On the theory that wherever there was a customs house local officials would find ways of enriching themselves at the expense of the national treasury, Vera Cruz had been declared the only port of entry on the Gulf Coast by Spain. The Republic of Mexico had not seen fit to rescind the declaration. It was a law that was either ignored or winked at wherever imports from abroad could be brought ashore, and nowhere was that truer than at Matamoros, the old and substantial town on the banks of the Rio Grande, fifty miles from Boca del Rio, the mouth of the river.

Because of their deep draft, oceangoing sailing vessels and steamships could not cross the bar there, nor could they have navigated the shallow river if they had. It was necessary, therefore, to lighter cargo ashore at Bagdad, a shanty town rendezvous of smugglers on the Mexican shore, and cart the goods overland to Matamoros.

The situation at Boca del Rio was further complicated by the fact that to the north there was only one break in the long, thin, 128 miles of sandy Padre Island, which paralleled the Texas coast like a barrier reef all the way to Corpus Christi Bay. That break occurred between Santiago Island and the southern tip of Padre Island, where a narrow but navigable channel led to a landward anchorage that was safe from the storms that raked the open Gulf. Appreciating its importance, the early Spaniards, who had a flair for such things, chistened it *El Paso de los Brazos de Santiago*—the Pass of the Arms of Saint James.

Across the three miles of shallow water of Laguna Madre, which separated Brazos Santiago from the mainland, they had lightered their goods in small boats to the sandy bluff at Point Isabel, from where they were forwarded by muleback and ox-cart over a dangerous, bandit-infested trail that, after winding through the dunes and salt grass swales for twenty-six miles, reached the Rio Grande at a point across from Matamoros—a laborious, roundabout operation that had been abandoned in favor of the hazardous and often abruptly terminated transferring of cargo at Bagdad, where ships caught in the open roadstead hurriedly had to put to sea to ride out a storm.

The Rio Grande, of course, had yet to see its first shallow-draft steamboats. It took the war with Mexico to bring them. When, in the spring of 1846, President Polk ordered General Zachary Taylor to march his army of regulars and hellbent volunteers, from Texas, Tennessee, Kentucky and half a dozen other states, across the disputed territory between the Nueces and the Rio Grande, it was tantamount to a declaration of war; and yet Taylor's orders, transmitted through the Secretary of War, express the unrealistic hope that hostilities might yet be averted. "In case of war," they read, "your main object will be the protection of Texas; but the pursuit of this object will not *necessarily* [the italics are supplied] confine your action within the territory of Texas."

Taylor reached the Rio Grande opposite Matamoros in late April and established an unfortified camp which he dubbed "Camp Texas." Above it on a makeshift flagpole the Stars and Stripes fluttered in the breeze for the first time on the Rio Grande.

On May 1, learning that Arista, the Mexican general, had crossed the river somewhere above him with his army and was moving to get behind him and cut his line of supplies, Taylor fell back from "Camp Texas," leaving Major Jacob Brown with five hundred men of the Seventh Infantry and two batteries to pin down the garrison at Matamoros.

On May 8, a few miles to the north, the two armies came to grips at Palo Alto, and again the following afternoon at Resaca de la Palma. Although Taylor was outnumbered three to one, he defeated the Mexicans and sent them reeling back across the Rio Grande in such panic that many of them were drowned. In the meantime Major Brown and his small force had been under bombardment from Matamoros for seven days without respite. An exploding shell mortally wounded Brown, but his men dug in and held their ground. Ammunition exhausted, they were still there when General Taylor and his troops returned from their victories.

Work on a fortified post on the site of "Camp Texas" was begun. It was named Fort Brown, for its fallen commander. Matamoros had become strangely quiet. The reason was disclosed when it was learned that General Arista was retreating to Monterrey, a hundred and more miles to the west, the most important town in northern Mexico, and that General Mejia, in command at Matamoros, had withdrawn the garrison and also was striking out for Monterrey.

The Americans crossed the river and took possession of Matamoros without meeting any resistance. The natives were happy to see the *Americanos,* happy that the shooting was over and particularly happy to discover that the newcomers had money to spend. Matamoros, with its trees and gardens, was a pleasant place and a far cry from the usual collection of sun-bleached adobes gathered around a dusty, wind-swept plaza. Zach Taylor's unmilitary volunteers, with their ingrained contempt for all things Mexican, found the pleasures of Matamoros interesting enough to draw them across the river from Fort Brown without regard for military regulations. There was so much running back and forth that Charles Stillman, an American, whose so-called importing and forwarding business had made him a wealthy man (his brick warehouse in Matamoros was bulging with contraband goods), established a ferry between the town and fort.

Stillman could smell a dollar a long way off. A shrewd, devious man, he managed to have a finger in many pies without calling attention to himself. In the bewildering ferment of Mexican politics, military commanders rising and falling with every shifting wind, he somehow invariably managed to emerge backing the current winner.

Having occupied Matamoros, General Taylor dispatched advance units up the river and, meeting little resistance, took possession of Camargo and Mier, respectively 170 and 200 miles above him, the latter of unhappy memory to all Texans.[1] The city of Monterrey, the capital of Nueva Leon, was his objective. He still had a long way to go.

Back in the States, Zach Taylor was becoming a national hero. Someone gave him the sobriquet of "Old Rough and Ready." It swept the country. But rash as he often was, he knew better than to attempt the long desert crossing to Monterrey without adequate transport. He needed mules, wagons if possible, subsistence for his men, ammunition. Such limited supplies as he was receiving were being lightered across Laguna Madre from Brazos Santiago to Point Isabel and forwarded from there to Fort Brown by mule train.

Washington could not afford to permit his appeal for aid to go unanswered. The Quartermaster General was ordered to assemble a fleet of steamboats and oceangoing steamships at New Orleans, take on cargo and proceed to Brazos Santiago at once.

It was taken as clearly indicating that the government was about to step up its war with Mexico. No one doubted the eventual victory. It might take a year or two, but that would be long enough to guarantee rich pickings for the boats that got into army transport. It was that prospect rather than any outpouring of patriotic fervor that was responsible for the coming together of steamboats from Mobile Bay, Red River, the Mississippi, along with deep-water vessels, both steam and sail that crowded the New Orleans levee.

The first loaded were the first to pull away. Daily, for several weeks, one boat after another headed downriver and through the delta to the open Gulf. The seagoing vessels struck out boldly to the southwest and the Rio Grande; the snub-nosed, fragile steamboats were not designed to fight the heavy seas and long rollers that crashed over their decks; the best they could do was to take the long way around and hug the Texas coast. Even so, if a storm caught them, they were likely to be swamped. Fortunately, they escaped that extremity.

Like homing pigeons coming in from the sea, the supply ships began arriving at Brazos Santiago. Days later the steam-

boats came limping in until the anchorage was crowded with
them. The big boats had come as far as they were going; it was
now up to the shallow-draft steamboats to get into the Rio
Grande the livestock and supplies that had been brought so far.
The only way to do it was to send them down the eight miles of
exposed open ocean on the windward side of Brazos Santiago
Island to Boca del Rio, the mouth of the river.

There was a great to-do as stores were unloaded and piled
up on the beach, mules put ashore and the whole given a military flavor by the presence of soldiery to protect the base. Steamboats were loaded for the run down to Boca del Rio. The *Corvette,* a side-wheeler built at Pittsburgh, and government-
owned, one of the few that were, was the first to go. At the
wheel was Captain Miflin Kenedy, lately taken into military
service.

Kenedy had earned his master's certificate as captain of the
steamboat *Champion* during the Seminole War, on the rivers
and West Coast of Florida. At war's end he had taken her all
the way up to Pittsburgh for a general overhaul. In Pittsburgh,
he advanced himself by gaining command of a new boat, the
Corvette, and brought her down to New Orleans on her maiden
voyage. He was only twenty-nine, however, when he caught his
first glimpse of the Rio Grande. It was to be a long and profitable association.

Miflin Kenedy was a Pennsylvania Quaker, of good family
and education, not given to profanity or strong drink, and
though he had cast his lot among rough men and was following
a rough calling, he remained a soft-spoken, gentle-mannered
man throughout his life. Because he never resorted to belliger-
ence to gain his ends, some men mistook it for weakness. It was
a mistake they never made twice.

Captain Kenedy put the *Corvette* over the bar at Boca del
Rio and took her up the fifty miles of unmarked, treacherous
channel to Fort Brown without mishap. Of the seven steamers
that followed, one struck a sandbar a few miles below Fort
Brown with force enough to open her seams. She sank in shallow water but most of her cargo was saved.

Now that he had transport, General Taylor moved his head-quarters upriver to Camargo, and ordered his army to follow, leaving only a small contingent of regulars to hold Fort Brown.

Five days came to be accepted as the average running time from Matamoros to Camargo, four miles up the Rio San Juan from its confluence with the Rio Grande. Frequent groundings and minor accidents quickly made it apparent that it was haz-ardous for a boat to proceed after dark. Consequently the owner-captains, who had placed their boats under charter to the gov-ernment, tied up wherever they chanced to be when night fell. They were learning something about the difficulties of river navigation with which their past experience had not acquainted them.

Heavy rain or cloudbursts hundreds of miles upstream could turn the usually placid, heavily silt-laden Rio Grande into a raging brown flood without warning, cutting away old bars and forming new ones. A day or two later the river might be low enough almost to justify the observation that a boat had to "nav-igate on its own sweat." To men used to the lush greenery of the Louisiana and Florida rivers, the barren, sunburnt valley of the Rio Grande had a grim, forbidding aspect unrelated to war.

On the Texas side the endless miles of chaparral and thickets of mesquite were unmarked by human habitation. Other than Fort Brown, which was to become the future Brownsville, the buildings at Davis Landing (Rio Grande City), opposite the mouth of the San Juan and adjacent to Camargo, supplied the only hint of American settlement.

The summer passed as General Taylor lay at Camargo, whip-ping his nondescript army into shape for the invasion of Mexico and the capture of Monterrey—"frittering his time away with plans for the invasion," his political enemies charged. It was the first gun in a campaign to undermine his popularity with the voters, which was beginning to cast its shadow over the White House. He was a Whig and the Democrats were in power, a po-sition they did not propose to relinquish.[2]

It wasn't lack of decision that was keeping Taylor bogged down at Camargo; his problem lay in the difficulty he was hav-

ing in putting an army in the field. Two thirds of his troops
were volunteers, most of them militiamen serving ninety-day
enlistments. Their time was often half over when he got them.
When their ninety-days were up, they were anxious to go home.
It followed that the steamboats were taking as many men down
the river to Brazos Santiago as they were bringing up.

He suffered his biggest loss in the departure of half of his
tejanos (Texans)—a wild, troublesome lot who had enlisted "to
kill Mexicans" and didn't give a damn about drilling and "riding formations." They were also his best men. But finally Taylor was ready to move. On September 20, he stood at the outskirts of Monterrey. After a bloody three-day battle that cost the
Americans almost five hundred in dead and wounded, the Mexicans capitulated. It put "Old Zach" in control of all north-
eastern Mexico. The President's political advisors convinced
Polk that the time had come to cut the old man down. Taylor
was ordered to confine himself to defensive operations only "in
territory already held by you."

But that was only the prelude to the humiliation he was to
receive. The blow fell with the announcement that he had been
superseded and that Major General Winfield Scott, Commanding General of the United States Army, would lead an invasion
into the heart of Mexico.

Scott was old, past sixty, a much bemedaled general jealous
of his prerogatives. He was ordered to assemble an army at
Brazos Santiago and, with suitable naval escort, take possession
of the port of Vera Cruz and from there strike inland to invest
Mexico City, the capital of the Mexican Republic. His call for
troops divested Taylor of the major portion of his command,
along with most of his artillery. But Taylor had one victory remaining to him, perhaps the most heroic of his military career;
and it was a battle not of his seeking.

Following the fall of Monterrey, he had pushed on another
fifty miles and taken possession of Saltillo, the capital of Coa-
huila. With his command reduced to fewer than five thousand
men, he was withdrawing from his advanced position, when
Mexican General Santa Anna caught him at Buena Vista, a

tight place on the Saltillo-Monterrey road, several miles north of that town.

The ubiquitous Antonio Lopez de Santa Anna, whose name was anathema to all Texans, had returned from his exile in Cuba with the connivance of the U.S. State Department and been elected president of Mexico. He needed a victory over the hated gringos to restore luster to his tarnished military reputation. It seemed to be within his grasp when he attacked Taylor at dawn on February 23, 1847, with upwards of fifteen thousand men.[3]

The battle lasted all day, the most fiercely contested of the Mexican War. For the number of troops involved the losses were heavy on both sides. Time after time Santa Anna sent his infantry charging down from the surrounding brown hills. When night fell, he had lost upwards of 2,000 men. He withdrew during the night, defeated but not without honor. The American losses amounted to 673 killed and wounded.

General Scott had reached Brazos Santiago the previous December, well in advance of his army, and established his headquarters aboard a damaged steamboat that had been turned into a floating hotel. Presently transports began arriving with men, supplies and munitions of war. From the Rio Grande came a procession of steamboats bearing troops that had been detached from Taylor's command.

The steamboats had never been busier, but their owners sensed that when the present activity was over, the war would be moving away from the Rio Grande. Among the privately owned boats, those that had escaped fire, explosion and snags were ready to fall apart. Here was an opportunity to unload them; by refusing to sign new charters, the Quartermaster's Department would be forced to buy them. The government was in no position to bargain. For several times their worth it bought the *Whiteville, J. E. Roberts, Brownsville, Hatchee Eagle, Troy, General Jessup, Colonel Hunt, Dragon, Colonel Cross* and several others, including the useless *Colonel J. Stephens,* a propeller. Three months later they lay tied up together at Brazos Santiago gathering rust.

Early in February everything was in readiness for the second invasion of Mexico. With his army safely aboard a flotilla of steamers and deep-water craft, General Scott set sail for Vera Cruz. It fell to him on March 29. Other victories followed— Cerro Gordo, Contreras-Molinas del Rey, Chapultepec—and on September 14, 1847, he marched into Mexico City with his victorious army. The war with Mexico was over, although it was not until February 2, the following spring, that a tentative treaty of peace was signed at Guadalupe Hidalgo.

Winfield Scott was an able commander and richly deserved the acclaim he received. But unorthodox Zach Taylor came out of the war the popular hero. At his request he had been relieved of his command after months of waiting. In November, 1847, he said farewell to his troops and came down the Rio Grande from Camargo for the last time aboard the steamboat *Colonel Cross*. Several weeks later he sailed for home from Brazos Santiago to become, despite his early reluctance to stand for the office, the twelfth President of the United States.

If, as his best biographer, Tom Lea, conjectures, young Dick King, twenty-three at the time, was the master of the *Colonel Cross* when she brought General Taylor down from Camargo, it would seem to have been the only time they ever met. It well could have been King's first trip as captain, for he had only recently received his master's papers. He was still very much an unknown quantity, but in the thirty-eight years that followed, he was to carve his name deep in the border history of south Texas. In his own lifetime he became a legendary figure, famous as the owner of the great King Ranch, so colossal that it dwarfed in size such outfits as John Chism's Jingle Bob, the giant XIT and the foreign-owned Matador. But he was a steamboatman, and he insisted on his title of captain to the day he died.

When Richard King first came ashore at Boca del Rio, he had a rating of second pilot. Young as he was, he had five years of steamboating behind him. By his own admission steamboating was all he knew. We are told that he had made his way to New Orleans, enlisted for the duration of the war and been shipped out to the Rio Grande in response to a letter from his friend Captain Miflin Kenedy.

This has to be taken on faith; there is no documentation for it.[4] Kenedy may well have written young King. They had served together as master and cub pilot on the Chattahoochee and Apalachicola rivers in Florida. If such a letter passed between them its appeal must have been urgent. It hardly could have held out the prospect of better wages than could be earned in the States; Kenedy was being paid one hundred dollars a month as master of the *Corvette;* the prevailing scale for even first pilots was seventy-five or less. That Kennedy could have expounded on the future prospects of the Rio Grande Valley seems equally unlikely, for he was never enthusiastic about its possibilities. In fact, it was at King's urging, not his, that they embarked in the steamboat business for profit after the war.

King's first duty on the Rio Grande was as second pilot of a wheezy old side-wheeler named the *Colonel Cross.* Only several weeks later he was transferred to the *Corvette* as first pilot. This was certainly Captain Kenedy's doing. It was the first of many favors he was to receive.

What drew these two men together and ripened their friendship into a bond that lasted throughout their lives, no one can say. In many ways they were as unlike as two men ever were— Kenedy mild of manner, educated, restrained; King, burly, hard-fisted, hardheaded, brash. Perhaps each found in the other qualities that he could not find in himself. Both were young men, Kenedy being only seven years Richard King's senior.

They were not saints. Far from it. Success did not come easily, but once they had started rising to the top, no man could stop them. Charlie Stillman, the wealthy and astute merchant prince of Matamoras, whose conscience was so flexible that he could see three ways at once, tried it and failed. Never one to overlook an opportunity to make a dollar, it must have occurred to him when the first steamboats appeared on the river that when peace was restored, Rio Grande steamboating could be developed into a very profitable business. He moved in quickly when the war ended and put a number of boats on the river in a determined effort to seize control of the traffic.

It was a business about which he knew little or nothing, and it proved to be a costly venture—money, he discovered, being no substitute for experience. Eighteen months later in an attempt to recoup his losses, he was to turn to his most successful competitors, young Captain Miflin Kenedy and Richard King, and take them into partnership. His money and their experience were to make an unbeatable combination. Under the firm name of M. Kenedy and Company they were to gain such a monopoly of the Rio Grande trade as no other river ever witnessed.

X

Border Bonanza

THE SHOOTING WAR had been over for three months before the U.S. Senate ratified the treaty of Guadalupe Hidalgo. Save for a small garrison at Fort Brown and Brazos Santiago, the troops were gone. In their place had come a horde of adventurous Americans who were convinced that the lower Rio Grande Valley, now that it was American soil, would boom with a resumption of the rich trade with the interior of Mexico.

Their optimism was well founded. Along the river itself, Matamoros was a town of eight thousand, larger than any in Texas, and Camargo claimed half as many. There were other towns—Reynosa, Mier and prosperous Rio Grande City. Behind them there was a vast hinterland of ranchos and a population of thousands gathered in such places as Monterrey, Saltillo, Torreón and many others, all needing a market for their products —hides, tallow, wool, cotton, lead, horses, mules and cattle. The natural movement of that trade was to the Rio Grande.

The changing face of the frontier was nowhere more noticeable than in the town that was growing up around Fort Brown. Several Matamoros merchants, Stillman among them, put up substantial warehouses on the river front. When the garrison was withdrawn, Fort Brown became Brownsville. In the meantime, however, the number of steamboats on the Rio Grande had decreased drastically. The government had withdrawn all of its boats and herded them together at Brazos Santiago in what appeared to be a steamboat graveyard. King's command, the *Colonel Cross,* was among them. The *Corvette,* Captain Kenedy's boat, sailed away for New Orleans. He was not aboard. Though both he and King were at loose ends, it did not occur to them to leave the country as other captains were doing. King went to Boca del Rio and converted a disabled boat into what he called a "hotel," with himself as staff of one. Apparently it was a rough sort of sailors' flophouse and grogshop.

Kenedy had gone off on his own and was promoting a new town up the river some thirty miles above Camargo, which he named Roma. He found it slow going. To "piece out," he began buying merchandise and transporting it by mule train into Mexico, going as far as Saltillo and Torreón. Not only was it profitable, but it gave him an opportunity to channel Mexican trade to Roma.

There was a scramble for bargains when the government announced that it was offering its boats for sale to the highest bidder on April 2, 1849. Prior to the time of the auction some of the boats had been disposed of at "private sale" to agents of Charles Stillman; and on the day of the sale his business partner, Samuel L. Belden (to make things look right), bought two more, the *Hatchee Eagle* and the *Troy,* paying $1,550 for the two boats. Captain Richard King bought his old steamer, the *Colonel Cross,* for $750, which was less than 5 percent of her original cost.

When all were back in commission it was revealed that Stillman, Belden and Company had what appeared to be absolute control of river shipping, being opposed only by the two boats operating under the firm name of Bodman and Clarke and by Captain Richard King's *Colonel Cross.* Stillman put the management of his steamboats in the hands of Captain Jim O'Donnell, the master of his (Stillman's) first little steamer, the *Tom Kirkman.*

There is no reason to believe that sentiment played a part in

King's purchase of the *Colonel Cross,* when he could have put his slender savings into any one of half a dozen other boats. They were all over-age, second rate. Having commanded the *Colonel Cross* it may be presumed that he knew how hard she could be pushed and what he might hope to get out of her. After giving her as much of an overhaul as his finances permitted, he secured a cargo and brought her up the river to Brownsville. Being his own captain and pilot, he could underbid the competition. Mexican merchants in Matamoros, rivals of Stillman's concern, welcomed the opportunity to throw their business to the independent boat.

It must have been a thorn in Stillman's flesh. Because of faulty handling, one of his boats broke up outside of Boca del Rio; another burned while tied up at Matamoros. If Charles Stillman knew little or nothing about steamboating, he knew how to read his ledgers. His boats were losing money. He disposed of two. They went into Mexican registry and disappeared from the Rio Grande.

Captain Jim O'Donnell considered himself fortunate if he could keep four or five Stillman steamboats running. Engines were breaking down. A broken part could not be replaced inside two months. To overcome that handicap he junked the little *Troy* and took parts out of her to repair the other boats.

In the meantime Dick King was not getting rich, but he was making a living keeping the old *Colonel Cross* on the move.

Practically all of the land embraced in the Brownsville townsite had been purchased by individual owners from Stillman. He had moved across the river, built a substantial home and a brick office building. Sometime in February, 1850, according to Harbert Davenport, in his *Notes on Early Steamboating,* Miflin Kenedy received word that Stillman wanted to see him. They met in Brownsville, and Stillman disclosed that he was not satisfied with the manner in which his boats were being operated. Impressed by the record Kenedy had established with the *Corvette*—two years on the Rio Grande without accident—he asked Kenedy if he would be interested in taking over the Stillman steamboat business on a partnership basis.

Though Kenedy realized it was a promising opportunity, he asked for several days in which to think it over. He felt that if King could be brought into the venture it would guarantee its success. He spoke to King. To his surprise, the latter said he was not interested in trying to pump life into what he called "Stillman's worn-out smudge pots." If Stillman was really serious about developing Rio Grande steamboating into a highly profitable business, let him put up the money for two first-class new boats specially designed for the work they would have to do. By "specially designed" he meant a heavy outside boat to make the run down from Brazos Santiago to Boca del Rio and up the river a few miles to a landing where its cargo could be transferred to a shallow-draft inside boat for the run up as far as Camargo and Mier. He would be interested if Stillman would agree to that.

What King had to say must have made sense to shrewd Charlie Stillman. Many conferences followed, and on March 1, 1850, the firm of M. Kenedy and Company came into being. There were four partners, each owning a quarter interest: Stillman, Kenedy, King and O'Donnell. Why Captain O'Donnell, who was being succeeded by Kenedy and King, was brought in as a partner can be interpreted several ways. Perhaps, as has often been said, it was an act of friendship and loyalty on Stillman's part, even though he was not noted for his generosity. More likely it was because by including O'Donnell he was, in effect, guaranteeing himself a half interest in the company and making it impossible for Kenedy and King to seize control.

King had some precise ideas of what the new boats should be. He incorporated them in a sheaf of rough drawings. Armed with them and letters of credit, Miflin Kenedy left for Pittsburgh to commission the building of the two boats, the heavy, outside boat to be named the *Grampus,* and the lighter boat, a sternwheeler for the river work, the *Comanche.*

Kenedy was not a stranger in that beehive of boatbuilding at the head of the Ohio; he knew where to go for what he wanted. At Elizabeth, a few miles up the Monongahela from Pittsburgh, he contracted with Samuel Walker and Son to build the *Grampus* and *Comanche,* and turned King's crude drawings over to

Billy King, the Walkers' chief designer. Several weeks later, after he had seen work begun, he left for home, the understanding being that M. Kenedy and Company was to accept delivery at Brazos Santiago.

While he was away, King and O'Donnell reduced the number of the firm's boats in operation to four and began building a warehouse and wharf at White Ranch, which was to be the firm's terminal on the Rio Grande, six miles from the mouth of the river, where cargo was to be transferred.

When the *Grampus* and *Comanche* were put into service, with several of the old boats to back them up, Rio Grande steamboating began to take on the aspects of a well-ordered business. It had been the custom for cargo arriving at Brazos Santiago in the holds of steamships and windjammers to be lightered ashore and then reloaded on the steamboats that were to take it up the river. M. Kenedy and Company cut costs by transferring freight directly from the oceangoing ships to the *Grampus*. The company followed the same practice at White Ranch, its terminal on the Rio Grande. The saving in time and money enabled it to establish rates that the independent boats could not meet.[1]

No figures are available to say what the profits of the first year amounted to, but when poor health forced Jim O'Donnell to withdraw from the firm at the end of 1852, he received approximately $8,000 for his quarter share for that year. Though O'Donnell died shortly thereafter, M. Kenedy and Company continued to pay his estate his full share of the profits until 1855, when the firm bought his quarter interest for an undisclosed sum. By then its profits had soared to $75,000 a year, some of which was expended on new boats. Its monopoly of the river business was complete, and it was not threatened until John Young and José San Roman brought the steamers *Guadalupe* and *Swan* to the Rio Grande in 1855. They proved to be annoying enough to induce M. Kenedy and Company to buy them out in 1857 for cash and an eighth interest in the firm.

Kenedy had married in 1852, and King two years later.[2] With Stillman for a neighbor, they had established their homes in

Brownsville. Both were already well-to-do, and with twenty years of steamboating still ahead of them, they could have had little reason to doubt that eventually they would be wealthy men. In their time they were to put more than a score of boats on the Rio Grande, most of them built to their express order. They had no interest in the vast tract of land that had been won for Texas by the war with Mexico: 169 miles across from Brownsville to Corpus Christi on shallow, unnavigable Corpus Christi Bay. Kenedy may have seen some of that land along the shore of Laguna Madre, north of Point Isabel; in his five years on the Rio Grande King had scarcely been out of sight of the river.

Of course, both were acquainted through hearsay with the perils of that vacant land between the Nueces and the Rio Grande designated on all maps simply as Wild Horse Desert— which was a misnomer; it was almost treeless and waterless, but it was not a desert in the usual understanding of the word. There were stretches of raw sand and thickets of mesquite and patches of granjeno, but mostly it was open, grassed-over llano, where wild horses and cattle born wild, or gone wild, roamed free.

In April, 1852, King and a party of armed men, numerous enough to guarantee their safety, set out from Brownsville to attend the first Texas State Fair at Corpus Christi at the invitation of Henry Kinney, the ubiquitous promoter of the town. Forty-five miles from Corpus Christi they bivouacked at Santa Gertrudis Creek, the first living water they had seen in several days. As he got down to drink, it certainly could not have occurred to Richard King that the very name of that trifling stream was to become so interwoven with his, even before his steamboating days were over, as to be almost synonymous.

The possibilities of that lonely land, where property rights, even life itself, could be purchased only by the gun, seem to have grown on King, for on July 25, 1853, at Rio Grande City, he purchased all existing rights to the Rincon de Santa Gertrudis grant—fifteen thousand acres at two cents an acre. His title was clear. The Act of Confirmation, passed the previous year, by the Texas Legislature acknowledged the validity of authentic Mexican land grants. A year later he bought the much larger de la Garza Santa Gertrudis grant—fifty-three thousand acres. He picked up other Mexican grants for the proverbial song. Without neglecting the steamboat business, he was putting together what was to become the great King Empire.

To establish a ranch in that lawless, unfenced sweep of country called for something more than just having title to the land. That was the easiest part of it; he would have to defend himself against the outlaw gangs and organized bands of cattle thieves, Texan as well as Mexican, who had made the Wild Horse Desert a haven for desperados. It was a challenge that only a man of his iron will could have elected to face. How he surrounded himself with fighting men, and how well he succeeded, is another story.

War-torn Mexico continued to be plagued by insurrections. The new boundary between the republics proved a boon to the *insurrectos;* when hard-pressed they crossed the river and found sanctuary on American soil. As soon as they had recruited their strength, they crossed back. To stop these incursions the United States established Ringgold Barracks at Rio Grande City. To M. Kenedy and Company fell the contract for keeping the post supplied.

While these violations of neutrality were of some local interest, they were soon lost sight of with the approach of a far more serious conflict. The grave portents came to a head when, despite Governor Sam Houston's impassioned appeals to the contrary, Texas seceded from the Union by popular vote on February 23, 1861.

When a declaration of war followed, all Union forces in the state were granted safe conduct to their lines. The *Mustang*, an M. Kenedy and Company boat, brought the United States troops downriver from Ringgold Barracks, along with the detail still at Fort Brown, to White Ranch, where they boarded the *Grampus* for Brazos Santiago. Colonel John (Rip) Ford and a company of Texas irregulars had evacuated the garrison there. All were put aboard a waiting steamship, after which Ford took possession of the military stores at Brazos Santiago and had them transported to Brownsville.

The lower Rio Grande was to become tremendously important to the Confederacy, but not until after the North had blockaded her other Atlantic and Gulf ports, and the Rio Grande was all she had left.

Miflin Kenedy and Richard King were not Southerners, but they were strongly for the Confederacy. Although a native of New York State, Stillman was a Southern sympathizer, but his loyalty was tempered by his consideration for his private fortune; he did not propose to come out of the war and find it swept away. He need not have worried, for ironically the war, instead of impoverishing him, was to make him wealthy beyond his dreaming.

Before New Orleans fell and the North gained control of the Mississippi, beef cattle by the thousands had been trailed out of Texas to Shreveport, on Red River, and either slaughtered there or sent down the river on the hoof to feed the armies of the Confederacy fighting in Tennessee and Virginia. Now it was cotton rather than beef that began finding its way down through east Texas to Brownsville and was hustled across the river to Matamoros, where it went in one warehouse door "Confederate" cotton and emerged from another labeled "Mexican" cotton. Identified as such on a bill of lading it meant that it could not be confiscated as contraband when a ship carrying it was boarded and searched by the far-ranging units of the U.S. Navy.

It was trickery that fooled no one. Whether it was reprehensible or an honorable means of outwitting a rapacious enemy depended on which side of the conflict you were aligned.

In the mistaken belief that by withholding its cotton from world markets the manufacturing industries of England and Germany would place such pressure on their governments that they would be forced to declare for the Confederacy, the South had waited in vain. With the value of its currency dropping and its need of gold and munitions becoming desperate, it belatedly changed policy and began an energetic and well-organized campaign to transport cotton two and three hundred miles overland to the Mexican border.

No one can say how many thousand bales of cotton, on which the Confederate government had fixed a tax of 10 percent, reached the unblockaded Rio Grande. The total must have been impressive to warrant the statement of an eyewitness, as reported by Davenport: "From 200 to 300 vessels ranging in size from a 20-ton schooner to a 2000-ton steamship were constantly anchored three to four miles from its [Bagdad's] beach, while hundreds of laborers engaged as lightermen in bringing merchandise across the bar from the Gulf to the harbor in the river." [3]

Trains of dusty, lint-covered wagons, ten or more at a time, under military convoy, moved down the Wild Horse Desert and across the Santa Gertrudis in such number that the trail was dubbed in popular parlance the Cotton Road. There was a dividend in every bale for M. Kenedy and Company. It had six boats in service and they were kept busy shuttling back and forth between Matamoros and Bagdad, or even venturing outside to the waiting fleet in good weather, taking downriver alleged "Mexican" cotton and bringing back cases and barrels of material masquerading on a manifest as farming implements, tools, sugar, etc., but which were in reality rifles, ammunition and assorted war material—all consigned to nonexistent Mexican merchants.

Matamoros was alive with speculators, all intent on defrauding one another and the Confederacy as well. Stillman was at home among them and more than their match. At his suggestion M. Kenedy and Company began buying cotton before it reached the Rio Grande. The great volume of business being conducted through the so-called back door of the Confederacy was proving to be nothing less than a gold mine. An interruption had come on February 25, 1862, when the U.S.S. *Portsmouth,* of twenty-two guns, dropped anchor at Boca del Rio. Stillman and his partners had answered that challenge by putting their boats under Mexican registry. Captain King took the *Grampus* down the river flying the Mexican flag at the jackstaff.

He had some anxious minutes, not knowing whether the *Portsmouth* would recognize the Rio Grande as international water or put a shot across his bow and order him to heave to. He went on unopposed, however, and since then there had been no interference with the Bagdad trade.

The war reached the Rio Grande in January, 1863, when Confederate Brigadier General Hamilton P. Bee, a Corpus Christi lawyer of little account as a military leader, occupied Brownsville with twelve hundred men, consisting of some infantry, four companies of the Texas Thirty-Third Cavalry and a battery, on orders by Major General John Magruder, commanding the Texas District, C.S.A., who contracted with M. Kenedy and Company to supply Bee with subsistence stores for six months, payment to be made in gold or cotton.

An ever-increasing quantity of cotton reached Matamoros to be transshipped as "Mexican" cotton. The firm's boats were never idle. But as the year wore on, the South received two staggering blows—the capture of Vicksburg and Lee's defeat at Gettysburg. The effect was felt as far away as Texas. Magruder, fearing that Union General Banks was about to invade Texas from Louisiana, hastily recalled his troops from the Rio Grande, leaving General Bee with a battery and fewer than a hundred men to hold the Brownsville sector. The Thirty-Third Texas Cavalry and other units that were being withdrawn from him were scarcely on their way when Bee was thrown into a panic by word that twenty-six Union transports had arrived at Brazos Santiago with an invasion force of ten thousand men. Actually the number was less than seven thousand, commanded by none other than Major General Nathaniel Banks.

Bee lost his head completely when his couriers informed him that Banks had crossed the ford at Boca Chico and was marching on Brownsville. Countermanding Magruder's orders, he recalled the departing cavalrymen, only to change his mind again and busy himself destroying all military stores, dumping his cannon into the river and setting fire to the eight thousand bales of cotton in the cotton yard. With Brownsville ablaze, he retreated to the north.

Banks entered the town on November 6 and did his best to save what was left of it. To avoid arrest as military prisoners all prominent Secessionists had fled to Matamoros. Stillman was already there. The partners received a stab in the back from an unexpected source. To ingratiate himself with the authorities across the river, Acting Governor Cortina turned over to the Union commander the M. Kenedy and Company steamboats that had been placed under bogus Mexican registry, which he had the right to do.

But Cortina was for sale to the highest bidder. Stillman convinced him that he had made an error. Cortina apologized to Banks for the "slight" mistake he had made, and the boats, with the exception of the *Matamoros,* were restored to their rightful owners.

Banks left the Rio Grande with the major part of his army in early 1864. Major General Francis J. Herron and three thousand men were left at Brownsville. Herron's command appeared to be strong enough to maintain the Union position, until Colonel Rip Ford and several hundred mounted men, of what the Confederacy was pleased to call its Western Expeditionary Force, swarmed over a Union outpost a few miles above Brownsville in reckless Ranger style, and drove the Union troops across the Rio Grande, taking a few prisoners. There were casualties on both sides.

Ford expected to be attacked in prompt reprisal from Brownsville, but the attack failed to come. He had upward of eight hundred men out in the chaparral, all first-class fighting men. Four days later he swept into the very outskirts of Brownsville, hoping to bait Herron into giving battle. Instead, the Union commander retreated down the river to Brazos Santiago and the protection of Union naval guns. Unopposed, Ford took possession of Brownsville on July 30, 1864.

Confederate cotton began flowing across the river to Matamoros again. Mexico was in turmoil, with the Imperialists of Prince Maximilian, the puppet Emperor, waging war on the armies of President Juarez. Ford was ordered to keep his eye on that struggle and hold his position at Brownsville. Between the

The *Antelope*—the Wells Fargo gold boat on the Sacramento and an all-time popular favorite. She was unique in being accident free.

The *Yosemite*. For years she ran opposite to the *Antelope* and later ended her days on the Columbia.

The *W. B. Dance* at the Fort Benton levee, the head of navigation on the Missouri River.

The *Lot Whitcomb* 1851, from an old drawing. The finest and fastest steamboat on the Columbia for many years.

The Hudson's Bay Company's *Beaver,* the first steamboat on the waters of the northwest.

The *Senator* from New York City that was brought around the Horn to Sacramento.

The *Delta King* was launched in 1926 as was the companion *Delta Queen*. During World War II the U. S. Government took over the *Delta King*. The *Delta Queen* later became an excursion boat on the Mississippi.

Steamboat wreck on the Missouri. Wrecks like this were often caused to collect insurance.

MOTHERS LOOK OUT FOR YOUR CHILDREN!
ARTISANS, MECHANICS, CITIZENS!

When you leave your family in health, must you be hurried home to mourn a

DREADFUL CASUALITY!

PHILADELPHIANS, your RIGHTS are being invaded! regardless of your interests, or the LIVES OF YOUR LITTLE ONES. THE CAMDEN AND AMBOY, with the assistance of other companies without a Charter, and in VIOLATION OF LAW, as decreed by your Courts, are laying a

LOCOMOTIVE RAIL ROAD!

Through your most Beautiful Streets, to the RUIN of your TRADE, annihilation of your RIGHTS, and regardless of your PROSPERITY and COMFORT   **Will you permit this?** or do you consent to be a

SUBURB OF NEW YORK!!

Rails are now being laid on BROAD STREET to CONNECT the TRENTON RAIL ROAD with the WILMINGTON and BALTIMORE ROAD, under the pretence of constructing a City Passenger Railway from the Navy Yard to Fairmount!!! This is done under the auspices of the CAMDEN AND AMBOY MONOPOLY!

RALLY PEOPLE in the Majesty of your Strength and forbid THIS

OUTRAGE!

Canalboat companies and stage coach interests united to frighten the public from riding on the railroads.

Henry Miller Shreve,
Father of the Steamboat;
he cleared the Mississippi
of snags.

Captain Richard King,
Rio Grande steamboat
magnate and creator of
the great King Ranch.

Captain Joseph La Barge, the famous Missouri River pilot.

Captain J. C. Ainsworth, the czar of Columbia River steamboating.

The New Orleans and Vicksburg packet *Natchez* that gained everlasting fame by her race with the *Robert E. Lee.*

The *Robert E. Lee,* one of the great Mississippi steamboats, famous in song and story.

The steamer *Jim White,* third of her name, the most luxurious of all Mississippi River steamboats.

Union army dug in at Brazos Santiago and his Texans there was constant fighting. There was no point in continuing the conflict; the South had lost the war. In the hope of effecting a truce on the border, General Lew Wallace, General Grant's personal envoy, arrived at Brazos Santiago and arranged a meeting between Ford and General Steele, who had succeeded Herron. They met at Point Isabel and an agreement was reached that became effective on April 1, 1865.

When news of Lee's surrender at Appomattox, on April 9, reached the border two days later, all semblance of civil law disappeared. Rip Ford's command crumbled as men deserted by the hundred—not to go home but to cross into Mexico to continue the war against the hated Yankees from there.

Several thousand bales of cotton had accumulated on the Brownsville waterfront. Matamoros speculators eyed it enviously. Formerly strongly for the South, they had switched their allegiance overnight to the North, as Stillman, King and Kenedy were to find it convenient to do. The price of cotton was still sky high. It wouldn't be for long. They wanted to get their hands on the Brownsville cotton before the Rebels destroyed it. Pulling strings, they induced General Steele at Brazos to attack the town. Ford met them with what men he could muster and drove them back. It marked the end of the shooting war on the Rio Grande.

Texas had escaped the devastation other Southern states suffered. No major battle had been fought on Texas soil. Being acquainted with the contentious character of its people, the task of "reconstructing" them and bringing them back into the Union as loyal citizens must have appeared to General of the Armies Ulysses S. Grant as a major undertaking, for he dispatched twenty-five thousand troops to Texas under command of, no less than, tough Major General Phil Sheridan.

In due course General Frederick Steele, at Brazos Santiago, was reinforced by several thousand battle-tested veterans, and on May 30 he marched into Brownsville. His orders were to restore civil law, confiscate all weapons and military stores and put down any pockets of Confederate resistance he might find. He found nothing; those who wanted to leave had fled, taking their arms with them. Brownsville was peaceful again—at least as peaceful as its location and turbulent character permitted.

Stillman had notified his partners in 1864 that he wanted to withdraw from the company, giving his failing health as his reason for retiring. With their approval he had sold his interest to James Walworth, long a close friend of all three. Several months later, however, Walworth died, leaving his entire estate to his wife. From her, for $50,000—which at this distance would seem to have been very hard bargaining—the two surviving partners acquired her interest in the firm, which they proceeded to reorganize; and in 1866 it became King, Kenedy and Company, strictly a steamboat business unconnected with their ranching operations.

If King and Kenedy were to retain the old company's monopoly of Rio Grande steamboating, it was imperative that they arrange to have their citizenship restored as quickly as possible. The terms of the general Amnesty Proclamation did not apply to them; being the owners of taxable property valued at more than $20,000, they were required to have their cases reviewed by the proper Union authorities and, if found eligible for citizenship, to be pardoned directly by the President of the United States. In some mysterious way it was quickly arranged. Before the summer was over the firm was under contract to the U.S. Quartermaster's Department to "transport military stores and supplies."

In 1866 Stillman left the Rio Grande to spend his remaining years at Cornwall-on-the-Hudson, in his native New York State. Before leaving he sold to Miflin Kenedy his de Los Laureles grant, some 50,000 acres, between King's holdings and Laguna Madre, to the east. Large though it was, it was less than a tenth the size of King's Santa Gertrudis with its 600,000 acres.

The old boats were worn out. Despite the dwindling trade with Bagdad and the postwar depression that was sweeping the nation, King and Kenedy bought four new Pittsburgh-built boats and had them on the Rio Grande by autumn, only to discover that they could not drum up enough business to keep them profitably employed. They were fortunate enough to dispose of two of them to the tottering Imperialist government of Mexico and placed another under charter to the United States, keeping only the new light-draft *Camargo II* under their own flag.

To add to the partners' concern the Texas Legislature had under advisement the granting of a charter to what its promoters called the Rio Grande Railroad Company. Nearer at home an extended drought had settled on the country; out on the Wild Horse Desert grass was dying, and there was so little water in the river that it was impossible for even the new *Camargo II* to get beyond Reynosa.

Undoubtedly they were too calloused by their past success to believe that the dropping off of business was more than a temporary setback. But 1866 proved to be no better. The Imperialist government of Maximilian collapsed when he faced a firing squad at Querétaro on June 9. The resulting chaos was felt on both sides of the Rio Grande.

Trade was just beginning to recover in early October when the worst hurricane in years struck the Gulf Coast, flattening everything at Bagdad and Brazos Santiago and reducing the old buildings at Point Isabel to kindling. At the White Ranch terminal it knocked down the warehouse and drove the steamboats *Camargo II, El Primero, Antonio* and *Enterprise* ashore, all total wrecks. Brownsville and Matamoros suffered heavily as well. It convinced both King and Miflin Kenedy that they could more profitably devote themselves to developing their great ranches.

They didn't completely divorce themselves from steamboating until two years later, when the company was dissolved and the names of King and Kenedy disappeared from the river. For twenty-two years, almost without a break, they had monopolized Rio Grande steamboating.

But the days when the commercial prosperity of the Rio Grande depended on the King-Kenedy boats belonged in the past. One by one the side-wheelers disappeared until only Captain Dan Kelly's little *Bessie* was left.

XI

The Wild Missouri

WHEN ST. LOUIS saw its first steamboat in August, 1817, thriving Louisville, Kentucky, was already an established steamboat town and could rightfully claim to be the most important river port between Pittsburgh, the head of navigation, and New Orleans. St. Louis was the acknowledged capital of the fur trade, but it was still a small town, with possibly three thousand inhabitants.

It was rich. There was, however, nothing in the nature of the fur trade to add appreciably to the future population of St. Louis; furs were marketed there and forwarded by keelboat to New Orleans. Their value, even at that early date, was tremendous; but the business was in the hands of a wealthy few, and it brought none of those varied industries to St. Louis that, a quarter of a century later, were to transform it into a bustling metropolis.

In 1819, the old French settlement on the bank of the Mississippi could hardly have imagined that in the next several decades its strategic position was to be an unconditional guarantee of its future growth and prosperity in the pathway of the greatest of all American adventures, the settlement of the West: the opening of the Santa Fe Trail as a great trade route, the mass migration of the pioneers to the Oregon country, the movement of the Mormons to Utah, the gold rush to California, and later, to Colorado—and in the end, most important of all, the breaking of the several thousand miles of wilderness through which flowed the Missouri.

Far from being unrelated, these episodes were all a part of the country's continuing movement westward, and in one way or another fanned out from St. Louis. It became the great central base of supplies for everything west of the Mississippi River, and back to it flowed the produce of that vast region between the river and the Rocky Mountains, stretching from the Mexican Southwest to the Canadian border. To maintain the preeminence that had been thrust upon it, cheap and reasonably fast transportation was necessary. The steamboat was the answer. When St. Louis belatedly recognized the importance of the steamboat and embraced it with enthusiasm, nothing could stop it from becoming the metropolis of the great valley of the Mississippi and the steamboat capital of the United States.

The mighty Missouri River, pouring its yellow flood into the Mississippi a few miles north of St. Louis, was well known to the pioneers of the fur trade. It pursued its uncertain course across the state whose name it bears to present-day Kansas City before it began its long swing northward to the faraway Indian country of the Dakotas and Montana. That east-west stretch of the river—that is, from St. Louis to today's Fort Leavenworth, known as the Lower Missouri—had long been navigated by keelboats and flat-bottomed Mackinaws. It was notorious for its sandbars and shifting channel. That it could be navigated by a steamboat was believed to be impossible, and it was not until the middle of May, 1819, almost two years after the *Zebulon M. Pike* reached St. Louis, that the first steamboat, the *Independence,* entered the Missouri; and despite many predictions that she would leave her bones on a sandbar or have her bottom ripped out by snags, she made her way upstream two hundred miles to the mouth of the little Chariton River and the settlement there and returned safely to St. Louis.

That same year the *Western Engineer,* a government boat under command of Major Stephen H. Long, with a party of

U.S. Engineers and troops aboard, made its way up to the original Council Bluffs, a few miles above today's Omaha. Her prow was carved in the shape of a monster; and by means of a flue, steam was conducted from the boiler and emitted from the mouth of the beast—this device being calculated to impress the Indians, which it did.

Hiram Martin Chittenden, in his authoritative *History of Early Steamboating on the Missouri River,* says five other steamboats were requisitioned by the government at that time for the purpose of transporting troops to establish a military post at the mouth of the Yellowstone River. Due to inexperience with navigating the Missouri, they were forced to turn back, only the *Western Engineer* reaching Council Bluffs. It should be explained that there were two Council Bluffs—the original council meeting place of the Maha Indians on the west bank of the Missouri, and the town of Council Bluffs, Iowa, across the Missouri from the city of Omaha, which was founded by the Mormons in 1840.

When Major Long decided that he had gone as far as he safely could, he made his first camp below the bluffs. When the soldiers who had been put ashore some miles down the river joined him, the temporary camp was abandoned and a semblance of a fortified post was established back from the river on the crest of the bluffs. This camp was known briefly as Camp Engineer before it became Fort Atkinson.

Although the *Western Engineer* had demonstrated that the Missouri could be navigated safely by steamboat well above the mouth of the Platte, one of its most important fur-producing tributaries, both the strongly entrenched American Fur Company of the Astor-Chouteau interests and Manuel Lisa and his Missouri Fur Company, the American's stiffest competition, refused to accept it as a practical and profitable means of transportation between their St. Louis headquarters and their upriver hosts. The keelboat had served them well in the past, and they continued to send their peltries and furs down the Missouri in that manner.

It wasn't only the tycoons of the fur trade who wrote off the steamboat as impracticable for the Missouri, an uncharted, unmarked river, with thousands of snags, uncounted sandbars and a channel that shifted with every stage of high water. It was a terrible indictment, and the years that followed were to prove how true it was.

Even on the lower river—that is, between St. Louis and the cluster of settlements that became Kansas City (Independence, Westport and Westport Landing) and Weston and Sibley—the steamboat was regarded with general apathy. By 1824 the Santa Fe trade was booming.[1] Thousands of tons of merchandise were moving back and forth across the state, moved by wagon, not by steamboat. Even after Colonel Henry H. Leavenworth erected Cantonment Leavenworth (later Fort Leavenworth) on the Kansas side of the river, it was not until 1829, two years later, that the *W. D. Duncan* inaugurated more or less regular steamboat service between St. Louis and the military post that had been built to protect the eastern end of the long trail to and from Santa Fe.

Of all our Western rivers that once enjoyed commercial importance, only the Missouri flowed through hostile Indian country. For two thousand miles, all the way from Fort Benton, Montana, to Fort Leavenworth, it was truly a wilderness river. Early maps show a number of "forts"; but they were only trading posts of the rival fur companies. North of Fort Atkinson there were no military installations, and none were built until the steamboat had proved that it could supply them with men and subsistence.

"Throughout the Indian wars of the Missouri Valley the steamboat played a part of the very highest importance," says Chittenden. "It was almost the exclusive means of transporting men and supplies along the river. Its use in the military service dates from the very beginning of steamboat navigation on the river, as well as from the first important step toward the military occupation of the valley."

The first Indian campaign west of the Mississippi River took place four years after the *Western Engineer* reached what was to become Fort Atkinson, when Colonel Leavenworth, with a considerable body of troops and Sioux allies, went upriver from that post to the Arikara villages to avenge the killing of a number of men in the employ of General Ashley, the fur trader. Two years later, in 1825, General Atkinson, accompanied by several hundred troops, left the fort that bore his name and made his way up the Missouri to a point about one hundred miles above the mouth of the Yellowstone. The announced purpose of this expedition was to make treaties with tribes he encountered and "impress on them the power of the United States." Of course, it was a military reconnaissance. Save for the journals of Lewis and Clark, the information Atkinson secured was the first definite knowledge the government had of that country and its Indian inhabitants, the western Sioux, Blackfeet and Crows.

Both Leavenworth and Atkinson had journeyed up the Missouri by keelboats. It was not until 1855, thirty years later, when General Harney was ordered to assemble a strong military force and establish bases of supplies to protect the emigrant routes across Nebraska (the Oregon Trail and the Mormon Trail) and inflict a crushing blow on the Oglala and Brûlé Sioux for the massacre of Lieutenant Grattan and his company, a few miles east of Fort Laramie, that steamboats were used for the first time to transport troops to the mouth of the Platte River and the Niobrara (the *Eau qui courre* of the French).

The steamboats had done all that had been asked of them, but the full measure of their importance had not yet been realized. Following General Harney's defeat of the Indians in the battle of Ash Hollow, peace appeared to have settled on the Northern Plains. For the Sioux it was only a time of waiting, of gathering strength for the far greater conflict with the white man that they regarded as inevitable. Their homeland was gradually being filched away from them by treaties that would not and could not be honored. They were being defrauded by government agents and cheated by white traders alike. The many injustices being visited on them should have cried a warning, but the military seems not to have been aware of the seething unrest that was about to erupt in violence and bloodshed.

The long-smoldering trouble came to a head on August 18, 1862, when the Santee Sioux in the valley of the Minnesota River, under the leadership of their noted chief, Little Crow, attacked the village of New Ulm and other settlements north of Mankato, murdering or taking captive the inhabitants, destroying property and spreading terror throughout the state. In three days upward of a thousand men, women and children were killed, with a property loss estimated at several million dollars.

State and federal troops were dispatched to the scene immediately. The outrages were checked, and the hostiles, defeated in a series of minor battles, retreated up the Minnesota River. Some of the white captives were killed, but the great majority were released unharmed. Several hundred Indians who had taken part in the massacre were made prisoner. They were tried by court-martial, and those found guilty were condemned to death. The sentences of many were commuted by the intervention of President Lincoln, but on December 26, 1862, thirty-eight were hanged at Mankato—the greatest mass execution to occur in the United States.

But Little Crow and many of his followers made good their escape and crossed the Missouri River into Dakota, where they spread disaffection among other Sioux tribes. The trouble was far from being ended, for this was what came to be known as the Great Sioux Uprising.

The Indians had taken advantage of the fact that the seasoned veterans manning the frontier posts had been withdrawn to fight the battles of the Civil War, then raging, and that they would have to face only untrained troops. But to their dismay they learned that the regiments of volunteers that took the field against them were excellent soldiers.

With General Sibley and two thousand men driving up the Minnesota River from the east and General Sully with as many more moving up the Missouri, the hostiles, numbering by now fully six thousand, resorted to the strategy of fight and run, dropping back after every engagement. They lost battle after battle, but the victories were not conclusive. Despite heavy losses the hostiles remained unsubdued and refused to make an all-out stand, until finally General Sully caught them on the Knife River; and in the battle of Killdeer Mountain, on July 28, 1864, hundreds were killed and their horses and other property either captured or destroyed.

Sully's victory at Killdeer Mountain (called Tahkahokuty by the Indians) is generally regarded as the culmination of the long campaign against the Sioux. In a way it was, but the various tribes of the Sioux Nation remained as defiant as ever, their spirit unbroken, and the great issue, which was whether they were to be forced to submit to the domination of the white man, give up their warlike habits and be cooped up on reservations, was not to be decided for another twelve years, when General Custer made his fatal mistake on the Little Big Horn and gave the Indians their greatest victory—from which they had to flee and which ironically marked the downfall of the Sioux Nation's power. After the Little Big Horn they were only a nuisance rather than a menace.

The military occupation of the Northern Plains was complete, and it had been largely accomplished by the constant use of steamboats. When necessary they had been pressed into service as fast dispatch boats; and for the movement of troops and supplies they had proven themselves indispensable. They had been asked to ply extremely dangerous waters, but only one major accident occurred, the destruction by striking a snag of a boat carrying timber and other supplies for the construction of a new post on the Yellowstone River, fifty miles above its mouth.

General Sully lavished high praise on the steamboats for the part they had played in the Indian wars. "It is impossible to estimate the great value in the military operations of this important line of communications. Forts and cantonments were strung all along the river from Fort Randall to Fort Benton, and all of them, as well as the troops in the field, depended for their support upon the riverboats. The conquest of the Missouri Valley would have been a very different matter had the government been deprived of this important aid in its operations."

Of all the steamboats that played a part in the long struggle, none won more fame than the *Far West*, Captain Grant Marsh.

With General Gibbon's command aboard, and also serving as
Major General Terry's headquarters boat, it ascended the Yellowstone as far as the Big Horn River several days prior to the
battle of the Little Big Horn. It was aboard the *Far West* that
the famous conference between Generals Terry, Gibbon and
Custer occurred. After the battle it was the *Far West* that
brought Major Reno's wounded down the Yellowstone to Fort
Abraham Lincoln, along with a pouch of dispatches, official and
private, relating to the Custer tragedy.[2]

Although the army leaned heavily on the steamboats in the
sixties and seventies, it did little or nothing to promote Missouri
River steamboating back in the days when it was universally believed that navigating that wild and unpredictable river by
steam was an impracticable dream that would end in disaster.
Even the fur companies, which had the most to gain if it could
be done, refused to consider it; and it was not until 1830, in a
long letter from Pierre Chouteau, Jr., to the firm's headquarters
in New York City, excerpts from which follow, that we have the
first evidence that the American Fur Company was seriously
considering putting a steamboat on the Missouri to serve its
posts on the upper river:

> Since the loss of our keelboat and the arrival of Mr. McKenzie,
> we have been contemplating the project of building a small steam-
> boat for the trade of the upper Missouri.[3] We believe that the
> navigation will be much safer in going up, and possibly in coming
> down, than it is by keelboat. The only serious drawback will be
> the danger of breakage of some important pieces of machinery,
> which it would be difficult and perhaps impossible to repair on
> the spot. However, after consultation with some of the ablest
> steamboat captains, we think that by having spare parts and a
> good blacksmith outfit on board, we may be able to overcome the
> difficulty. . . . If we succeed it will be a great advantage to our
> business. The expenses we are annually put to in the purchase
> of keelboats and supplies, and in advances to *engages* before their
> departure, are enormous, and have to be repeated every year.
> With the steamboat we could keep all our men in the Indian
> country, where we could pay the greater part of their wages in

merchandise instead of making the large outlay of cash which we are now constantly required to do.[4]

The boat would make the voyage to the upper river every spring. By starting from here [St. Louis] at the beginning of April with the full season's outfit of merchandise it would probably be back in early June, and bring with it a portion of the peltries. The finer furs could still be brought down in the ordinary way. The merchandise would all reach its destination before ice closed in in the fall, which we now sometimes fail to do, to our great loss. . . . Such a boat as we require we think will cost $7,000, in Cincinnati or Marietta, but as we shall want a number of duplicate parts and extras the cost may amount to $8,000.

Our plan, promising as it seems to us, has its difficulties, and we submit it to you for approval before taking definite action.

John Jacob Astor was the real head of the company, although his son, William B. Astor, was its president. While the New York headquarters managed the finances and marketing for the firm, in the West the production of furs and profits was in the hands of Bernard Pratte and Company, of St. Louis, of which Chouteau was the guiding spirit. He has been characterized as an impatient, impulsive man; but it is to be doubted that, having long scoffed at the idea of steamboats being able to operate successfully on the Upper Missouri, he had done such a complete about-face on the spur of the moment. Writing that "the finer furs could still be brought down in the ordinary way [by keelboat]" indicates that he still entertained some grave doubts about the safety of steamboat transportation on the Missouri River.

The New York headquarters approved Chouteau's suggestion. He journeyed to Cincinnati at once and arranged to have the boat built there, the contract specifying that it was to be completed and delivered at St. Louis by May 15 of the following year, 1831. She was a small boat, 130 feet overall, a side-wheeler, powered by a single engine. (It might be noted that the first double-engined steamboat, the *Platte*, did not appear on the Missouri until 1838.)

Appropriately, Chouteau named the fur company boat the

Yellowstone. When she left St. Louis on her maiden voyage it was expected that she would be able to reach the mouth of the Yellowstone. Owing to unforeseen circumstances she did not get away from St. Louis until early in June, and by the time she reached Fort Leavenworth the first of the Missouri River's so-called two annual spring floods had passed, which meant that she would be too late to take full advantage of the second runoff, which was caused by melting snows in the mountains far to the west. The first runoff, or "flood," was due to the melting of snow in the Missouri Valley.

The presence aboard of Pierre Chouteau, Jr., and Kenneth McKenzie, the American Fur Company's chief trader, was proof of the importance attached to the first voyage of the *Yellowstone.* She ran only by daylight, a custom that Missouri River steamboats were to follow for years. To have done otherwise on a river filled with snags, boils and sandbars, and unimproved by a single aid to navigation, would have been suicidal.

When in 1832 the government began appropriating money for the improvement of the "Western Rivers," in which the Missouri was included, Captain Shreve began clearing the Mississippi of snags; but nothing was done for the Missouri. In fact, it was neglected until 1838, when Shreve's two old snag boats, the *Heliopolis* and the *Archimedes,* ascended that river for over three hundred miles, removing 2,245 snags and cutting 1,710 overhanging trees from its banks. That same year U.S. Engineers under command of Captain Robert E. Lee made a survey of the Lower Missouri as far up as Westport (Kansas City), looking to its general improvement.

Much has been made of the hazards of navigating the Mississippi, but the number of steamboats destroyed on the Missouri, 70 percent by striking snags (295), is evidence enough that the Big Muddy was by far the more dangerous of the two rivers. The number of steamboats lost from all causes on the Missouri totaled 400, which exceeds the number lost on the Mississippi. Of course, Missouri River steamers were, as a whole, much smaller; few of them could rate comparison with the big packets and "floating palaces" on the St. Louis–New Orleans run. But after a late and fumbling beginning, they became very numerous.

If the reader of Western narratives has frequently encountered the descriptive line, "the plains were black with buffalo," and has come to accept it as basically true, it is no greater exaggeration to say that in 1859 the Missouri River was "black with steamboats."

In the beginning there was little if any legal supervision covering the operation of steamboats, but the frequent accidents and disasters that befell them soon resulted in a whole body of laws, state and federal, being enacted. Frequent boiler and hull inspections and other safety measures became mandatory. Carefully kept records of arrivals and departures helped to make steamboating a well-ordered business. Surprisingly, records show that in 1859 more boats left St. Louis for Missouri River points than for the upper and lower Mississippi. In that year, 308 arrivals were recorded at Fort Leavenworth and 48 at Sioux City.

The little *Yellowstone* did not have any traffic of that nature to contend with; she had the Missouri to herself. She met the second runoff of the year some distance below the mouth of the Platte and made the most of it, but it passed her by the time she reached the Niobrara, and a few miles above that river she grounded in low water. Efforts were made to back her off, but she was so heavily laden that she could not be moved. Burning with impatience at the delay, Chouteau sent two men upriver in a skiff to Fort Tecumseh for lighters (flat-bottomed Mackinaws).

The story is told that every day Chouteau climbed the bluffs overlooking the river, pacing back and forth as he watched for help to arrive. The bluffs have been known ever since as the Chouteau Bluffs.

At last three boats came down the river and took off enough of the Yellowstone's cargo to enable her to reach Fort Tecumseh, located across the river from Pierre, the present-day capital of South Dakota.

As she lay at Fort Tecumseh the *Yellowstone* was still far from Fort Union, the American Fur Company's principal post, three miles above the mouth of the Yellowstone. But the experiment

of sending a steamboat far up the Missouri had been so successful that no attempt was made to go farther. By leaving St. Louis
earlier the following year, Chouteau was convinced that Fort
Union could be reached without great difficulty.

With the river beginning its annual summer drop, and his
plans completed for building a new post at Fort Tecumseh,
farther back from the river, he boarded the *Yellowstone* for St.
Louis and reached it without mishap. Getting an earlier start
the following spring, he came upriver again in the *Yellowstone*.[5]
When he reached Fort Tecumseh the new post was ready for his
inspection, and out of respect for him it was renamed Fort
Pierre.

After a short delay, he boarded the *Yellowstone* and ordered
her pointed upriver. Allowing for the meandering of the Missouri it was better than four hundred miles to Fort Union, but
with the river standing at a favorable stage, she reached her
destination safely, an achievement that was to convince Pierre
Chouteau, Jr., and the heads of the American Fur Company that
with the steamboat to do their bidding they could monopolize
the fur trade of the Upper Missouri, buying out their formidable competitors and forcing the small fry out of business—a
prospect that certainly was encouraged by the triumphant return of the *Yellowstone* to St. Louis in the remarkable running
time of one hundred miles a day.

By 1833 the firm's plans were so far advanced that two boats,
the *Yellowstone* and the *Assiniboine,* were dispatched up the
Missouri. The *Yellowstone* went no farther than Fort Union;
the *Assiniboine* tried to reach Fort McKenzie, the most distant
of the company posts at the mouth of the Marias River (later
Fort Benton), and was caught by low water and compelled to
remain there all winter. The American Fur Company was now
embarked on its program of annually sending steamboats upriver to its distant posts, a practice it maintained until it went
out of business years later. To hasten its complete control of the
trade, it absorbed Manuel Lisa's Missouri Fur Company and
purchased the several so-called nuisance posts that the firm of

Campbell and Sublette had established in the American's territory to draw off what trade they could.

It was on the *Yellowstone,* in 1833, that Maximilian, Prince of Wied, the second of the famous naturalists to explore the Upper Missouri country, arrived at Fort Union as the guest of Pierre Chouteau, Jr.[6] Before the summer was over he had adventured by canoe and keelboat as far as Fort McKenzie, collecting specimens and studying the fauna and flora of the country. His *Travels in the Interior of North America,* originally published in German, was hailed as the first accurate scientific knowledge of the region. His pertinent observations about the color and life of the northern posts and the men engaged in the fur trade have become only the richer with the passing of time.

The *engages* and *voyageurs* were almost exclusively French-Canadians or Creoles from Louisiana. They were a hard-working class, obedient and cheerful, satisfied with their lot, and "presented a phase of pioneer life on the Missouri which has long since become wholly extinct." The pay was poor, the food plentiful but of the coarsest kind. They had no physicians, no nurses and only the simplest of medicines. Feats of strength and endurance were their common characteristics. Civilization rode forward on their brawny backs and arms. They have been forgotten, even their names are lost. But scores of them occupy the unmarked graves that line the banks of the Upper Missouri.

XII

—◆———◁🄲🄲◷🄾▷———◆—

· The River of the Naturalists

MAXIMILIAN WAS NOT THE FIRST NATURALIST of royal blood to
explore the great basin of the Upper Missouri. Friedrich Paul
Wilhelm, Prince of Württemberg, made several trips to the
United States and ascended the Missouri in the company of fur
traders to Fort Atkinson for the first time in 1822–1824. His credentials were of the highest, and he had been entertained in St.
Louis by two of the elder Chouteaus, Pierre, Sr., and August.

When Prince Paul left Fort Atkinson his party included a man
named Schlape, whom he had brought from Germany to serve
as servant and hunter, a wilderness ranger variously referred to
as "Rodger" or "Bell," and a halfbreed named Mombrun, an
experienced hunter who proved himself both courageous and
faithful. For an outfit he had three or four horses and a like
number of mules, but although his party was small and scantily
provisioned, he visited the Omaha and Ponca Indians, explored
the valley of the Niobrara River, Ponca Creek and White River,
returning to the Missouri at Fort Recovery, a post of the Missouri Fur Company, where he was welcomed by Joshua Pilcher,
the company's noted agent.

Prince Paul was only twenty-five, and although for the past
five years he had devoted himself almost exclusively to an in-

129

tense study of the natural sciences, he was not a naturalist or geologist of professional rank. By some he is held to have been no better than a dedicated amateur; but he saw more in his travels and journeyed farther than most of his contemporaries, going almost all the way to the Rocky Mountains on one occasion and bringing back information of priceless value. Perhaps his most important achievement was the friendly relations he established with the various Indian tribes with whom he came in contact.

Lloyd McFarling in his *Exploring the Northern Plains* says that Prince Paul became acquainted with Toussaint Charboneau and his Indian wife Sacajawea (of Lewis and Clark fame) and their son Baptiste Charboneau, and that when the prince returned to Europe he took the boy with him to be educated at his expense; young Charboneau "returned to the plains and mountains of the United States to become a guide, interpreter and fur trader." [1]

With some justification the Missouri has been called the River of the Naturalists. By 1843 the eyes of the European and American scientific world were focused on the unexplored and still largely unknown American West and Northwest. Following Prince Paul and Prince Maximilian, Thomas Nutthall and John Kirk Townsend, the American naturalist, had reached St. Louis in 1834, where they joined Captain Nathaniel Wyeth's expedition of settlers and missionaries bound for the Columbia River, which was financed by Boston interests and known as the Columbia Fishing and Trading Company.

It was into a wet and sodden world, the last of the winter snows still going off and pleasant spring weather some weeks away, that on March 24 Nutthall and Townsend disembarked in St. Louis from the steamboat that had brought them from Pittsburgh. Nutthall was an experienced wilderness traveler, but it was Townsend's first contact with the frontier. After consulting Captain Wyeth, they spent a day outfitting themselves for the long journey into the wilderness beyond the Missouri.

They stowed their gear aboard the *W. D. Duncan,* which was to take them to Independence, where they were to complete their outfitting for the take-off for the Oregon country. They

were impatient to be on their way, and when they learned that
there was to be a delay of several days because of necessary repairs to the *W. D. Duncan,* they informed Wyeth that they
would set out at once on foot, cataloguing the birds and flowers
along the river, if the steamboat would pick them up when it
overtook them. Wyeth being agreeable to their plan, they left
St. Louis the following morning, after an all-night rain.

Keeping close to the river, they fought their way through the
wet underbrush and the ankle-deep mud. The trees had not
leafed out as yet, and none of the early spring flowers were in
bloom, to Nutthall's disappointment.

Being buffeted all day long by a cold, raw wind and bivouack-
ing at night without shelter, when they could not find a settler's
cabin and hopefully a hot meal, made it a trying experience. In
the hardwood groves below St. Charles they saw numerous
pileated woodpeckers, parakeets and, overhead, flocks of sand-
hill cranes and northbound Canada geese. On the open prairies
flocks of plovers wheeled in the wind. It was a scant reward for
the energy they were expending, and when they heard a steamboat blowing for the landing at Boonville, they hurried to the
river hoping it might be the *W. D. Duncan* with their baggage
and Captain Wyeth. That proved to be the case. They were
taken aboard and continued to Independence where Wyeth's
wagon train was already assembled. They bought several pack
animals, saddle horses and such other necessaries as they were
going to need.

Independence was a wild, raw, booming town, figuratively
bursting at the seams as it tried to keep up with the spiraling
Santa Fe trade. The landing was piled high with boxes and
barrels of merchandise; the seemingly bottomless mud of its
streets was churned into clinging muck by the constant passing
to and fro of heavy freighting outfits.

The town proper was located some distance from the landing.
The latter was to be washed away in the great flood of 1844 and
replaced with a sandbar that ended the town's usefulness as a
river port. The trade shifted to Westport Landing, making it
the jumping-off place for the West.[2]

Nutthall and Townsend were eager to begin their long adven-

ture across the plains. Rain and hail delayed them for several
days, but after a belated start they soon ran into good weather.
Wyeth led his expedition, consisting of 50 men (not including
the several missionaries), with 140 horses and mules and a score
of cattle for the emergency subsistence of his party, up the valley
of the Kaw. He was accompanied by Milton Sublette, the noted
plainsman and the brother of William Sublette. Sublette had his
own modest outfit of twenty men and three times that many
horses.

It was understood that the two companies were to travel together as far as Wyoming's Green River, where the mountain
men were to gather for the annual rendezvous; but ten days out
of Independence the leg injury that Sublette had suffered some
time previously, from an Indian arrow, took such a serious turn
for the worse that he was forced to return to the settlement. The
expedition went on without him. By the time it reached the
Platte the new grass was coming strong, providing ample forage
for the livestock, and owing to the wet spring the plains were
carpeted with a riotous display of wild flowers.

It became the daily routine of the two naturalists to range far
ahead of the train, Townsend fearing that the birds would take
flight at its approach, thereby depriving him of the opportunity
to fill his game bag with the specimens he wanted to take back
to Philadelphia and present to the great Audubon. Nutthall was
equally anxious to collect the plants he wanted before the horses
crushed them.

Although they wore the heavy boots, leather breeches and
hard white wool hats of the frontier, their garb could not conceal the fact that they were two innocents wandering through
wild Indian country in which white men went armed and with
due regard for the safety of their scalps. The two naturalists,
absorbed in their work, appear to have been blissfully unaware
of the dangers that surrounded them.

Their mishaps were many, often ludicrous, but they survived
and ultimately reached the Columbia, from where they embarked in a sailing vessel for the then Sandwich Islands and,
making the long trip around the Horn, returned safely to Phila-

delphia. Nutthall brought back five hundred plants that were new to science, and Townsend returned with "more than seventy birds" to dazzle Audubon. Townsend had kept a careful journal of their wanderings, and when it was published in 1839, the full extent of their contribution to the advancement of American ornithology and botany was realized.

During the winter of 1832–1833, Sir William Drummond Stewart, the titled Scot and sportsman of some distinction, arrived in St. Louis with the announced intention of adventuring into the Far West to enjoy what he termed "the pleasures of the chase." Judged by his cultured speech, flamboyant manner and utter ignorance of the country, he appeared to be the most unlikely material out of which an accomplished plainsman of the first rank could be made.

Stewart came with letters of the highest recommendation to William Sublette from J. Watson Webb, the financier and newspaper publisher, and others. Presumably Bill Sublette arranged for him to go with the company's train to the annual rendezvous, if not in 1833, then surely in 1834. If so, it has escaped Stewart's most devoted biographers, Mae Reed Porter and Odessa Davenport. To quote them: "The first dependable knowledge we have of Stewart's whereabouts in 1834 is of him, in the company of Jim Bridger, riding in a northerly direction to that year's rendezvous (which was to be held on Ham's Fork, a clear pleasant stream flowing into the Green River)."

He and Bridger may have been with Captain Bonneville's expedition, which is admittedly only a conjecture, but he certainly did not travel with Bill Sublette's caravan from Independence that spring, which, although leaving Independence a few days after the departure of Wyeth's train, overtook and passed it before it reached the Laramie River. When the rendezvous was over and Wyeth proceeded on his way to Oregon, Captain Stewart went with him.

Far from being an encumbrance, Stewart, with his expert marksmanship, quickly proved his worth as a hunter.

It was the first of at least four journeys Stewart was to make across the plains to the Shining Mountains and beyond. The last one, made in 1843, was undertaken as a grand farewell to a land he had come to love. Financially, he was at last in a position to gratify his wishes. The outfit he assembled in St. Louis was the most extravagant ever put together—the best blooded horses, tents, and such physical comforts as the plains had never seen, including a commissary stocked with European and American delicacies, preserved fruit, condiments, aged cheese, and an assortment of the finest wines.

Stewart had not previously exhibited any interest in the sciences, and while this last journey into the land of the wild Indian was largely for fun, he nevertheless brought to St. Louis to accompany him such learned men as Dr. Charles Mersch, a naturalist formerly of Luxemburg; Friederich G. L. Luders and Charles A. G. Geyer, from Germany; and Alexander Gordon of Scotland, all well-known botanists, their enthusiasm aroused by the discoveries of Maximilian, Prince Paul, Townsend and Nutthall and the pioneer work of John Bradbury, of the Liverpool Botanical Society.

The fur trade was by then on the way to disappearance. Stewart had known it in its heyday. But if he is to be remembered it is not for his involvement in it, or for his slight contribution to the advancement of science; his greatest claim on history is that he gave Alfred Jacob Miller, the Baltimore painter, to the West. Miller was a far better painter than Catlin or Bodmer, and he put on canvas the best record we have of the days of the mountain men.

From Germany in 1839 came Dr. Frederick Adolph Wislizenus. He was a scholarly man, well versed in the natural sciences, and a practicing physician. In the little town of Mascoutin, Illinois, he got his first taste of life in the West. "Feeling the need of mental and physical recreation," he wrote years later, he gave up his practice in Mascoutin and crossed the Mississippi to St. Louis "determined to make a journey to the Rocky Mountains and the wilder parts of the West."

From Pierre Chouteau, Jr., he received permission to join a small caravan that soon would be leaving Westport for the annual rendezvous, that year on the Popo Agie, a branch of the

Sweetwater. Taking passage on a steamboat, he went up the Missouri and reached Westport in time to join the train. It was one of the first, if not the first, sent out by the company in which the trade goods were carried in carts, two-wheeled affairs, each drawn by a pair of mules, of which in this instance there were four, carrying nine hundred to a thousand pounds of merchandise, including a number of barrels of whisky.

The faint trail the caravan followed from Westport to Grand Island and the Forks of the Platte was soon to be carved deep in the prairie sod by thousands of oxen and prairie schooners and be remembered for all time as the Oregon Trail. It went up the North Fork of the Platte, passed Fort Laramie, the trading post established by William Sublette and Robert Campbell, doing business under the name of Rocky Mountain Fur Company, and on to South Pass and the Popo Agie. Dr. Wislizenus left the caravan there and continued beyond as far as Fort Hall, the gateway to the Oregon Country, built by Captain Wyeth. Turning back at that point, he retraced his way across the Laramie Plains, then south along the Front Range of the Rockies to the Santa Fe Trail, by which he returned to Westport. After several trips to Mexico and Europe, he settled down in St. Louis, where he practiced medicine until his death in 1889, several years after becoming blind.

Wislizenus' contact with the Oglala Sioux on the South Fork of the Platte, in 1839, is interesting for the fact that in 1846, seven years later, Francis Parkman, the famous historian, while gathering the material that appears in his *The Oregon Trail*, lived for some time in their village, the band at that time under the leadership of Whirlwind, who had succeeded old Bull Bear.

In all the written history of the West no better description of the building of a bullboat is found than occurs in Chapter 7 of Wislizenus' *A Journey to the Rocky Mountains in the Year 1839*. The bullboat he describes is not the round, tublike so-called bullboat used extensively by Indian women on the Upper Missouri. To quote him:

Small trunks of some wood that bends easily are split; out of these a boat-shaped frame-work is made with some crosspieces inside; this is firmly bound with thongs of buffalo leather and willow bark, and all gaps are stopped with withes; and buffalo hides, sewed together, with the hair inside, are stretched as taut as can be over the whole. Then it is dried in the air, and the outside daubed over with a mixture of buffalo tallow and ashes. Our canoe [sic] was covered with three buffalo hides, and was about fifteen feet long by a width in the middle of five to six feet.

He neglects to say that only the hides of buffalo bulls were used—hence the name.

The wretched little *Gallant,* on which John James Audubon and his party arrived in St. Louis in 1843, did not represent the progress in speed and passenger comfort that Mississippi River steamboating had made. Even on the steamers plying the Lower Missouri a marked improvement had occurred.

Audubon was sixty-three, but still vigorous and fond of a dram. His *Birds of America* had brought him fame and some measure of prosperity. In New York, he had accepted the generous offer of the Chouteaus to transport him and his party— consisting of Edward Harris, a young gentleman farmer and amateur ornithologist of Moorestown, New Jersey (who had inherited a sizable fortune and was able to indulge his scientific interests); Isaac Sprague, an artist; John G. Bell, the ornithologist and taxidermist; and Lewis M. Squires, a young man of no particular calling—to Fort Union and return on the firm's new steamboat, the *Omega.*

It should be interjected here that the American Fur Company had sold its western division to Pratte, Chouteau and Company in 1834, and that in 1838 the firm name had been changed a second time to Pierre Chouteau, Jr., and Company. But habit being what it was, the original name survived in common usage and is so referred to by many writers.

St. Louis was growing. Having entertained so many noted visitors, it was beginning to achieve a sense of sophistication, but without losing the flavor of its generous French hospitality. In one of his letters Audubon speaks of it as "this very pleasant town." It pointed with pride to the new sixty-room Glasgow House. The interior arrangements of "this new and commodious edifice," said the *Missouri Republican,* "in point of comfort and convenience are not surpassed by any similar establishment in the Valley of the Mississippi."

Audubon and his party put up at the Glasgow House at first, but not for long. In a letter to James Hall (brother-in-law of John W. Audubon) he wrote:

> . . . will leave it [the Glasgow] the day after tomorrow, as it is too good for our purses. . . . The markets here abound with all the good things of the land, and of nature's creation. To give you an idea of this, read the following items: Grouse, two for a York shilling; three chickens for the same; Turkeys, wild or tame, 25 cents; flour $2.00 a barrel; butter, sixpence for the best—fresh and really good; Beef, 3 to 4 cents; veal, the same; pork, 2 cents; venison hams, large and dried, 15 cents each; potatoes 10 cents a bushel; Ducks, three for a shilling; Wild Geese, 10 cents each; Canvas-back Ducks, a shilling a pair; vegetables for the asking, as it were; and only think, in the midst of this abundance and cheapness, we are paying at the rate of $9.00 per week at our hotel, the Glasgow, and at the Planters we were asked $10.00.

The *Omega* was a more costly steamboat than her predecessors, the *Yellowstone, Assiniboine, Trapper* and *Emily.* She had had her trial runs and, something being found amiss, had been put in drydock to have the fault corrected, and was there when the Audubon party arrived in St. Louis. The trouble, whatever it was, could have been corrected in a few days, but in a dispute over wages the workmen had laid down their tools, and it was not until April 25 that she finally began the long trip up the Missouri, with, in addition to the other passengers, a hundred or more trappers aboard, most of them drunk or just recovering from a protracted debauch.

In his correspondence with Harris, back in New York, when his plans for the expedition up the Missouri were taking shape, Audubon had written persuasively: "Mr. Chouteau goes with us to the Yellow Stone." Although he doesn't say which one of the Chouteaus was to accompany them, it seems obvious that it was Pierre Chouteau, Jr., the president of the fur company, to whom he was referring. If there was such an arrangement it must have been tentative, for it is not mentioned again. Pierre Chouteau, Jr., preceded Audubon's party to St. Louis, where, says Harris, "Audubon was extremely kindly received by Mr. Chouteau and his partners."

But, whatever his intentions may have been, Pierre Chouteau, Jr., did not accompany them up the Missouri. The discouraging reports he had received from the company posts that spring may have convinced him that he was needed in St. Louis. Being an astute man, he undoubtedly realized that the lush years of the fur trade were about over.

Although it was for structural reasons that developed, which had nothing to do with the shrinking trade, the *Omega*'s maiden voyage to the Upper Missouri was to be her last as well as her first. But she was to have the distinction of being officered by two of the foremost men in the history of steamboat navigation on the Missouri River: Captain Joseph Sire, master; and Captain Joseph La Barge, her pilot.[3] Of Captain Sire, Audubon said: "Mr. Sire, the gentleman who will command the steamer we go in, is one of the finest-looking men I have seen for many a day, and the accounts I hear of him correspond with his noble face and general appearance."

Of Captain La Barge he has nothing to say. Uniformly, he refers to him as "one of our pilots." La Barge is ignored both in Audubon's *Journal* and in *Up the Missouri with Audubon*, by Edward Harris. If this treatment does not spring from some enmity, about which nothing is known, it at least indicates an absence of respect for a worthy man whose name, in his world, was as worthy as theirs. Perhaps it is not surprising that Chittenden, in his *Life and Adventures of Joseph La Barge*, dwells on how the crew of the *Omega* resented the master-and-servant air with which Audubon treated them.

"The impression which the celebrated scientist made upon the crew and those who were entertaining him was quite unfavorable," says La Barge. "He was very reserved, and when he did hold intercourse with members of the crew it was generally in an overbearing manner which alienated their good will . . . his hunters rendered him inefficient service, and his journal is full of complaints at their failure to keep their promises."

Audubon retaliated by humiliating them. Captain La Barge was his target on one occasion. Here is the incident in La Barge's own words as it appeared in the *Missouri Republican,* found by Chittenden:

> On one occasion he [Audubon] asked me if I had ever seen any black squirrels during my voyages on the upper Missouri River. My answer was that I had often killed them. "Do you know what a black squirrel is?" he asked. I replied that I knew what I called a black squirrel, and would try to get him one at the first opportunity. A few days later we were windbound. Seeing that we would be compelled to remain tied to the bank most of the day I took my gun and started around to look for a black squirrel.

The *Omega* must have passed the Black Snake Hills, the site of Roubidoux' trading post, where the town of Saint Joseph was soon to take root. La Barge continued:

> I was fortunate. I ran across a very fine one and shot him. He proved to be a fine large buck. I brought him aboard. The first person I met was Mr. Bell, taxidermist of the Audubon party, who remarked, after examining the squirrel, that it was certainly a very fine specimen. He called Mr. Audubon's attention to it, who examined the animal carefully, and then said to me: *"That is what you call a black squirrel, is it? I expected as much. It is very strange that people born and raised in a country do not know the names of the animals and birds which it produces."* After the squirrel had thus been criticized for some time, I remarked that I would take it down to the cook and have it baked for dinner. "No, no!" said Mr. Audubon, "Mr. Bell will take care of it"; then walked off.
> Some few days after this one of his assistants called to me to show me a painting Mr. Audubon had finished that morning. . . . On entering the room I saw the drawing of the squirrel just finished. The assistant then told me that Mr. Audubon had remarked that it was the best specimen of a black squirrel he had ever painted.

By federal law it was a crime punishable by fine and imprisonment to transport alcohol and alcoholic beverages (whisky and rum) into the Indian country. On the Missouri River the two principal points of inspection to prevent its introduction were at Fort Leavenworth, where the military did the inspecting, and at the American's post at Bellevue, on the Nebraska side of the river below today's Omaha, where widely known Peter A. Sarpy was the company's capable agent. In an attempt to keep peace between the Sioux and the Potawatomis, Fort Croghan, a small military post (the farthest north on the Missouri) had been established several miles above Bellevue and a government agent placed there (at Bellevue) who was in charge of Indian affairs and also charged with stopping whisky smuggling into the Upper Missouri.

Various accounts of what happened when the *Omega* arrived at Bellevue exist, all differing: Audubon and Harris saw it one way, La Barge another. Chittenden, who is seldom in error, presents the fantastic story that in the dark, shallow hold of the *Omega* a small tramway ran down both sides from stem to stern and circled around from port to starboard at the ends, so that barrels of whisky could be concealed on one side of the hold while the other side was being inspected, and then pushed around out of sight when the inspector turned his attention to the opposite side of the hold. This is sheer fantasy. Perhaps the only accurate account is that found in Captain Sire's log.

He says that when the *Omega* reached Bellevue he found that both Sarpy [4] and Daniel Miller, the Indian agents, were away on some errand up the Platte; that he unloaded the merchandise consigned to the post and then steamed up the river several miles and tied up for the night; that early in the morning, as he was getting under way, several shots were fired across his bow and that he brought the *Omega* to at once, seeing that the shots came from a small party of army dragoons from the fort. The young officer in charge insisted on making an examination of the boat before she would be permitted to proceed, Agent Miller having entrusted that responsibility to the military before leaving Bellevue.

Audubon had a permit to carry a small amount of liquor for himself and his party, to be used for medicinal purposes, but that could not be stretched to cover the barrels of whisky the *Omega* was carrying. Anyone at all acquainted with the fur trade knew that it could not be conducted without whisky to debauch the Indians and sell to them at an incredible profit.

Audubon says that he volunteered to return to the fort with the officer and present his credentials to Captain Burgwin, who was in command—this subterfuge being for the purpose of giving Captain Sire time to conceal the contraband he was carrying. Of course, Captain Sire had had days in which to conceal it as he steamed up the river, being fully aware that his boat would be inspected when it reached Bellevue.

According to Chittenden, Audubon borrowed a horse from the officer and rode to Fort Croghan, where the commandant, Captain John Burgwin, was much taken aback on learning the identity of his famous visitor. Of the occasion Audubon says: "I was on excellent and friendly terms in less time than it has taken me to write this account of our meeting."

He took Captain Burgwin back to the *Omega*, where he was treated to an elaborate luncheon, which included a generous sampling of choice beverages from Audubon's private stock. After which the steamer was "inspected" and permitted to proceed.

It shed some light on the manner in which these so-called inspections were conducted.

But it was not always thus. A year later Sire and La Barge got into difficulties with the new agent at Bellevue, and the matter went to court in St. Louis. The United States Attorney refused to bring the case to trial, however, unless he could put La Barge on the stand. La Barge made himself very scarce until the case was dropped.

Undoubtedly some whisky was confiscated on the Missouri, but it was the small, independent trader who suffered, not the American Fur Company and the opposition Union Fur Company boats.

The frequent stops for wooding and for cleaning the river mud out of the boilers gave Audubon and his party almost daily opportunities for going ashore to hunt for birds and quadrupeds, many of those they secured proving to have been hitherto unknown to science.

On May 20, they saw their first buffalo. In the days that followed they saw hundreds of them. Two days later, as the *Omega* was passing the point where later Fort Randall was built, a number of Indians appeared on the east bank (Sire identified them as Santee Sioux), and when the boat refused to stop for them they opened fire on her. "The bullets tore through the cabins and pilothouse, but by the greatest good luck no one was hurt," says Sire. A high wind that afternoon drove the *Omega* into shallow water and she was soon fast aground. There she remained for that day and the next until she was pushed off with poles.

On May 26, she reached the Great Bend, which was twenty-six miles around and only three miles across. Audubon's party was put ashore to walk the short distance and be picked up when the steamer came along. On this tramp across the Bend they saw their first prairie dog village. Audubon and Harris were delighted at the antics of the little marmots. They tried to take several for specimens, but their marksmanship was not up to it.

They were then not more than seventy-five miles from Fort Pierre. Low water impeded their progress after they were in sight of the post, and it was not until May 31 that they reached it, thirty-six days out of St. Louis.

Their experience with low water was very much on their mind, and their concern about what lay ahead of them for the rest of the journey was not lessened when they saw the steamer *Trapper,* a company boat, moored across the river, waiting for the crew that the *Omega* had brought up to take her down to St. Louis. The *Trapper* had been caught by low water the previous fall and had been forced to remain where she was until the big rise in the spring. Harris comments: "We crossed the river to where the *Trapper* lay to put on board her our Mate Mr. Durac and our black Pilot Desiree who has undertaken to Pilot her down without an assistant, a pretty serious undertaking as he will be obliged to stick at the wheel the whole time the boat is running or from daylight to dark." [5]

But the *Omega* discharged half of her cargo and most of the trappers at Fort Pierre, thus lightening her for the journey to

Fort Union. Captain Sire assured Audubon's party that he would land them there in no more than twelve days, a promise he fulfilled even though he stopped for a day at the Mandan villages near the mouth of Grand River, to permit them to go ashore as they were anxious to do.

Smallpox had all but destroyed the Mandans. Those who were left had integrated with their old enemies the Arikarees. In their journals both Audubon and Harris speak of the filth in which the survivors were living.

At Fort Union their host was Alexander Culberson who, with Kenneth McKenzie, was the most important fur trader on the Upper Missouri. He left them free to pursue such diversions as appealed to them, killing buffalo, elk and deer and, in the name of science, slaughtering a great number of birds. But he was responsible for their safety and he undoubtedly kept a watchful eye on them. Audubon painted a great number of mammals and a lesser number of birds. He was gathering material, of course, for his projected *Quadrupeds of North America.*

In the autumn they began the long journey back to St. Louis by Mackinaw boat, under the command of Etienne Provost, a veteran of thirty years' experience in the Great West. They reached St. Louis October 19.

The Missouri was now about to engage in the sterner business of advancing civilization. Settlers, pioneers of the plow and the shop, were moving into the Missouri Valley; settlements were taking shape, towns being laid out. Soon there would be a steamboat 'round every bend.

XIII

The Steamboats Lead the Way

PRIOR TO 1846, steamboating on the Upper Missouri—that is, north from Fort Leavenworth—had been confined almost exclusively to the annual voyages of the boats of what was still popularly known as the American Fur Company. In 1844 it sent a new boat, the *Nimrod*, up to the northern posts. Captain Sire having retired from the river, the command fell to La Barge. He continued with the company in 1845 and 1846 in command of the *General Brooks*. In the winter of 1846 he was sent to Cincinnati to oversee the building of the steamboat *Martha*.

After having been her master for two years, a disagreement developed between him and the Chouteaus and he left their employ, and in September bought the *Martha* for $12,000, the first boat he ever owned. After running her independently for the remainder of the season, he sold her at a profit and she went south to run in the sugar trade of Bayou La Fourche. He immediately contracted for a bigger and better boat and named her the *St. Ange,* honoring the memory of St. Ange de Bellerive, the first governor of Upper Louisiana. A contract was offered him by the Quartermaster Department of the Army and he began hauling military supplies from St. Louis to Fort Leavenworth. Troops going to the South and Southwest to take part in the

War with Mexico were being dispatched from Fort Leavenworth. The flow of men, armament and supplies up the river
resulted in boom times for the steamboats.

The *St. Ange* was returning from her second trip when she
ran into a severe rain and wind storm that delayed her for hours.
It proved to be the luckiest of misfortunes, for instead of tying
up in St. Louis before dark, it was midnight when she steamed
out of the mouth of the Missouri for the short run to St. Louis.
The bright glow in the sky in that direction had been observed
for some time and dismissed as the reflection of just another fire.
But as the *St. Ange* moved down the Mississippi, it was seen that
a major conflagration was taking place. The whole length of the
levee was wrapped in flames, and back from the waterfront the
main business section of the city was beginning to burn.

It was a night of terror for St. Louis that was referred to ever
afterward as The Great Fire. It began about 10:00 P.M. on May
17, 1849, and burned out of control throughout the night and
into the early morning. Captain La Barge steamed past the city,
looking for a safe place to land and, finding none, turned back
and, crossing the river, tied up at Bloody Island.[1]

In the city, ten square blocks were left in ashes. Along the
levee a large fleet of steamboats was moored, among them the
White Cloud, Eudora, Belle Isle, Julia and the *Edward Bates.*
The fire onshore first spread to the *White Cloud.* A strong northwest wind was blowing, and in a few minutes the *Eudora,*
moored astern of her, was blazing. The *Edward Bates* then
caught fire. Someone may have cut the *Bates* adrift in the hope
of saving other boats, or her hawsers may have burned. She
drifted out into the river, but the wind quickly bore her back to
shore, and like a flaming torch she went scraping down the levee,
setting afire everything she touched. Several boats had been cut
adrift. But the *Bates,* as though commanded by some fiery de-
mon, brushed into them, setting them afire. As the mooring
lines along the levee burned through, the current caught the
boats and swept them down past the city in the most costly pyro-
technical display the Mississippi was ever to witness.

In all, twenty-three steamboats were destroyed, three barges

and a number of small craft. The total value of boats and cargo
lost was estimated at $440,000. Approximately 50 percent of the
loss was covered by insurance; but not more than half of this
was paid, as some of the companies were unable to meet the
heavy losses and were forced to liquidate.[2]

One of the steamboats destroyed by the fire was the *Martha*,
which Captain La Barge had sold to the fur company. She
burned with a full cargo aboard for the upper river posts.

Pierre Chouteau, Jr., through Captain Sire, prevailed upon
La Barge to make the voyage for the company, in the *St. Ange*,
at least as far as Fort Pierre, as soon as he completed his contract with the government. Although it was the middle of June
before the *St. Ange* got away from St. Louis for the long trip
north, with low water facing her on the upper reaches of the
river, she made the round trip without accident.

In midsummer of 1849 one of the worst outbreaks of cholera
swept the Missouri Valley. Thousands died in the cities and
small settlements that had sprung up. Hundreds died on the
steamboats, mostly on the four-hundred-mile run from St. Louis
to Westport and Fort Leavenworth. Hoping to combat the
spread of the pestilence, it became the rule to stop a boat as
soon as death occurred and inter the body of the deceased at
once.

With greatly increased traffic on the Lower Missouri, the
number of accidents began to multiply. The *Edna* had exploded
at the mouth of the Missouri, snuffing out the lives of forty-two
German emigrants. Snags and whirlpools sent a dozen boats to
the bottom, usually with some loss of life. It had become the
rule rather than the exception for eight to ten steamboats to
leave the St. Louis levee every day for Kansas Town (the com-
plex of Independence and the Westports). The Gold Rush to
California was in full swing and hundreds of eager gold seekers
were going overland by way of the Santa Fe Trail or by cutting
south to the so-called California Road across Indian Territory
that Captain Randolph Marcy had marked in 1848.

Great as their number was, it was dwarfed by the thousands of
families that were converging by covered wagon on the eastern

marge of Kansas for the take-off to the Oregon Country. By a thousand different routes they had driven across Iowa and, on reaching the Missouri, had been ferried across. Some continued west to Fort Kearney, Nebraska, where they waited to join a train that had set out from western Missouri, but the great majority turned south and followed the river to Westport, where the big trains were organized, captains elected, and experienced, buckskin-clad plainsmen engaged to pilot the caravans through to South Pass or beyond.

All of this activity was pouring money into the pockets of steamboat owners. Far from being the least profitable of the many-faceted bonanza was the steadily growing upriver traffic being supplied by the Mormons. The religious sect had received such harsh treatment in Missouri that it had left the state and migrated to Illinois and established the town of Nauvoo, where they were treated kindly at first, the general feeling being that they had been persecuted in Missouri. But after two years, public opinion turned against them. The temple at Nauvoo was burned, and Joseph Smith, the founder of the Latter-day Saints, and his brother Hyrum were dragged from their cell in the Carthage jail, where they had been placed, charged with violence against the state, and slain in cold blood.

Ironically, the Carthage mob in killing Joseph and Hyrum Smith did more to advance the Mormon cause than anything else could have done. It set the seal of martyrdom upon the founder of the church; it healed internal dissensions; it intensified the high resolve to succeed; and finally it opened up the way for the one man who above all others was qualified to carry the movement to success. This was that dynamic and gifted leader of men, prophet Brigham Young.

Joseph Smith was a dreamer who wrapped himself in mysticism; Young was down-to-earth, practical and farsighted. It was apparent to him that there was no sanctuary on the soil of the United States for Mormonism and the Church of the Latter-day Saints. Inspired by the report of the committee he had sent out to explore the country beyond the Rocky Mountains, he convinced his followers that on the shores of Salt Lake, in territory then under the sovereignty of the Republic of Mexico, they would find a permanent home, where they could prosper and build a New Zion.

In July of 1844 the exodus from Illinois began. By handcart and wagon they crossed Iowa to the Missouri River and gathered on the east bank of the river at Council Bluffs, with a great number crossing to the west bank where the future city of Omaha was sprouting. Some reached the great encampment by water, going down the Mississippi by steamboat to St. Louis and up the Missouri to their destination.

For almost a decade this gathering of the Mormons at Council Bluffs and Omaha continued. Then as now, they were thrifty people. They needed supplies, merchandise, and had the money with which to pay for what they needed. Mormon missionaries were busy in England, Scotland, and on the Continent, and were so successful that hundreds of proselytes were arriving in the United States, bound for the Council Bluffs encampment.

La Barge found that doing business with the Mormons was so profitable that for two years he never went north of Council Bluffs. On one trip in 1851, he steamed up the Missouri on the *St. Ange* with assorted cargo for Council Bluffs and over two hundred Mormon converts. The *Sacramento* was just behind him with four hundred. On April 9 of the following year the worst disaster in the history of Missouri River steamboating occurred at Lexington, Missouri, as the *Saluda,* a side-wheeler with two boilers located on the guards, tried to round the point just above town. She was carrying a full load of assorted cargo and two hundred Mormons bound for Council Bluffs.

As usual at that time of the year, the river was very high and the current running so strong that Captain Francis Belt, the master of the *Saluda,* found that he could not get her around the point. After trying repeatedly he dropped back to Lexington and tied up for two days waiting for the river to drop. But conditions did not improve, and impatient at the long delay, he ordered steam built up until the boilers were carrying every pound they could stand. The lines were cast off and the *Saluda* moved out into the stream, but the wheels had made only several revolutions when both boilers let go in a terrific explosion that reduced the boat to splinters and filled the air with the dead and the maimed. Over a hundred bodies were recovered.[3]

Captain La Barge and his wife suffered a personal loss. The pilot of the *Saluda*, Charles La Barge, was his brother, and the second pilot, Louis Guerette, was her brother.

It was only several months later that Captain Edward Salt-Marsh, brought his new boat the *Sonora*, a Howard-built boat just off the ways at Jeffersonville, Indiana, to St. Louis. She was a splendid boat, 163 feet overall, a three-decker, with side wheels and double boilers. La Barge was invited to inspect her and fell in love with her at once. Although intended primarily as a cargo carrier, her passenger accommodations had not been neglected. La Barge bought her several days later for $30,000, which indicates that he was finding steamboating profitable. He took the *Sonora*, the finest boat the Missouri had seen, to Fort Union that year under contract to the Chouteaus. The voyage was without incident, and that fall he put her in the New Orleans trade for the winter.

Since the steamboat was the only reasonably fast and cheap means of transportation, it followed that the new towns that were springing up were for the most part river towns. St. Joseph, Omaha, Council Bluffs and Sioux City were showing definite signs of prosperity. A dozen other settlements were taking shape, some of them destroyed by the vagaries of the shifting river. Others soon failed and have long since been forgotten. Leavenworth became an organized town and, because of its strategic position in the shadow of Fort Leavenworth, was destined to become an important river port.

The government had inaugurated mail service of a sort on the Missouri as far up as Omaha, but it was shrouded with uncertainty and subject to unconscionable delays. The first postmaster at Omaha carried the mail for the town in his stovepipe hat. It was the steamboats that kept the small river towns in touch with the outside world. When a boat tied up for the night at one of the settlements the word spread quickly and the whole population moved down to the bank. It was the most exciting event of the week, for there was sure to be news of what was happening down the river and entertainment as well. Among the Negro roustabouts there were always a few who could sing, dance and strum a banjo. Of course, those boats that dispensed liquor over a counter did a brisk business. If there chanced to be a preacher aboard, which often was the case, he never failed to take advantage of such opportunities to go ashore and in the flickering light of a log fire exhort his audience to advance the work of the Lord.

The purchase of Fort Pierre in 1855 marked the first step in the military conquest of the Upper Missouri Valley by the Army of the United States. The quantity of furs received at Fort Pierre had been dwindling, proof that the surrounding region had been worked out; the company's main interest now was Fort McKenzie and beyond it to the head of navigation on the Missouri, a point which yet had to be determined, but necessarily somewhere below the Great Falls of the Missouri.

At Pierre, the change-over from trading post to army outpost was accomplished without incident. To take the government commissioners and army officials up the river on this important voyage, the Chouteaus again turned to Captain La Barge and his new boat, the *St. Mary,* in which he owned a quarter interest. He was accompanied by Charles Chouteau, the son of Pierre Chouteau, Jr., who superintended the transfer of company property at Pierre to a new post at the mouth of the Chantier Creek (better known as Shonkin Creek), a few miles below the future Fort Benton.

The great fire that had scourged the St. Louis levee was still fresh in the minds of steamboatmen, when, on February 27, 1856, another calamity struck the boats that were wintering there. The winter had been severe and the ice was three to four feet thick. It was firm, and rivermen who were watching it did not expect it to show any signs of breaking up for another four or five weeks. Having witnessed the annual breakup for years, they believed they knew what to expect. But their experience and calculations went for nought when a sudden rise in the river up above shattered the ice. Once it was broken, it began moving with the current, slowly at first and then piling up in temporary jams, which in turn were smashed by the tremendous force of the river.

Soon the icefield was brushing against the steamboats moored along the levee, snapping their iron hawsers as though they were merely string, and carrying the boats downstream to destruction.

The Missouri *Democrat* published this account of the havoc by an eyewitness:

The ice at first moved very slowly and without any perceptible shock. The boats lying above Chestnut Street were merely shoved ashore. Messrs. Eads [the bridge builder] & Nelson's Submarine No. 4, which had just finished work at the wreck of the *Parthenia*, was almost immediately capsized and became herself a hopeless wreck. Here the destruction commenced. The *Federal Arch* parted her fastenings and became at once a total wreck. Lying below were the steamers *Australia, Adriatic, Brunette, Falls City, Altona, A. B. Chambers,* and *Challenge,* all of which were torn away from the shore as easily as if they were mere skiffs, and floated down with the immense fields of ice. The shock and the crashing of these boats can better be imagined than described. All their ample fastenings were as nothing against the enormous flood of ice, and they were carried down apparently fastened and wedged together. The first obstacles with which they came in contact were a large fleet of wood-boats, flats, and canal-boats. These small fry were either broken to pieces or were forced out on the levee in a very damaged condition. There must have been at least fifty of these small water craft which were destroyed, pierced by the ice or crushed by the pressure of each against the other.

In the meantime some of the boats lying above Chestnut Street fared badly. The *F. X. Aubrey* was forced into the bank and was considerably damaged, the noble *Nebraska,* which was thought to be in a most perilous position, escaped with the loss of her starboard wheel and some other small injuries. A number of the upper-river boats, lying above Chestnut Street, were more or less damaged. Both Alton wharf-boats were sunk and broken in pieces. The old *Shenandoah* and the *Sam Cloon* were forced away from the shore and floated down together, lodging against the steamer *Clara,* where they were soon torn to pieces and sunk by a collision with one of the ferryboats floating down. The Keokuk wharf-boat maintained its position against the flood and saved three boats below, viz., the *Polar Star, Pringle* and *Forest Rose,* none of which was injured.

After running about an hour the character of the ice changed, and it came down in a frothy, crumbled condition, with an occasional heavy piece. At the end of two hours it ran very slowly, and finally stopped about 5½ o'clock P.M. Just before the ice stopped and commenced to gorge, huge piles, twenty and thirty feet in height, were forced up by the current on every hand, both on the shore and at the lower dike, where so many boats had come to a halt. In fact these boats seemed to be literally buried in ice.

If the ice breakup of 1856 was not as spectacular as the Great Fire, or as costly to the owners who had lost their boats, the result was the same, the earnings of years swept away in a few hours. But the far greater conflict that was to set neighbor against neighbor and turn the state into a battleground was already casting its shadow before it.

Missouri was a slave state, although perhaps as many as 40 percent of its people were antislavery. Geographically, the Missouri River, flowing east to west across the state, was roughly the dividing line between the proslavery element to the south of the river and the antislavery stronghold to the north.

President Pierce had no sooner signed the Kansas-Nebraska Act, which in effect repealed the Missouri Compromise of 1820, than armed conflict began to determine whether Kansas should be free or slave. The Kansas-Nebraska Act divided the territory of Nebraska into two parts, the southern portion of which (about one half) was named Kansas, and it was left to the settlers of those two territories to decide whether they would have slave labor or not.

The first move was made by the proslavery element residing in or near Weston, Missouri. Responding to the fiery eloquence of U.S. Senator David R. Atchison, the outspoken advocate of slavery, they crossed the Missouri and established the town of Leavenworth, thirteen days after the signing of the Kansas-Nebraska Bill. Fourteen months later, the Missourians founded a second town and named it Atchison.

The free-staters had not been caught napping. In 1854 they founded the towns of Lawrence and Lecompton. The fight for Kansas had begun. Far away in Boston, Massachusetts, the New England Emigrant Aid Society, possibly the most powerful antislavery group in the United States, outfitted three hundred men, armed them with rifles, and hurried them off to what was soon to become "bleeding Kansas."

If the free-staters continued to receive reinforcements, so did the proslavery faction. Presently thousands of men were engaged in an internecine struggle the like of which the slavery question produced nowhere else. Bands of armed guerrillas ravaged the western counties of Missouri and eastern Kansas. The savage excesses of one side were matched by those of the other. Houses and barns were burned, towns looted; men were called to the door of their homes at night and shot down for no better reason than they were suspected of favoring the other side.

Steamboats on the four-hundred-mile stretch of the Missouri between St. Louis and Fort Leavenworth were fired at and stopped, with passengers and cargo at the mercy of the bands of guerrillas. For safety's sake, it became the habit of riverboatmen to anchor in midstream for the night.

Missouri River steamboating was about to embark on the greatest, and last, decade of its commercial importance. Barely forty years had passed since the crude little *Independence* had demonstrated that the Lower Missouri was navigable for at least two hundred miles. Now the goal was Fort Benton, the recognized head of navigation, 3,100 miles from St. Louis. The *Spread Eagle* and the little *Chippewa* were to make it to Brule Bottoms, the former site of Fort McKenzie, fifteen miles below Benton, in 1859. The following year the *Chippewa* and *Key West* made it all the way.

It was an achievement, but of far greater importance to Missouri River steamboating was the arrival at St. Joseph of the first railroad to reach the banks of the Missouri. Although it was inadequately financed and its rolling stock second-rate, the Hannibal and St. Joseph Railroad was to work a profound change on the commerce of the Missouri, rescuing it from the

domination of St. Louis. For the cluster of towns around Kansas
City and the growing settlements to the north, it meant a saving
of hundreds of miles, lower transportation costs and quicker
service. Naturally, St. Joseph became the most important river
town between St. Louis and Benton.

The long, cruel War between the States was at hand. Many
steamboats were taken into government service, at a profit to
their owners. Other boats reaped a harvest transporting troops
and military supplies. But even richer pickings came with the
discovery of gold in Montana and the frantic rush of thousands
of men and some women (the latter largely of the kind one
would expect) to the diggings.[4] The best way to get there was up
the Missouri by steamboat to Benton and on from there by
stagecoach. Freight to Benton was twelve cents a pound and
cabin passage one-way three hundred dollars. How profitable
this business was for the steamboats can be judged from Captain La Barge's statement that one round trip in the *Octavia*
netted him $45,000. That figure he never equaled even in the
Emilie, the finest boat he ever owned, which cost him $60,000.[5]

Of course, with others it was a different story. Greedy owners,
determined to get a share of the rich pickings, took the gamble
of sending their boats up the Missouri under the guidance of
inexperienced pilots, with the result that at least one out of
every five boats that left St. Louis for Fort Benton failed to
reach it. Nor did they ever return; somewhere along the thousands of wilderness miles of shifting channels, sandbars, whirlpools and snags, disaster overtook them. Years later, whitening
bones of their superstructures could be seen projecting above
the swirling water. Usually they had struck with force enough
to topple their stacks, break their backs and twist their upper
works askew.

No attempt was ever made to raise the wrecks. Indians
stripped them of whatever appealed to their savage taste, and
what remained was left for the river to disintegrate.

In the meantime, Fort Benton was booming.

XIV

Big Years at Fort Benton

In 1845 Alexander Culberston had built a new post for the American Fur Company on the Missouri, twelve miles above where the modern city of Fort Benton now stands, and named it Fort Lewis for Meriwether Lewis. Its purpose was to trade with the Blackfeet tribes (the Piegans, Bloods, Blackfeet and the Gros Ventres of the Prairies). This was trade that the company had lost through the mismanagement and sinister conduct of Alexander Harvey and Francis Chardon, at Fort McKenzie. Both men were long-time, valued employees of the company, but when they were placed in charge of Fort McKenzie, their savage instincts ran away with them, culminating in the planned robbery and massacre of a band of Blackfeet who had come to trade. Six Indians were killed, as many more wounded, two children made prisoners. The loot from this outrage amounted to 22 horses, 350 robes, along with guns and bows and arrows. The Blackfeet began a war of vengeance. Harvey got out of the country. Chardon burned the fort and established a new post down the Missouri at the mouth of the Judith River, which he named Fort Chardon. But the trade was ruined. He was dismissed and in the spring capable Alexander Culbertson was sent up to see what he could do about repairing the situation.

Culbertson abandoned and burned Fort Chardon and established the new post, already mentioned, which he named Fort Lewis. The site proved unsatisfactory, and a few months later he moved down to the fine open bottom where Fort Benton was to take form. In its new location the name Fort Lewis was retained for several years, and it was not until Christmas night, 1850, with a great feast and grand ball (Culbertson's Blackfoot wife had supplied a number of young women for the occasion) that it was rechristened Fort Benton for Senator Benton, "who had so often rescued the Company from its own malefactions." [1]

The Blackfeet tribes trusted and respected Culbertson, but they could not be enticed to trade at Fort Benton, although it was ideally located for them, especially for the Piegans. Culbertson suspected that, far to the north, the powerful Hudson's Bay Company was doing its best to attract them to its posts. From the few Gros Ventres who came to trade, he learned that the Bloods, Piegans and Blackfeet had been scourged by an epidemic of smallpox and had fled to the mountains to escape the ravages of the disease. Discounting the proclivity of Indians to exaggerate, the tales he heard were fantastic.

Fearing the worst, but determined to find out for himself what the situation was, he left Fort Benton with a single companion at the approach of cooler weather, intending to go as far as the Three Forks of the Missouri if necessary. His fears were realized; he found villages of fifty and sixty lodges from which the inhabitants had fled, leaving the bodies of the dead, men, women and children, on which the scavenger birds and wolves were feasting.

It was the same wherever he went. In his report to the company, Culbertson estimated the mortality among the three tribes—Bloods, Piegans and Blackfeet—at not less than six thousand. For some unknown reason the Gros Ventres escaped the epidemic.

When the disease had run its course, Culbertson persuaded the chiefs to visit Fort Benton. He feasted them and gave them appropriate presents. It healed the breach, and when spring came Fort Benton began to do a brisk trade, which was to grow over the years and, by the time it saw its first steamboat, make it the most important of all company posts.

Because the Missouri River was the mainstream of travel into the Indian country of the Upper Missouri Valley, the Bureau of Indian Affairs established its agencies for the various Plains tribes on or adjacent to the river—that is, north from the Poncas at the mouth of the Niobrara. Most of the agents were ordained ministers, for it seems to have been the judgment of the Bureau that because a man had worked in the vineyard of the Lord it peculiarly fitted him to administer the affairs of a tribe of wild Plains Indians. The great majority proved to be outright rascals and totally unfit to perform the duties for which they had been appointed, which was to have been expected, since the appointments were part of the political patronage system.

The agents were charged with advancing the cause of peace, seeing that treaties were observed and that government annuities were received properly and devoting themselves to the general welfare of the tribe. Actually, they principally devoted themselves to feathering their own nest, so that after several years they could retire with a competence. What they were doing was an open secret; even the Indians were not fooled. They knew they were being cheated out of their full share of the annuity goods the government had sent them. It was not a little matter; the value of the annuities loaded aboard a steamboat at St. Louis or St. Joseph ran from fifty to seventy-five thousand dollars. Before they reached their destination, a third or more were concealed and went into the warehouses of the fur company. Later they were sold over the counter for the furs and peltries the Indians brought in. It meant that they were buying back their own goods with the fruits of their hunting and trapping.

They were ignorant savages but they were not stupid; they knew what was being done to them. It is not necessary to look further to understand the open hostility of all the tribes north from the Niobrara to the Great Falls. That this methodical cheating of the Indians could have gone on year after year without the collusion of the company is unthinkable. Few historians have cared, or dared, to take a hard look at the record; but the trouble that occurred at Tobacco Garden, at the mouth of Tobacco Creek, on the north bank of the Missouri, eighty-eight miles below the Yellowstone, in 1863, is indictment enough.

No single incident involving Missouri River steamboats and the distribution (and disappearance) of Indian annuities has received as much attention as what is always referred to as "the Tobacco Garden affair." Two Indian Agents, Samuel M. Latta for Sioux, Crows and Mandans, and Dr. (Reverend) Henry W. Reed for the Blackfeet tribes, were among the principals in what occurred, and in their lengthy reports to the Commissioner of Indian Affairs they gave their version of what had taken place. Henry A. Boller, a passenger on the *Robert Campbell* at the time, published his eyewitness account in his *Among the Indians,* which attracted some attention at the time. It is inaccurate, and like the reports of Latta and Reed, it excuses their conduct and criticizes Captain Joseph La Barge, the master of the *Robert Campbell,* for the action he took. In much the same vein is the material found in Charles Larpenteur's journal, *Forty Years a Fur Trader.* Larpenteur was better known in the Indian country for his consistent failures than for his achievements. But his book had the blessing of being edited by the eminent Dr. Elliott Coues and was widely accepted as authoritative. Had La Barge accepted Dr. Coues' challenge to tell his side of the story at that time, instead of waiting for a quarter of a century to state his case, the controversy would have been decided in his favor.

As has been previously stated, the first steamboats to reach Fort Benton were the small, light-draft *Chippewa* and the *Key West,* on July 2, 1860. In the next two years at least seven steamers tied up at the bank in front of the post, there being no landing or levee as yet.[2] In the meantime, a score of steamers made their way upriver as far as Cow Island, 130 miles below Fort Benton, where they were stopped by low water. There passengers were put ashore and cargo piled up on the bank, the remainder of the journey to be completed by keelboat and Mackinaw.

The situation changed when the little *Deer Lodge* was brought up the river. She could carry only sixty tons, but she made a fortune for her owners, scuttling back and forth between Cow Island and Fort Benton. Grudgingly steamboatmen were forced to admit that with the improvements they had introduced their boats had become too big for the upper river. But the bigger the boat the more passengers and freight it could carry, so they refused to trim their sails; everybody wanted to get rich in a hurry.

An old photograph made in 1863 shows seven steamboats tied up at the new wharf at Fort Benton. In high water they could make it all the way without difficulty. They came up laden to the guards. More often than not, until the middle sixties, they went down light, the running time to St. Louis not more than two weeks. The passenger business grew steadily, however. There was an estimated 18,000 people in the Virginia City district. Men who had done well and wanted to send their wives and families east for a vacation put them aboard one of Oliver and Company's stages for Fort Benton and sent them down the Missouri by steamboat. It was a safe and pleasant way of getting them home.

Every day men were arriving in Fort Benton from the mines, among them some who had struck it rich and were getting out of the country with their gold, and others whose luck had failed them and who had had enough of the diggings. No one can say how much gold the steamboats carried down the river. Usually a man put his dust in the boat's safe; but not always. One figure survives that is accurate: in 1866 the *Luella* had in her safe $1,250,000 in gold.

The boats arrived at Fort Benton only in the spring, when the river was high. They left on the return trip a week or ten days later, and after they departed there was no way of getting out of the country until the following year except by Mackinaw boat. With the hostility of the Indians what it was, it was foolhardy to travel down the river in an open boat. But parties of eight to eighteen men tried it. The majority made the long journey safely. Others, to the number of three hundred, were killed. In the summer of 1863 one party of twenty-one men and

three women went down the Missouri in a Mackinaw. At Apple
Creek, in the vicinity of today's Bismarck, they were attacked
by Indians. In a battle that lasted all day, every member of the
party was killed. Dozens of such incidents could be cited.

At Fort Benton a townsite had been surveyed; new buildings
were going up. Sitting at the head of navigation, it was freely
predicted that Fort Benton was destined to become a great inland seaport. A look at some statistics shows that some of this
optimism was warranted. In 1865, 1,000 passengers, 6,000 tons
of merchandise, and 20 quartz mills were received at Fort Benton. Two years later forty steamboats passed Sioux City bound
for Fort Benton before June 1. The profits for a successful voyage became enormous. The reported earnings of some of the
boats for that year were as follows:

St. John	$17,000
Tacony	$16,000
W. J. Lewis	$40,000
Peter Balen	$65,000
Octavia	$40,000

In Virginia City, Judge W. B. Dance, N. P. Langford and a
group of speculators were so impressed that they conceived the
idea of establishing a rival town at the mouth of the Musselshell,
which would be a hundred miles nearer the diggings than Fort
Benton and which could be reached by a practically water-level
road. They named their projected town Kercheval City and received a charter from the territorial legislature. They built a
wharf, but to their chagrin the steamboats passed without stopping. Kercheval City and other similar ventures were to die
aborning. The only business Fort Benton lost was to the specially built Mackinaws that carried four or five hundred men
a year down the Yellowstone.

The voyage down the Yellowstone began at the mouth of Yellowstone Canyon, which was not more than a hundred miles to
the east from Virginia City and reasonably easy to reach. It was
less than a third of the distance to Fort Benton and meant a
saving of $25 to $30 in stagecoach fare. That was almost equiv-

alent to the total cost of getting down to St. Louis by Mackinaw boat. With deck passage down the Missouri fluctuating between $150 and $175, the saving was considerable.

For greater safety against Indian attack, the boats left the mouth of the canyon in flotillas of eight or more at a time. They were built on the spot. The firm of Lyman and Tomlinson had set up a sawmill and it was busy the year round whipping out planks. The average length of the boats was about forty feet, large enough to accommodate a score of passengers and their baggage and provisions. They were roofed over "with double planks placed at an angle the better to bounce [off] Indian rifle balls which might be fired at them." [3] For further protection the gunwales were double-planked and had apertures from which guns could be fired. When a man booked passage on one of the Mackinaws it was with the understanding that he would come armed with a rifle and take his turn at the oars when called upon.

October was the time of departure. It was a perilous business shooting down the white water of the Yellowstone at a hundred miles a day until the canyon was passed. There were accidents, drownings, but the boat companies could always find men who were willing to risk their lives to save a few hundred dollars. Some of the boats ran night and day until they were below the Niobrara. The majority tied up after dark and got away before daylight. Few escaped being fired on by Indians. Those who left the territory by one of the overland routes were likely to be robbed by road agents; by the Mackinaws they might lose their life as well as their gold. The reasonably safe way was by steamboat.

It is only against the background of continuing Indian unrest and hostility, which was not to end until after the Custer debacle on the Little Big Horn, in 1876—and then only because the Plains Indians were a crushed people and had no choice but to submit to the domination of the white man—that the so-called Tobacco Garden affair can be put in focus. It was not an isolated incident, as some would have it, but the outgrowth of the continued exploitation of the Sioux, in this case the Two Kettles band, by their agent and the fur company.

In the spring of 1863 La Barge chartered the steamboats *Shreveport* and *Robert Campbell* for a voyage to Fort Benton. He put his brother, Captain John La Barge, in command of the *Shreveport,* the smaller of the two boats, and took charge of the *Robert Campbell* personally. The cargo and passenger list of the *Shreveport* was made up almost exclusively of machinery, merchandise and people bound for the mines; the *Campbell,* when she finally got away from St. Louis, was loaded with government annuities for the Sioux, Crows, Blackfeet and Assiniboins, and some other freight, making a cargo of nearly five hundred tons. The *Shreveport* left port in the latter part of April. Due to the failure of the annuities to arrive, it was forty days later before the *Robert Campbell* started up the river. The Missouri was so low by then that there was little likelihood that she could reach Fort Benton.

Among the *Campbell's* passengers were the aforementioned Indian agents, Samuel M. Latta and Henry W. Reed. Henry A. Boller, the writer, and Alexander Culbertson and his wife were also aboard. There were some thirty passengers in all, and the number increased at the various landings up to Sioux City.

The *Campbell* reached Fort Pierre on June 20 and found several bands of Sioux assembled to receive their goods, among them two hundred or more of the Two Kettles. The latter were enraged over the recent killing, with little justification, of eight of their band by the soldiers at Fort Randall.[4]

The *Shreveport* had cleared Fort Pierre ten days previously and proceeded up the river.

La Barge, who had dealt with Indians for a quarter of a century, warned Agents Latta and Reed that the situation was precarious. But they refused to heed his advice, and after some parleying the distribution of the goods began. All of them were not put ashore, however. According to La Barge fully a third were still aboard the boat when Latta ordered the gangplank lifted. The Indians were not deceived; they knew they were being cheated. They appealed to La Barge, whom some of them had known for years, to have justice done them. He was helpless to do anything; he was responsible for the boat and its safe navigation, but he had nothing to say about the disposition of the annuities.

Whether the Indians understood his position is debatable, but they warned him they would follow the *Robert Campbell* all the way to Fort Union and fire on it at every opportunity. He took them at their word and barricaded the vulnerable parts of the boat with bales and boxes of cargo. All arms aboard were made ready for an attack. It was a wise precaution because at every stop for wooding, Indians appeared and fired at the crew.

Latta made no explanation for holding back such a large share of the goods that rightfully belonged to the Indians gathered at Fort Pierre. In his official report he does not mention that part of the annuities were held back. Neither does Reed, the agent for the Blackfeet.

The *Shreveport,* which had gone up the river in advance of the *Campbell,* had been unable, because of the low water, to get beyond Cow Island. She had discharged her cargo on the bank and returned downriver. She met the *Campbell* below Bismarck and was stopped by La Barge. Part of the cargo of the larger boat was transferred to the *Shreveport,* the two boats then proceeding up the river together, the *Shreveport* sometimes being ahead and sometimes astern.

One day Louis Dauphin, the well-known French-Canadian hunter, who was employed to provide the *Campbell* with fresh meat, had been ranging along the shore in advance of the boat, when he ran into a party of Indians and saved himself by taking to the water and swimming downstream to meet the boat.

"You are going to have trouble at the Tobacco Garden," he told La Barge. "There are at least fifteen hundred Indians gathered there and they intend to capture the *Campbell.*"

It was toward noon when the two boats hove in sight of the Tobacco Garden, and there, true to Dauphin's prediction, "they beheld on the south shore a large body of Indians assembled with the evident purpose of stopping them. There was no use in trying to run a gauntlet like that, and accordingly the boats made fast to the opposite sandbar, the *Shreveport* about one hundred yards below the *Robert Campbell*." (This quotation and the following version of what took place are culled from the statement La Barge made to his biographer, Hiram Martin Chittenden.)

XV

Boom and Bust

AT THE TOBACCO GARDEN the Missouri makes a sharp turn to the west for several miles; hence its banks are referred to as the north and south banks. In low water there was only one navigable channel, which ran between the sandbar in midstream and the south bank. The two boats made fast to the sandbar. It placed them near enough to the Indians onshore to make conversation possible. La Barge asked what they wanted. They replied that they wanted the balance of their annuities; they wanted no trouble, simply their just dues.

Latta refused them the goods, but, as he stated in his report, "requested the Captain to send his yawl and bring aboard some of the chiefs and head men that we could have a talk and . . . make them a present of sugar, coffee, tobacco, etc., and by this means quiet them."

The Indians likewise wanted the yawl to be sent out, but wanted the agent to go with it. They would then send their principal chiefs back with him to the boat, where everything could be talked over.

La Barge refused to order the yawl out; he was convinced that once the Indians had Latta in their hands his life would be forfeited unless they got their goods, and very likely the crew that took him ashore would be killed.

"Why, I'll go," Latta told him. "I am not afraid."

"All right, if you can get seven men to volunteer," the Captain informed him. "I will not order them to go."

The agents asked Miller, the mate of the *Campbell,* to call for volunteers. He had no difficulty getting the required number. Latta had gone to his cabin on the upper deck. When he was informed that the yawl was ready to shove off, he sent down word that he had suddenly been taken ill and could not go. With the redoubtable Andy Stinger at the tiller, the yawl headed for the shore.[1] It struck head-on and was quickly swung around by the current and lay alongside the bank.

The yawl was attacked at once. Two Indians leaped into it, brandishing their lances, and killed two of the oarsmen. A third was seriously wounded, and a fourth was killed by a bullet. Stinger had leaped into the water. Working his way along the river side of the yawl, he got it away from the bank in time to save his own life and the lives of two of the crew who had flung themselves on the floor.

Seeing what had happened, La Barge did not hesitate. There were two small howitzers on the *Campbell* and one on the *Shreveport.* He ordered them to be fired at once. From behind the barricades of crates and boxes those passengers who were armed turned loose a fusilade. A number of Indians were seen to fall before they could scatter; their horses broke away, screaming.

It was all over in a few minutes; the big encampment disappeared and not an Indian could be seen. That was the Tobacco Garden affair—four white men, eighteen Indians and a large number of their ponies killed. It was a tragedy that would never have occurred but for the corruption of one man, Samuel M. Latta, the Sioux agent, and his silent partner, the fur company, the only possible customer for the goods that had been withheld from their rightful owners.

In the East many well-meaning people, who had banded together to befriend the Indians, severely criticized La Barge for having fired on the savages. But seeing members of his crew being shot and killed before his eyes, he would have been condemned by men who were acquainted with conditions along the frontier had he failed to do what he could to save as many as possible.

Fifteen miles up the Missouri from Tobacco Garden he stopped to bury the dead on the riverbank, with crosses erected to mark their graves. His difficulties were far from over, for when the *Robert Campbell* reached the mouth of the Yellowstone she found only two and a half feet of water on the bar, and she could not get over it. By sparring, the lighter *Shreveport* was able to make it. Fort Union was only six miles away. Agents Latta and Reed agreed that the only way out of the impasse was to store the annuities in the fur company's warehouse at Fort Union for the winter.

La Barge was not concerned about the Sioux annuities that had been held back, Latta having receipted for the whole on arriving at Fort Pierre; but Reed could not be asked to receipt for the Crow and Blackfeet goods until they reached their destination at Fort Benton, which La Barge was under contract to do.

Aside from the matter of freight charges, which amounted to some $16,000, there was the value of the merchandise, for which the government could and would hold La Barge responsible. Also he didn't relish putting himself in the hands of the fur company, which he had been bucking for the past two years. But there seemed to be nothing else to do. He made an arrangement with William Hodgkiss, the company's agent, and five days were consumed in transferring the cargo to the warehouse.

Full receipts were given him by Hodgkiss, and these were witnessed by Captain W. B. Greer, U.S.A., who was stationed at Fort Union with a company of troops. In addition La Barge secured from Reed a statement of the circumstances covering the storing of the annuities, in order that he might be able to give the government the fullest explanation possible. When that business was completed, the *Campbell* and the *Shreveport* turned their prows down the river.

La Barge reached Fort Union in the spring of 1864 with the *Effie Deans,* which he had bought in partnership with John S. McCune, president of the Keokuk Packet Company, for $40,000. She had left St. Louis on March 22, with 49 passengers and assorted cargo of 160 tons, the tonnage having been held down to that figure to leave room for the annuity goods he expected to pick up at Fort Union.

The first man he fell in with at Fort Union was Captain Greer. The latter knew why he was there. "I don't believe you will find much," he told La Barge. "The company has traded nearly all of it for robes."

There was a new agent at Fort Union, a man by the name of Rolette. Hodgkiss, the former agent, had died during the winter. Rolette began by refusing to turn over the goods until the sum of $2,000 was given him for storage. The figure was preposterous and was demanded in the mistaken belief that La Barge would refuse to take the goods. The sum was offered, however, whereupon Rolette stated that as a prior condition the receipts given by Agent Hodgkiss would have to be turned over to him. This La Barge refused to do. He was convinced by now that the goods were not there, and he harried Rolette into admitting that, under instructions of Commissioner Dole, of the Bureau of Indian Affairs, transmitted through the company, he had delivered a large share of the annuities to the Gros Ventres and to other Indians. The balance, therefore, could not be delivered except under surrender of the previous year's receipts.

Captain La Barge asked to see the receipts given by the Indians to whom the goods had been delivered—an invariable rule in handing out annuities. Rolette could not produce any, nor could he present the alleged instructions from the Commissioner, his excuse being that the order had come by messenger and had been delivered orally.

La Barge had heard enough. He knew that the large quantity of goods had been traded out to the Indians by the company, constituting an unqualified theft from the government. He went on his way and that winter journeyed to Washington to thresh out the matter with the Bureau. His evidence was such that he was relieved of having to pay for the "lost" annuities, but his bill for freight charges and demurrage, amounting to $26,620.58, was not allowed. All he ever received was $7,206.55, amounting to a loss of almost $20,000.

The whole system of dispensing amnesty goods to the Plains Indians was so badly conceived and administered that it could not fail to result in the wholesale corruption of government contractors and Indian agents. What occurred at Fort Union was the pattern, not an isolated example, of what happened elsewhere. Indian agents had no warehouses in which to store the goods they received, which compelled them to depend on the facilities of the traders, an arrangement that opened the door to graft and dishonesty at the expense of both the government and the Indians.

Unfortunately, the untutored Indian could not distinguish between the skulduggery of the agents and the government that employed them. As a consequence it was that vaguely understood source of power called "the government" they held responsible for the bad faith, broken promises and exploitation that confronted them.

Of course, under the best of circumstances it would have been impossible to take over Indian lands, rob them of their birthright and expect them to like it. With more and more settlers moving into the Upper Missouri Valley, and new military forts being built, it was increasingly clear to the great Sioux Nation that that was the white man's ultimate goal. Sitting Bull, the astute leader of the Hunkpapa Sioux, summed it up in a few words. "We do not want any trouble with the white man; all we want is to be left alone and be permitted to live like Indians." [2] It was too late for that.

New treaties were made with the various tribes that included the bribery of increased amounts of annuities. The military leaders took a dim view of them. "It is beyond question that such a system of treaty-making is, of all others, the most unpolitic . . . and aside from stimulating breaches of peace, is always attended with fraud upon the government and upon the Indian," said General Pope. General Alfred Sully was equally critical. "This system of issuing annuity goods is one grand humbug," said he. Tough old General Harney had previously expressed himself in similar vein.

A number of so-called peace commissions had met with the Sioux tribes over the years and accomplished nothing other than the system of giveaway. In 1866 the government tried again. It was officially known as the Northwestern Treaty Commission. It was composed of Newton Edmunds, Governor of Dakota Territory; General S. R. Curtis, an officer of the Iowa Volunteers; Orrin Guernsey, the Rev. Henry W. Reed, the former agent of the Blackfeet; and several others. While it was supposed to negotiate new peace treaties, its principal purpose was to secure a railroad right-of-way across Indian lands.

If there was one thing the tribes did not want it was a railroad, and seething with unrest as they were at this time, nothing could have been calculated to further inflame them than talk of one. Only in their colossal stupidity could politicians in faraway Washington have voted funds for such a ridiculous adventure. Any faint hope of success it might have was damned by the calibre of the men appointed to the Commission. But they gathered in St. Louis plentifully supplied with money and prepared to make the long voyage up the Missouri in style. Wanting the best, they contracted with Captain La Barge to convey them up the river at a rate of three hundred dollars a day, in a brand new boat, the *Ben Johnson,* which he chartered for the trip.

La Barge was ordered to tie up early each evening and make a late start in the morning. The *Ben Johnson* stopped at every landing, a fact which Chairman Curtis noted in his journal. When put in the record, it would speak for the thoroughness with which the junket had been conducted. To the Captain and his crew the voyage appeared to be nothing more than an excursion for pleasure at government expense. If the commissioners had any serious business to transact, there was no sign of it; they whiled away their time reading, playing cards and stuffing themselves with the choicest foods. They had several tons of presents for the Indians aboard, but they were never broken out. In fact, they saw and talked with very few Indians.

On board, acting as interpreter for the Commission, was Larpenteur. When his book was published it included the statement that "The great Peace Commission was a complete failure." That was the opinion of all knowledgeable men in the Upper Valley. They regarded it with contempt and predicted that instead of accomplishing anything worthwhile it would aggravate an already explosive situation. Nothing untoward happened, however, until the *Ben Johnson* neared the mouth of White Earth River, some seventy miles below Fort Union. Catching sight of two hunters on the shore, Chairman Curtis ordered the boat stopped and invited the two Indians on board. They belonged to the Yanktonais band, the most belligerent of all the Sioux tribes. Their main camp was a few miles up the White Earth River. Curtis requested them to have their people move down to the mouth of the river and wait for the arrival of the steamboat, where a council with gifts for all would be held.

When the *Ben Johnson* arrived at the mouth of White Earth River it found a village of six hundred lodges, which meant about three thousand Indians, awaiting it. Remembering Tobacco Garden, La Barge urged Curtis not to permit the Indians to come aboard. He was overruled. The steamer had no sooner tied up than several hundred Indians reached the deck. Chairs for the chiefs and a table had been set out, but all was pandemonium. The commissioners retreated to their staterooms and locked themselves in.

La Barge had kept the engineer at his post with steam up and sent the mate to the bow with an ax, his instructions being to cut the rope at the first tap of the bell. La Barge gave the signal, the line was cut, the wheels began to turn backward and the boat slipped quickly away from the bank. "The sudden move astounded the Indians," says La Barge. "Those on shore seized the line before they discovered that it had been cut. I knew they would not dare to fire, for fear of shooting their own people. Those on the boat were panic-stricken and began to leap overboard. I caused the nose of the boat to be held close to shore so that they could get to land without drowning. In a few minutes the boat was clear of them. No further attempt was made to treat with these Indians, and we went on up the river."

The commissioners spent some time at Fort Union conferring with delegations of Crows, Assinboins and Gros Ventres who had been brought down on the small steamboat *Miner* from their camps on the Musselshell. The Indians were in a sullen mood and would not sign any treaties. When it was seen that it was a waste of time to treat with them any further, arrangements were made to return them to their hunting grounds on the *Amanda,* a small government boat.[3] The river was by now so low that it was impossible for the *Ben Johnson* to proceed farther. She turned around and began the leisurely return downriver.

Most of the goods intended for the Indians were still on board. Part of them were put off at Yankton. But the following night, as the *Ben Johnson* lay tied up at Sioux City, La Barge was awakened by the sound of freight being moved ashore. He investigated and was informed that the goods were being removed at Chairman Curtis' order. The stealth with which the operation was being conducted was prima facie evidence that the merchandise being piled up on the wharf—the property of the United States—was on its way to disappearance, to be sold for the private enrichment of one or more of its trusted servants.

The Great Peace Commission returned to Washington, with nothing accomplished, and was quickly forgotten.

Even though the ensuing year opened with the threat of a general uprising of the Plains Indians, 1867 proved to be the record year in the history of Missouri River steamboating. Forty-three boats arrived at Fort Benton, the finest of them owned by the Kountz Line, the Peck Line, the Fort Benton Transportation Company and the fast boats of the Northwestern Transportation Company, the Chicago and Northwestern Railroad subsidiary, operating out of Sioux City. It was the feast before the famine. By 1870 most of them were gone. Those that remained confined themselves to running between Chamberlain and Benton. Even that lucrative business was soon to disappear. The railroads had driven the steamboats off the Upper Mississippi and were now about to drive them off the Missouri.

The U.S. Report of Navigation for 1880 lists 366 steamboats plying the Missouri River. That figure is misleading, for it includes all of the little cargo carriers plying between St. Louis and Kansas City. The Missouri Pacific Railroad, which largely parallels the river for most of that distance, had reached Jefferson City in 1856, but did not build to Kansas City until 1866. It had little effect on the river business because the boats reached points beyond the end of track, such as Leavenworth and Atchison, which made the transfer of freight from rail to boat at Kansas City unnecessary. Elsewhere it was an entirely different story. The Mormon-financed Utah Northern Railroad had reached Virginia City and pulled a great share of the trade of western Montana away from Fort Benton. But what really hurt was the arrival of the Sioux City and Pacific (a Northwestern affiliate) at Sioux City in 1868, followed by the arrival of the Illinois Central two years later. With its two railroads Sioux City became a more important river port than St. Joseph and Omaha.[4] It ruined the formerly important St. Louis trade with the Upper Missouri Valley. But when the Northern Pacific reached Bismarck in 1883, it virtually ended the river trade below that point. If a final blow was needed, it came when Jim Hill's Great Northern drove into Montana and reached Helena in 1887.

Although it had nothing to do with steamboating, Fort Benton committed a form of civic hara-kiri by refusing to give Hill a right-of-way through the town. He responded by bypassing it and heading for Great Falls, which welcomed him with open arms and went on to become the most important town in Montana, while Fort Benton was left to wither on the vine.

The last of the downriver steamboats pulled away from Fort Benton for St. Louis in 1890. Whether it was the *W. B. Dance* or the *Ben Johnson* is a matter of argument. Within a period of thirty years the great business of the river had reached its pinnacle and vanished; the fur trade had lost its importance; the railroads had come and the Plains Indians had been subjugated. It had not taken very long.

Unlike the railroad, which could not pull up its tracks and move when business faded, the steamboat could go anywhere. But when steamboatmen began looking around for a river from which the trade had not vanished, they were unable to find one. It was the same all over: the steamboat was an anachronism, a relic of an era that was gone. The bitter admission ushered in a sad day for the marine insurance companies. With increasing frequency boats began to burn or sink, leaving the underwriters to bear the load. Old-timers like La Barge could only shake their heads; they had seen it all.

XVI

Steamboat Days in the Northwest

WHEN FURS WERE THE ONLY TRADE of the great and wonderfully rich wilderness area now encompassed in the states of Oregon, Washington and the maritime regions of the Province of British Columbia, its only means of contact with the outside world was by its rivers and the sea. The area's remoteness from a market, and the dangers to be encountered in reaching one, must forever stand as a monument to the indomitable spirit and courage of the men who successfully pitted themselves against what often proved to be the tragic consequences of such a desperate undertaking.

Whether the market was China, Australia, the eastern seaboard of the United States or England, oceans had to be crossed. The trade called for stout ships, and although they were capably handled, many were lost at sea. And the commerce of the great Pacific Northwest was also dependent on the brigs, barks and schooners. There was no other way; what sail had meant to the prosperity of coastal New England was even more all-important to the Oregon Country (Oregon and Washington) and the bordering waterways of British Columbia. As a consequence, boats of every size and style cluttered the Columbia River and its tributaries as well as the Strait of Juan de Fuca and the expanse of Puget Sound. This was no more than fifty-eight years after the first oceangoing vessel crossed the bar at the mouth of the great unknown river of the West, then called the Oregon, on May 11, 1792.

She was a full-rigged ship of 212 tons burden, with two decks and ten guns. She was out of Boston, and her master was Captain Robert Gray. He ascended the river for some fifteen miles and spent several days taking on fresh water and trading with the Indians who swarmed about his ship in canoes. On May 19, he dropped down to the mouth of the river, went ashore, raised the American flag, planted some coins under a large pine tree and formally took possession in the name of the United States. He named the river Columbia after his ship. Three years later at least fifty ships were trading in Northwestern waters, the majority owned by the Hudson's Bay Company, which was firmly established at New Westminster and fast-growing Vancouver, B.C.

In 1836 the H.B.C. fleet received a notable addition in the coming of the *Beaver*—always affectionately remembered as the *"Old Beaver"*—the first vessel powered by steam to ply those waters.

In her architecture and depth of hold the *Beaver* was a steamship, not a steamboat in the tradition of the steamboats of the Mississippi and its tributaries. She was a sturdy lady and was to become remarkable for her longevity. She survived accidents and fire for forty-eight years until she piled up on the rocks at the entrance to Vancouver harbor in 1888. She had long since become a marine relic, dwarfed in size and magnificence by the fast liners that tooted her out of the way.

The *Beaver* was built at Blackwall on the Thames. She was a side-wheeler, but her wheels were not attached and she was rigged as a brig for her ocean voyage. Her length was 101.4 feet, her beam 20 feet. Her engines and boilers were built by Bolton and Watt. She proved her seaworthiness and speed by reaching the Columbia after a passage of 163 days.[1]

The first steamboat built in Oregon was the namesake of the first vessel to enter the Columbia River: the *Columbia*. She was a little side-wheeler built at Upper Astoria and made her trial run on July 3, 1850. She was only 90 feet long. Her non-condensing engines were of French make and had been brought up by ship from San Francisco.

The honor of being the first steamboat to ply the Columbia belongs to her. She left Upper Astoria at noon and reached Portland at 3:00 P.M. the next day. After lying there two or three hours, she proceeded up the Willamette River to Oregon City, arriving at eight o'clock that evening, where "a great celebration took place." [2] In passing the little settlement of Milwaukie, the steamer *Lot Whitcomb,* a much more pretentious boat, could have been observed as she stood on the ways, nearing completion.

The *Lot Whitcomb* was launched on Christmas Day, 1850. She was a commodious side-wheeler, 160 feet long, and was named for the founder of the town, who was one of her owners. Her machinery had been brought out from New Orleans to go into a Sacramento River boat, but Whitcomb had bought it and shipped it north. As a further indignity, he induced the captain (J. C. Ainsworth) and engineer (Jacob Kamm) of the now engineless boat to come to Oregon with him at top money, to take charge of the *Lot Whitcomb* when she was completed.

Captain Ainsworth and Engineer Kamm had several thousand dollars due them in back wages, by the time the *Lot Whitcomb* came off the ways. Promoter Whitcomb settled that by giving them stock in the company, in lieu of cash. He was selling a great amount of stock in the boat. It was very profitable for him and his partners, but when the bubble burst the investors got little or nothing.

When the boilers for the *Lot Whitcomb* were unloaded at Milwaukie, they were in twenty-one pieces. There were no boilermakers in Oregon at that time, but with the self-confidence that was to be characteristic of their long and distinguished careers, Ainsworth and Kamm went to work to put the boilers together, first having to forge the tools with which to do the job. They succeeded so well that although the *Lot Whit-*

comb encountered many difficulties, it was never from her boilers.

With her graceful lines and tall twin stacks, she was a beautiful boat and would have been so acclaimed even on the Mississippi. Her staterooms were on the main deck, with pilothouse and texas above on the hurricane deck. She proved to be an expensive boat to run, but in her day, and long afterward, her equal was not seen on the rivers of Oregon.

Her first work was on the Astoria route, making two trips each week. A few weeks after this service was inaugurated, she ran on the rocks opposite Milwaukie, carrying away her right wheel, wheelhouse and guard, and tearing a hole in her hull. When repaired she continued on the lower river, connecting at Ranier with the Cowitz River Canoe and Batteau line. Having great power, she made an excellent towboat, and handled nearly all of the sailing vessels that came up the Columbia.

That fall the steamship *Goldhunter* was brought up from San Francisco by the proprietors of the Portland townsite, who were forced into buying her to combat the scheming of Whitcomb. He ran his boat from Milwaukie to Astoria, ignoring Portland, for a time refusing to stop there at all. The *Goldhunter* carried several cargos of Oregon products, mostly grain to San Francisco, and gave the future metropolis of Oregon such a boost that Whitcomb was obliged to recognize it.

Minority stockholders of the *Goldhunter,* dissatisfied with their investment in her, forced her sale, and she went to Mexico to run between Tehuantepec and San Francisco. The *Lot Whitcomb* then took over the Portland business. But she did not remain on the Columbia for long. In 1854 she was bought by the California Steam Navigation Company. On August 12, with Captain George Flavel, the famous bar pilot, in command, she steamed out over the bar. When she was outside, Captain Ainsworth resumed command. The steamship *Peytonia* was waiting to tow her to San Francisco Bay. It proved to be a rough trip, and the *Lot Whitcomb* reached her destination with three feet of water in her hold. On the Sacramento her name was changed to the *Annie Abernathy,* and as such she ran for many years between Sacramento and San Francisco.

Old Oregon had been officially organized as a territory in 1848, embracing at that time everything between the 42nd and 49th parallels, west of the Rocky Mountains. The temporary seat of government at Champoeg was removed to Salem, the permanent capital. The treaty of joint occupancy, of 1846, had ended the boundary dispute between the United States and Great Britain, made famous by the battle cry of "Fifty-four forty or fight." The two countries agreed that the 49th parallel was to be recognized as the international boundary, and that everything to the south of it was the undisputed territory of the United States. But under the joint occupancy agreement, the Hudson's Bay Company was to be permitted to continue its operations on American soil.

This treaty was in effect when Dr. John McLoughlin, the chief factor of the H.B.C., built Fort Vancouver on the north bank of the Columbia, a few miles east of the mouth of the Willamette, where he reigned for twenty years.

The tidal wave of emigration that had been flowing westward over the so-called Oregon Trail for years had peopled the hitherto wilderness valleys of the Columbia and Willamette with thousands of Americans. More were arriving every year. Perhaps no other mass migration of human beings will ever equal it for the high character, determination and industry of the individuals who composed it.

They had come to Oregon believing they would find it a land of plenty. For the great majority that dream was being realized: the soil produced bumper crops; great stands of the finest timber awaited the ax; cattle, horses and other livestock multiplied, and with careful breeding developed into finer animals than were to be found in the Midwest, from which most of the pioneer Oregonians had come. But distances were great; there were few roads; if a man hoped to find a market for what he produced, it had to be by water.

Steamboat navigation was limited to the lower rivers by such natural obstructions as the Cascades on the Columbia and the Falls on the Willamette. If boats could be placed above them, vast and as yet untouched regions would be opened to commerce.

Facing a challenge, the rewards of which promised to be lucrative, it was not long before small boats were dragged over
the rapids at the Cascades and a way found around Willamette
Falls. As they advanced ever deeper into virgin territory, the
recognized "head of navigation" changed so frequently that no
one could be sure where it was located.

In 1851, the diminutive *Hoosier* became the first steamer to
operate above Willamette Falls. Originally a ship's longboat,
she had been lengthened and supplied with a pile-driver engine
and boiler.[3] She ran for a long time between Canemah and upriver points.

The *Hoosier* was followed by the *Washington* and later by
the *Multnomah,* the most famous and profitable of the pioneer
steamers operating on the upper Willamette. It was not unusual
for her to bring down from a thousand to fifteen hundred bush-
els of wheat at a trip. Albany was believed to be as far up the
river as it was safe for a steamer to go, but Captain Leonard
White took his boat up to Corvallis without difficulty, and was
rewarded by the local authorities with the gift of a square block
of land in the town.

Both as pilot and master, Leonard White was a daring and
outstanding navigator, taking craft, of which he was master,
far beyond the limits established by his competitors. Although
the Willamette above Corvallis was narrow, crooked, swift and
encumbered with driftwood and logs, he took the *Fenix* (local
spelling for Phoenix), a new boat, all the way to Harrisburg in
1855; and two years later, in the *Clinton,* he accomplished what
was believed impossible by reaching Eugene.

Transferring to the Upper Columbia in 1858, in the following ten years he opened navigation farther to the north and east
than ever before, at one time going up the Snake River, beyond
Lewiston, as far as the mouth of the Grand Ronde River.

In 1865, at Colville Landing, Washington, on the Upper
Columbia, Captain White set something of a record, even for
himself, by building a small stern-wheeler and equipping her
with a second-hand engine, with the boilers out of the old *Jennie Clark,* the first stern-wheeler seen in Oregon, and from

which Captains Ainsworth and Kamm had put together their fantastically rich and powerful Oregon Navigation Company. Fittingly, White named his boat *Forty-Nine*. A gold strike in the Big Bend had brought several hundred mad men to Colville Landing, all anxious to get to the diggings at once. It was December, no time to undertake such a voyage, but White collected the fares and told them to get aboard. One-way passage was $25; freight $200 a ton.

Few men would have dared to face that wild stretch of the Columbia at any time of the year. For ten days, in which he never left the wheelhouse, Captain White brought the *Forty-Nine* through the Little Dalles and Little Rock rapids on lines and got through floating ice in Lower Arrow Lake to the Kootenay. There, he encountered solid ice and could go no farther. He discharged his passengers, who proceeded on foot, and turning around before she was frozen in, the *Forty-Nine* returned to Colville Landing. She was the first, and for a long time the only, steamboat to cross the 49th parallel. As a pathfinder, the Columbia never produced Captain Leonard White's equal.

On skids, several small boats had been dragged up and over the rapids at the Cascades and were running the middle Columbia as far as The Dalles. Just above The Dalles was Celilo Falls, an impassable barrier to navigation, In a few miles the river drops eighty feet. There was no getting a boat over the falls, but there was talk of taking one around them. Nothing was done about it, and meanwhile Robert R. Thompson and his partner, E. F. Coe, were enjoying the fruits of their government contract to transport supplies to Fort Walla Walla and other upriver posts. Portaging around the falls and forwarding goods by a fleet of batteaux had become a very profitable business. How profitable can be judged by the fact that their forwarding charges amounted to a hundred dollars a ton, which even the Quartermaster Department found exorbitant. To reduce costs to the government, without reducing their profits, Thompson and Coe built the small steamer *Colonel Wright,* named for the commandant at The Dalles, and put her in the water at the mouth of the Des Chutes River, above Celilo Falls. As might have been expected, the man into whose hands they entrusted her was Captain Leonard White.

The freight rate to the government was reduced to eighty dollars a ton. Even so, Thompson and Coe made so much money that the following spring they put the steamer *Tenino* on the same route, both boats making three round trips weekly. By connecting with the boats of the Oregon Steam Navigation Company at The Dalles and again at the Cascades, passengers could be landed in Portland thirty hours after leaving Walla Walla, a feat that was then considered remarkable.[4]

When the *Columbia* proved to be too slow to compete with the *Lot Whitcomb,* her engines were removed and put in the *James F. Flint,* which was being built at the Cascades by the Bradfords and Van Bergen. After completion she was hauled over the Cascades to run to The Dalles. Disappointed with her earnings, her owners brought her down to the lower river the following spring, and that September she sank opposite Mult-nomah Falls. After being abandoned for the winter, she was raised and taken to Vancouver, B.C., and renamed *Fashion.* Not long afterward she blew a boiler bolt, scalding her engineer to death. Her engines were removed and she ended her days as a barge in the coal trade on Puget Sound.

These pioneer boats, with the exception of the *Lot Whitcomb,* were all small, ugly ducklings, completely lacking in marine grace of line and looking very much as though their works above the waterline had been hammered together by the crudest kind of frontier carpentry—which was undoubtedly the case. Although they were ugly and cheaply built, they served a useful purpose. Without exception they were wood-burners, short single-stackers, and excitement attended them as they chugged up and down the rivers, belching smoke and sparks.

In 1851, the commercial possibilities of Puget Sound had be-gun to be recognized, and a port of entry was established at Olympia, the great expectation being that with flourishing San Francisco in desperate need of more and more timber, a great coastwise trade between the Sound, with its boundless forests of fir and spruce, and the California metropolis was certain to develop. The premise was correct, but it was not to come over-night. Although the collector opened his office in February it was not until November 19 that he recorded his first clearance, when the brig *George Emery* took out a coasting license.

That such a potentially rich wilderness, containing the great-est stand of conifers in the United States, with its mild winters, copious rainfall and a figurative thousand miles of waterfront on its bays, inlets and streams, into which felled timber could be dumped and herded into booms and moved to the nearest sawmill, could long fail to escape the ax and the saw was un-thinkable. Such minor excitements as the Fraser River gold rush, and the much greater one to the Klondike, would come and go without leaving any lasting effect on the economy of the Sound, which is bound inseparably to its many natural re-sources, with none more important than timber and its by-products.

That the commercial possibilities of Puget Sound were not going unnoticed was indicated earlier that year (1851) when the schooner *Mary Taylor*, which had enjoyed a favorable repu-tation as a pilot boat on the Columbia River bar, left the river to trade on the Sound. On board when she came north on her first trip were L. B. Hastings and Francis W. Pettygrove, the founders of Portland, and their party. They cruised leisurely about the Sound, looking for a site on which to establish what they hoped would be another Portland. They finally came ashore on the Olympic Peninsula, staked off a settlement and named it Port Townsend. The location was well chosen. It was on the Strait of Juan de Fuca at the entrance to the Sound proper, and less than a hundred miles to the open ocean. It was to become, for a time, the territory's most important seaport. Port Townsend is a prosperous small city today, but it was des-tined early in its history to be overshadowed by a rival settle-ment, less than fifty miles distant, which was still unborn when Port Townsend was founded. That, of course, was Seattle.

In the early summer of 1851, two men, David Denny and John N. Low, reached the little settlement of Olympia, having come overland from Portland, where they had left the wagon train, captained by Denny's brother, Arthur A. Denny, to recuperate from the long journey across the plains, while they went ahead to search out a likely place where all might settle. At Olympia, Denny and Low embarked on Puget Sound in Captain Robert Fay's schooner. Late in September they sailed into Elliott Bay. Satisfied that they had found the place they were seeking, they dispatched a letter by Captain Fay to the group waiting at Portland, telling them to come at once, and began building a cabin on the south headland of the bay. They were the original settlers of today's Seattle.

Within two months the other members of the party, five families, consisting of twelve adults and an equal number of children, arrived at Alki Point on the schooner *Exact*. They laid out a town and, optimistically, named it New York, obviously believing that from such a small acorn another great metropolis would grow. Fortunately, when the brig *Lenora* arrived, seeking a load of piles for San Francisco, the difficulty of loading at Alki Point caused the pioneers to seek a more practicable shipping point. This was done, with the help of the friendly Duwamish Indians. New York was dropped and the location named Seattle, for the chief of the Duwamish.[5]

Other settlers soon arrived, and Seattle began to prosper when Henry Yesler came up from Portland and built the first steam sawmill on Puget Sound. In 1856, Seattle was attacked by bands of hostile Klikitats and Pyallup Indians. With the aid of the guns of the U.S. sloop-of-war *Decatur,* the Indians were driven off with some losses. No further hostilities occurred in the vicinity of Seattle. In the following seven years, however, in other parts of the territory, the various tribes were an almost constant menace. After the massacre of the Marcus Whitman missionaries in the Walla Walla Valley in 1847, and the resulting Cayuse war, in which the Indians were severely punished, several army posts were established and a number of blockhouses built by the settlers to which they could retreat when hostilities threatened. But isolated farmhouses and small emigrant trains continued to be attacked and men, women and children murdered.

Undoubtedly a general uprising of the tribes along the Columbia and its tributaries, and on the Sound, numbering fifteen or more, was kept in abeyance because they had no common language and could communicate only by using the trading language of the white traders, known as the Chinook jargon, which was a curious mixture of French, Russian, English and Chinook. Despite that difficulty, Kamiakin, the able and intelligent chief of the Yakimas, organized to sweep all whites from the Columbia River and Puget Sound basins. Although it was well conceived militarily, Kamiakin followers were too few in number and too poorly armed to win. The sporadic campaign began with the failure of the attack on Seattle, in January, 1856, and ended shortly after the unsuccessful attempt to capture Fort Cascades, on the Columbia, in which a few whites and a number of Indians were killed. The retreating Indians, under Chief John of the Spokanes, were pursued and rounded up by Colonel George Wright and his troops. On September 11, 1858, at The Dalles, Wright executed sixteen of his prisoners. Whether justified or not, it was the sort of retaliation that the Indian mind could understand. It broke the back of all resistance to the encroachments of the whites. They could hardly have foreseen that those encroachments were only the beginning. When the fisheries became commercially important, even the Indians' right to catch salmon when and where they pleased would be grievously curtailed by a so-called Open River Policy, with its canals, locks and dams.

At that time, 1858, had anyone suggested that the hordes of salmon that went up the Columbia on the yearly runs to spawn were a fabulous asset, comparable only to its wheat and timber, he would have been dismissed as harebrained. Several attempts had been made to ship Columbia River salmon to San Francisco, but they had arrived in unsalable condition. To have sent them down properly iced might have been successful. It was a long and uncertain voyage, however, dependent on the wind and weather. And ice was expensive. The probable returns, measured against the costs, promised so little that the experiment was not continued. In the meantime, the Indians continued to cling to their precarious perches at Celilo Falls and caught salmon by the thousands, to be smoked or salted.

The Hudson's Bay Company established several fisheries on the lower river to catch and salt salmon for export, but it was never more than a minor operation. In fact, salmon as a potential source of wealth did not receive serious consideration until 1867, when four Down-Easters from Maine—the three Hume brothers, William, George and Robert, and Andrew Hapgood, a tinsmith—settled at Eagle Cliff on the north bank of the Columbia in what is now Wahkiakum County, Washington, and opened what they called a fish cannery, the first in the Pacific Northwest.

The Humes were shrewd, ambitious Yankees, with a keen appreciation of a dollar; their partner, Andy Hapgood, the tinker (or tinsmith as he preferred to be called), had come along because in his spare time, during the long, cold Maine winters, he had discovered, invented or devised what he called a secret process by which lobsters could be put in sealed tin cans and shipped down to Boston. His secret appears to have been nothing more than that he found by packing raw lobster in a can and sealing it with solder, and then cooking the contents with steam, the meat would keep indefinitely.

Unfortunately New Englanders continued to exhibit a decided preference for fresh lobster. Sometimes the cans exploded, which did not improve sales. Then, too, the supply of the crustaceans was often limited. When the lobstermen began to realize that they were undermining themselves by having the product of their labor sold in cans, the Humes and Hapgood decided to pull up stakes and transfer their business to the Pacific Coast. They tried the Sacramento River first, but the run of salmon proving to be unsatisfactory, they moved north to the Columbia.

It was the beginning of a multimillion dollar industry that came on with a rush. The Hume-Hapgood pack for the first year amounted to four thousand cases of forty-eight cans each, all hand-soldered. Within twenty years there were thirty-five canneries along the river, of which the Humes owned twenty.

By then the process of sealing the cans hermetically by machinery had been invented.

At first no attempt was made to grade the different kinds of salmon being packed, but it did not take astute Bill Hume long to discover that the chinook, the king of all salmon, would fetch a higher price when marketed as the Royal Chinook. Presently the American housewife could buy her choice of Royal Chinook, silver, blueback (or sockeye) and chum salmon at varying prices. Without opposition, Astoria, built largely on piling, had become the capital of the canning industry. With its numerous saloons, brothels and deadfalls it was tough, rowdy and immoral, and over it hung the stench of dead fish and the offal from the canneries, in which thousands of Chinese did the inside work, gutting and cutting up fish and packing them in the tin containers. When a machine was invented to do most of their work, it at once was dubbed the Iron Chink.[6]

Contrary to the popular belief that the great fish wheels on the Columbia produced the major portion of the salmon taken in the semiannual runs, it was the men fishing offshore—Swedes, Danes, Norwegians and Finns—who kept the ravenous canneries supplied. The Indians contributed very little, even after the Warrens and Seuferts opened their canneries between Celilo and The Dalles. The white man had usurped their land and their rivers, and all they had left was a quickening retreat into obscurity. On gala occasions future generations of whites would parade a few of them in their tribal dress to lend color to whatever they were celebrating, a shabby tribute to the race they had dispossessed.

XVII

The Great Steamboat Monopoly

COLUMBIA RIVER and Puget Sound steamboats did not escape the sinkings, burnings and explosions that occurred so frequently on the Mississippi and other rivers. The first notable disaster was recorded in January, 1852, when the steamer *General Warren* went to pieces on Clatsop Spit at the mouth of the Columbia.

The *General Warren* was an old boat, and although powered by steam, she was also schooner-rigged. En route from Portland to San Francisco, she passed out of the river late in the afternoon of January 28, in charge of Captain George Flavel, the well-known pilot, who left her soon after crossing the bar, turning the command over to her master, Captain Charles Thompson. The *Warren* stood out to sea with a stiff breeze blowing from the south.

The weather continued to thicken. Shortly after midnight the foretopmast of the *Warren* was carried away. It convinced Captain Thompson that his safest course was to return to the Columbia. The ship was making water. Deeply laden with grain, her cargo had begun to shift, clogging the pumps. The Columbia was sighted in the morning, but Captain Thompson was unable to communicate with the pilot boat until midafternoon.

High seas were running and another hour passed before Pilot Flavel was able to come aboard. The graphic account of what followed is quoted from E. W. Wright's *Marine History of the Pacific Northwest:*

> He [Flavel] objected to taking the steamer in, stating that it was too late, and with a strong ebb tide running, unsafe to make the attempt. But as the vessel was leaking, and the passengers were fearful of drifting into worse dangers northward, they crowded around him, begged so earnestly, and even taunted him with cowardice, so that he finally said: 'If you insist I will try to take you in, but will not be responsible for what may happen.' He then ordered the pilot schooner to accompany the steamer, and at 5:00 P.M. crossed the bar, the wind meanwhile dying out so that the schooner could not follow. The steamer was making water faster than ever and was so unmanageable that it was difficult to control her movements, and with a strong ebb running she made so little headway that Flavel requested the Captain to anchor. Captain Thompson informed him that the steamer could not live in such a sea, and that she must be beached immediately.
>
> This statement surprised Flavel, who had not until then realized how thoroughly worthless the old tub was, and he obeyed the Captain's wishes and headed for Clatsop Spit, beaching her at 7:00 P.M. In a short time the sea was breaking over her. At 9:00 P.M. everything abaft the foremast had been carried away, but as yet no lives were lost. Everyone was mustered forward hoping that the wreck would hold together until morning, when they could expect relief from shore. At 3:00 A.M. the steamer was breaking up so rapidly that Captain Thompson determined, as a last resort, to launch a boat and send for assistance. Captain Flavel was asked to take charge, and volunteers were called for to man her. Most of the people on board preferred to take their chances by remaining on the steamer than to rush into what had the appearance of certain death in the breakers, which were then running so high that it seemed impossible for a boat to live.
>
> Ten men responded to the call for a crew [and] by mere chance cleared the wreck, and a few hours later reached Astoria, where they found the bark *George and Martha*. Her master, Beard, immediately started for the scene of the disaster with a large whaleboat, but when they reached the spot where the doomed

vessel had been the night before, she had disappeared from view; and the bloated corpses of the unfortunate passengers and crew, which drifted ashore on Clatsop Beach, were the only evidence of the disaster. Forty-two men and women and two children had perished.

Accidents began to multiply. The steamboat *Gazelle* exploded as she lay at the wharf at Canemah, killing twenty, passengers, officers and crew. The U.S. revenue cutter *Lincoln* went ashore at North Beach. Nine men perished. The *Marie* also piled up there, and again nine lives were lost. Accidents were costly, but the river and coastwise boats were making so much money for their owners that for every one that was lost, two or three new boats were launched. Competition began to pull down freight and passenger rates. Instead of costing a hundred dollars, the first-class passage to San Francisco from Portland fell to seventy-five dollars.

The first American-owned steamboat on Puget Sound appeared in 1853, when the little *Fairy* began running between Olympia and Seattle. In January of that year the new H.B.C. steamer *Otter* arrived at Victoria from England to share the work the old *Beaver* was doing. She was twenty-one feet longer than the *Beaver,* but when her masts and sails had been removed, she was very much like the older boat in appearance. She was a sturdy boat, and although she ran for many years, she never supplanted the *"Old Beaver"* in the public's affection.

Late in 1852 fifty delegates representing settlers living north of the Columbia River met at Monticello to petition Congress to divide Oregon Territory at the Columbia River, stressing the difficulty and time consumed in reaching the "distant" territorial capital at Salem, and declaring that such a division would enable those citizens living north of the river more quickly to organize a successful defense against an Indian uprising. To quote the memorial, what they asked was that "all of that portion of Oregon Territory lying north of the river and west of great northern branch thereof, should be organized under the name and style of the Territory of Columbia."

Congress received the petition favorably. In the course of committee hearings the name Columbia was dropped and Washington substituted. The petitioners not only were granted all they had requested but much more besides. The boundary designated in the act was to run along the Columbia to its intersection of the 46th parallel, near the mouth of the Walla Walla River, then due east to the summit of the Rockies. This included, of course, a large part of what was to become Idaho Territory when it was subsequently detached from Washington Territory in 1863. Olympia was designated the capital, and to govern this new wilderness empire, President Franklin Pierce dispatched Major Ingalls Stevens, a West Pointer and veteran of the Mexican War, to the scene. Late in the year, Major Stevens reached Olympia without fanfare and began organizing a territorial government.

Shearing off the upper half of old Oregon had no noticeable effect on the people living south of the Columbia. Oregon was prosperous and growing. Already she was talking about statehood, and six years later she was to achieve it.

Portland was expanding so fast that Oregon City, once the most important town in the territory, had been pushed back into second place. Milwaukie had failed to respond to the valiant efforts of Lot Whitcomb and others to promote it; farther up the Willamette, the prosperity of Salem, Corvallis and Eugene was definitely tied to booming Portland.

The Willamette Falls Company, backed and controlled by the San Francisco–Portland banking house of Page, Bacon and Company, embarked on an extensive promotion opposite Oregon City in 1853, with the definite intention of overshadowing the old town across the Willamette. Thousands of dollars were spent in building a basin and bulkheads and making other improvements. But from the start the company's operations were beset with one misfortune after another. Its first boat burned as she stood on the stocks at Oregon City; the next, the *Gazelle,* exploded, as has been mentioned, less than three weeks after she was put in service; a few months later the third, the *Oregon,* sank, proving a total loss. These reverses drove the company from the river, and in 1861, during a spring freshet, their ware-houses and other property went floating downstream.

If the H.B.C. steamers *Beaver* and *Otter* enjoyed a remark-able longevity, so did the American-owned *Goliah*. Although she was never engaged in the Columbia River trade, she ran on Puget Sound for years, where she won the sobriquet of *"The Indestructible Goliah."* With the lumber business booming, she is said to have towed half of the dozens of coastwise vessels that entered the straits bound for Nanaimo, on the British side, and nearly all that went to the American sawmills.

The *Goliah* was built in New York in 1852 as an oceangoing tugboat. After her arrival on the Sacramento River in 1853, she underwent many changes. She was alternately lengthened, short-ened, then lengthened again, and again shortened. At one time staterooms were added. They had been removed when Captain Flavel brought her north. On the Sound, she was stripped down for the purpose for which she was originally intended. When she was forty-one years old, she was still the workhorse of the Sound.[1]

Making use of the old portage trail around the Cascades, Joseph S. Ruckel and Harrison Olmstead, the owners of two small steamboats on the Portland–Cascades run, gave Oregon what has been called its first railroad, when they laid a mile and a half of wooden rails over which horses and mules pulled trains of four or five small cars. The cars were loaded above the Cascades and unloaded below. One of the cars was reserved to accommodate passengers.

The innovation was so successful that several years later a more circuitous but better route was established, measuring some four miles, and the rails were sheathed with strap iron to reduce delays and increase speed.

The tramway improved business at The Dalles, and it was further increased when a second tramway was built around Ce-lilo Falls to the mouth of the Deschutes River. It became a com-mon occurrence for the Umatilla House, its leading hotel and reputedly the best in Oregon at the time, to be taxed to capacity.

The fame of the Drovers' Cottage in Abilene, Kansas, and

the Dodge House at Dodge City in their rambunctious cowtown days was no greater than that enjoyed by the Umatilla House. It had 123 rooms and two bathrooms, which was par for the time and place, with a toilet in the basement. Its dining room was enormous, as was the quantity of food it served. In the parlance of the river, "you could always get your shirt filled at the Umatilla House."

It has been said, and with much justification, that the steamboat era on the Columbia began with the arrival of John C. Ainsworth and Jacob Kamm, the two men who had been brought up from California by Lot Whitcomb to take charge as captain and engineer of the boat he was building at Milwaukie, and ended with them. After leaving Whitcomb's employ, they had continued to run together as master and engineer on other boats.

Ainsworth, whose business judgment was excellent, had learned his steamboating on the Upper Mississippi, first as purser, then as pilot and captain. Kamm was a thrifty Swiss. Saving their money and establishing credit, they were able to improve their financial position by buying an interest in several boats. Kamm had captured the Oregon City mail contract, and through his close association with Abernethy and Clark, the California freight forwarders, he and Ainsworth were assured that their boats would have cargo to handle. All of this was in preparation for the move they made in 1858, when they formed a pool of four small boats doing business under the firm name of the Union Transportation Company. From this humble beginning were to evolve in turn the all-powerful Oregon Steam Navigation Company and a later Oregon Railroad and Navigation Company.

Kamm had designed and built the first stern-wheeler on the Columbia, the little *Jennie Clark*. From her speed and the ease with which she handled, Captain Ainsworth was convinced that she was the best type of steamer that could be put on the Columbia. With the financial backing of J. W. Ladd, of the Portland banking firm of Ladd and Tilton, they built a much finer stern-wheeler at Oregon City and named her the *Carrie Ladd*, in honor of their backer's daughter. She was launched in October, 1859. The following February, with Captain Ainsworth at the wheel, she made her first run up to the Cascades and back in record time. She so clearly outclassed her competition that four pioneer steamboatmen joined the pool, turning their boats over to Union Transportation Company direction.

Ainsworth was still a young man, barely thirty-eight, and although of benign appearance, like all would-be monopolists he was ruthless.[2] The program on which he was embarked called for the complete elimination from the Columbia and Willamette of all steamers not flying his house flag from their jackstaffs. Owners with good boats would be given an opportunity to come into the company. Those who refused would find passenger and freight rates slashed at the points from which they were getting business. If that didn't bring them to terms, he was prepared to buy their boats or subsidize them for keeping them tied up. He did not have to go to the latter extreme very often.

The Union Transportation Company merged into the Oregon Steam Navigation Company. Some competition developed on the Cascades run when the steamer *Julia* was brought down from the Sound. The O.S.N. ended that by buying her, and thereafter the *Julia* and the *Carrie Ladd* ran on alternate days, averaging two hundred passengers per trip. But as prosperous as the O.S.N. was, Captain Ainsworth's monopoly was not complete. Up above Celilo Falls, Thompson and Coe, with the *Colonel Wright* and the *Tenino,* their government contract and their outrageous freight and passenger rates, were coining money so fast they couldn't count it. They were monopolists themselves, and they were not interested in the overtures Ainsworth made them. But he had to have them in the fold, and he convinced his associates that because of the peculiar position Thompson and Coe enjoyed they would have to be given a greater share of stock in the company than was originally intended.

The two parties came to an agreement in 1862, in time to reap the profits of the greatest year in Columbia River steamboating. Gold had been discovered on the Salmon River in

Idaho. Thousands of frenzied gold hunters, anxious to get up the river, thronged the boats. Freight piled up at the Cascades so fast that the primitive railway there could not handle it. Getting around the Cascades was not only a great hindrance to river transportation, but the one link needed to give the Oregon Steam Navigation Company domination of the Columbia from Astoria to Fort Walla Walla.

By now Captain Ainsworth's plans were so well-known that he knew he could not open negotiations for buying the tramway without being asked many times its real worth. He did not hold back, however; one of his tenets of success was that when you needed anything badly enough you went out and got it, no matter the price. Put Bradford and J. S. Ruckel, the principal owners, stood him off for a time and succumbed only after they had driven up the price. For cash and O.S.N. stock, the Portage Railway came into the possession of the corporation.

To improve what he had bought, Captain Ainsworth went to San Francisco and ordered sixteen miles of iron rails and two diminutive locomotives; he was going to have a real railroad around the Upper and Lower Cascade Rapids.[3] When he returned to Portland, he began thinning out the O.S.N. fleet. The oldest and poorest boats were retired; he could see no point in keeping three boats on a run, the business of which two could handle. His policy was the best possible service at the lowest possible cost to the corporation. Company boats would leave on schedule and they would arrive at the destination on schedule, weather permitting. It was an innovation that the traveling public appreciated. Captain Ainsworth did not stop at that; he insisted that the continued success of the Oregon Steam Navigation Company depended on keeping the goodwill of the people of Oregon. It was a position that certainly improved the public image of the company and quieted its critics who were crying "monopoly."

Under Captain Ainsworth's direction, it soon became obvious that the Oregon Steam Navigation Company was making its stockholders wealthy men. That was common knowledge. It followed that others wanted to get in on such a good thing, and

led to the formation of the well-financed Peoples Transportation Company. They put the fine steamer *John H. Couch* on
the Astoria run, running opposition to the O.S.N.'s *Julia.* Captain Ainsworth immediately slashed the Astoria–Portland fare
to twenty-five cents, including a free meal. After two weeks of
that the Peoples Transportation conceded it had made a mistake; the *John H. Couch* and their two other boats were bought
at a sacrifice by the O.S.N. Others tried to cut in and failed.
There was no bucking the monopoly.

Much has been written about John C. Ainsworth, his detractors picturing him as a ruthless despot, who closed the river to
men of small means and drove many to failure and bankruptcy,
which was true enough. But Ainsworth's defenders tell a different story. To them, he was one of the great developers of Oregon, bringing order out of chaos on its navigable rivers and
providing the state with the best possible service. That can
hardly be denied, for the man had a genius for organization.
Of course, in the process he became a millionaire, which, to
some, attached a certain odium to him.

To say that Jacob Kamm, his long-time partner and asso-
ciate, was equally responsible for the success of the O.S.N.
would not be true. John C. Ainsworth *was* the Oregon Steam
Navigation Company. In his time no man was refused passage
on one of its boats because he did not have the money to pay his
fare. He was carried free and dined free. That many of these
temporarily embarrassed individuals afterward squared their
indebtedness to the company does not appear on its records. If
they did so, it was done voluntarily: there were no bills. It was
in line with the Captain's policy of fostering and keeping the
goodwill of the public. Twice he reduced the fare from Portland to The Dalles. It is small wonder that the O.S.N. had more
friends than enemies.

When it had become so strongly entrenched that it could do
about as it pleased, it began retiring its old steamers and building new ones, three of them finer and more luxurious than anything the Northwest had seen. The *Oneonta* was the first, a
true Mississippi River-type steamboat. Under the superinten-

dence of Jacob Kamm, she was built at the Cascades by master builder Samuel Forman. The second was the *Wide West,* called by many "the perfect stern-wheeler." She was the pride of the O.S.N.'s chief engineer John Gates. When she was launched at Portland, so much wheat was glutting the warehouses at the Cascades that she was rushed into service as a freight boat, making a round trip daily between Portland and the Cascades, and it was not until some weeks later that her cabins were completed and her really gorgeous furnishings installed.

The *Wide West* was a big boat for the Columbia, 218 feet overall, with a beam of 39½ feet. She had a deep hold, 8 feet, and was capable of carrying a deckload of 550 tons.

The *Wide West* was followed by the fine steamer *R. R. Thompson,* which was her equal in every respect. For twenty years she was unsurpassed in speed and elegance. By then, the great decline of steamboating had begun.

Three transcontinental railroads were making a determined bid to reach the Pacific Coast: Jim Hill's Great Northern, the recently resuscitated Northern Pacific; and up from Salt Lake City, the Oregon Short Line, a Union Pacific subsidiary, was pointing for the Columbia. At home, in Oregon, the demand for rail connection with California became so great that the legislature voted a handsome subsidy for building it. Two Portland groups started laying rails simultaneously, one on the eastern bank of the Willamette and the other on the west side of the river. Scenting rich pickings, flamboyant Big Ben Holladay, the so-called Napoleon of the Plains, who had made several million dollars stagecoaching, hurried to Oregon. With scandalous corruption he took over the East Side Line and forced the West Side Line to capitulate. A year later, although he had built only some twenty miles of track, he had sold several million dollars worth of bonds to English and German investors. Suspecting that they were the victims of a gigantic swindle, they sent young Henry Villard to Oregon to look out for their interests.

Villard, a dynamic young man of German descent, had won some recognition as a financial genius. What he found in Oregon was a shambles. He forced Holladay to turn the projected

Oregon and California Railroad over to him. Work on the road was resumed. Making the most of his success, Villard got control of the Northern Pacific.

Captain Ainsworth had had some ideas of his own about building a railroad from the Upper Columbia, where it would connect with his boats, to Huntington, in eastern Oregon, where it would meet the Oregon Short Line when it arrived there. But now he envisaged a move that would be more profitable for his stockholders—he was always thinking of his stockholders, of which he was one; he would lay his plans for connecting the Oregon Steam Navigation Company with the Oregon Short Line before Henry Villard, and sell the O.S.N. to the Northern Pacific.

Villard liked the idea; it would not only help the Northern Pacific to reach Portland ahead of its rivals but give it command of the Columbia as well. John Ainsworth had executed the greatest coup of his career. The Northern Pacific bought the O.S.N. for a whopping price, and under its new title of the Oregon Railroad and Navigation Company, Villard incorporated it on June 14, 1879, for $6,000,000.

Captain Ainsworth is not listed among the incorporators, although his son George is. Jacob Kamm's name is also missing.[4] Retiring from the river, John Ainsworth invested heavily in Tacoma real estate, which brought him handsome returns. For the last fourteen years of his life, he resided in Oakland, California, where he engaged in banking and several oceanfront real estate ventures.[5] He had been a part of Columbia River steamboating in its beginning, was largely responsible for its best years, and left it in its decline. It was to continue for two decades, but its importance and glory were gone.

Today, with its canals, locks, dams and a thousand-foot jetty at its mouth, the Columbia is a tamed river. Ocean liners from the world around discharge and take on cargo at the Portland docks. The few steamboats that ply its waters are remarkable only for the nostalgia they arouse.

XVIII

Lonesome River

WITH FEW EXCEPTIONS, it is impossible to locate on a modern map the score of river towns and landings that were of some importance in the years when gold mining flourished in the basin of the lower Colorado. They are gone, and so are the steamboats that served them.

In that vast mountain-desert region, the desert has many names: Mojave, Colorado, Yuma, Arenoso and the different llanos. But they are all one, and they stretch away southward to end in the Great Sonoran Desert of northern Mexico. Through them threads the red, silt-laden Colorado, the longest of America's Western rivers. Dams and irrigation projects have changed it out of all semblance to what it was in the 1850's, when nearly the entire commerce of the territory was by water communication. That was necessarily so, for there were only three east-west roads across Arizona to California. The most important followed for a great distance the trail Father Kino had blazed from Sonoita, on the Mexican border, in 1699, to the mouth of the Gila River, where Yuma now stands, and named it El Camino del Diablo (the Devil's Highway). For sixty years it remained unused until, in 1774, Captain Juan de Anza, commandant of the Presidio of Tubac, and Padre Francisco Tomas

Garces, the Franciscan missionary, with a company of soldiers, marched over it under orders from the Spanish government to break a road from Sonora to the West Coast.

Instead of going down the Gila, as Father Kino had, De Anza cut through the desert far to the south. On reaching the site of today's Yuma, he crossed the river, struck on westward through the Algodones Sand Hills and the glaring white wastes of the Colorado Desert to the pueblo of Los Angeles. Although De Anza's route was longer than Father Kino's, with even less water, it was fairly beyond the range of Apache raiding parties. This was reason enough for Spaniards and Mexicans going from Sonora to California to prefer it, and for years they passed over it by the thousand. It continued to be the one recognized route across southern Arizona until the War with Mexico, when Lieutenant Colonel Philip St. George Cook and the Mormon Battalion, with its train of wagons, marched overland from Santa Fe to San Diego in 1846, taking possession of the Presidio of Tucson as it advanced.

Cook's route took him along the northern border of Mexico to the San Pedro River and then north along that trifling stream to what is now Benson. From there he went on to Tucson and west to the Colorado, below Yuma. Cook's Road, as it became popularly known, was used by hundreds of emigrant trains bound for the California gold diggings.

With its entrance into the Union, California began to press Congress for overland mail and stage service. In 1857 appropriations were made, and James B. Leach began construction of a wagon road from El Paso to the army post at Fort Yuma, located on the hill overlooking the old river crossing. Where it served his purpose, Leach followed De Anza's old Devil's Highway.

The other important road pointing for California crossed Arizona Territory far to the north. This was Beale's Road, from Fort Defiance, New Mexico, to the Colorado River, and closely followed the 35th parallel.[1] This route had previously been surveyed by the government for a railroad line. This, however, was some years before the War between the States was to erupt. But already there was growing agitation both in the

North and in the South for a transcontinental railroad. The proslavery majority in the Congress were determined that if the government undertook such an enterprise the rails should be laid through the Southern states, crossing the Mississippi in the vicinity of New Orleans, or no farther north, in any event, than Memphis, Tennessee. The North insisted on a northern route to California, and the North won when President Lincoln signed the Pacific Railroad Act on July 1, 1862.

Lieutenant Beale and, before him, Lieutenant A. W. Whipple, the original surveyor, must have done their work well, for when the Atchison, Topeka and Santa Fe Railroad built across Arizona to the Coast, in 1883, it followed Beale's Road. As a trace over which merchandise and humanity moved, it was less important than the Mormon Road; the territory's principal thoroughfare was Leach's El Paso to San Diego wagon road. Related as Leach's was to De Anza's El Camino del Diablo, it led the Boundary Commission to state in its report issued in 1857, "during the few years that this road [El Camino del Diablo] was much traveled, over 400 persons were said to have perished of thirst between Sonoita and Yuma, a record probably without parallel in North America."

If that figure sounds incredible, it should be remembered that an estimated 60,000 persons, bound for California, had crossed the Colorado at Yuma before the end of 1852. In the fall of 1849, Lieutenant Cave Counts, in command of the military detail escorting the members of the Boundary Commission down the Gila River to Yuma, stated that "2,000 wagons were on the road in the 185 miles between the Pima villages and the Colorado."

When Leach's Road was declared open for travel, in 1858, there were long stretches of it that were as cruel and merciless as in De Anza's time; and none took a greater toll of human and animal life than the hundred and some scorched, waterless miles of drifting sand of the Colorado Desert, which the westbound traveler encountered after crossing the river at Yuma. The trail through that wasteland was soon marked with the bleached bones and dead bodies of thousands of mules, oxen and horses.

To lighten their loads so that they might keep on going, untold scores of the argonauts abandoned some or all of their possessions. For many that was not enough, and they died and were buried beside the trail without reaching the El Dorado they were seeking.

The first mail and stage service over Leach's Road was operated by the San Antonio and San Diego Stage Company, early in 1857. Although the company had received a government subsidy of $148,000 on the mail contract, it offered a very limited, semimonthly service. In its advertisements it guaranteed that passengers and express matter would be "forwarded in new coaches, drawn by six mules over the entire length of our line, excepting from San Diego to Fort Yuma, a distance of 180 miles, which we cross on mule back," which meant that passengers from the East, bound for the Coast, on reaching Yuma were compelled to face the rigors of that true *jornada del muerte,* the Colorado Desert, on muleback, stopping overnight at the company stations, a journey that in favorable circumstances required four days.

Conditions improved vastly when the San Antonio and San Diego Stage Company was superseded by John Butterfield and his Overland Mail Company, in December, 1858. His coaches ran all the way through from Tipton, Missouri, the end of track on the Missouri Pacific Railroad, west of St. Louis, to San Francisco. Twice-weekly mail service was inaugurated.[2]

It remains one of the great ironies of the westward rush of the Forty-niners to the gold fields of California that when they hurried on after crossing the Colorado River they were putting behind them an El Dorado that would have rewarded them with more of the yellow metal than most of them were ever to find on the Mother Lode.

No one can say with any authority when gold was first discovered in the sands of the Colorado. Presumably it occurred soon after Padre Francisco Garces, the noted explorer and missionary, arrived at the junction of the Colorado and the Gila, in 1780, with three other priests, twenty soldiers, twenty colonists and twelve laborers, the soldiers and civilians accompanied by their families, and established the two missions of San Pedro y San Pablo de Bicuñer and Purisima Concepción, the latter on the hill where, after many years, Fort Yuma was to stand. In fact, some of the material used in constructing the fort was salvaged from the ruins of the old mission. Mission San Pedro y San Pablo was built a short distance up the river about at the present site of Laguna Dam.

Tales of gold discoveries and rich stores of gold buried by the padres, when Indian hostilities threatened, are entwined with the folklore history of all of the old Spanish missions. San Pedro y San Pablo de Bicuñer was no exception. The Yumas, or Quechans, as they preferred to call themselves, revolted in 1781, killing the priests and most of the male inhabitants, and destroying the missions. The few men who escaped death, together with the women and children, were held for ransom and were rescued a few months later by an expedition from Sonora commanded by Lieutenant Colonel Pedro Fages.

The Spaniards made no further attempts to colonize the Colorado River valley, but after Mexico won its independence from Spain, in 1821, the tales of a great quantity of gold buried at Bicuñer, which had been kept alive over the years, brought numerous parties of placer miners up from Sonora to search for it. It is not of record that they found any buried treasure, but they began working the gravel between the mission ruins and the river with gratifying results. These were the famous Potholes, from which the California Division of Mines reported that a minimum of $2,000,000 was extracted. Across the river, the equally rich Laguna placers were discovered. A few years later, gold was found in other places up the valley, and by the middle forties, placers were being developed at La Paz and Ehrenberg and lode mining at Picacho, Wickenburg and three or four other camps. But their only means of communication was largely by pack train. If their potential riches were to give the territorial economy the boost it sorely needed, some reasonably fast and cheap means of transportation had to be found.

There was the Colorado River. It entered the territory in the north and flowed down its entire length. Although it carried more silt to the cubic yard than any other river on the continent, including the Mississippi, its current was swift and its channel continually shifting. It served no useful purpose, and there seemed to be little reason to hope that it ever would. Credit for doing something about it belongs to Major Samuel Heintzelman.

In 1850, Heintzelman had arrived at the Colorado River, crossing it with troops, and built Fort Yuma on the west bank of the river, its purpose being to protect travelers on the California trail against Indian attack. His nearest point of supply was San Francisco. Everything the post needed had to be brought down the coast of California and up the Gulf of California to Mexican Puerto Ysabel, in the delta at the mouth of the river, by oceangoing steamers and sailing vessels. There, freight had to be unloaded and forwarded by pack train or poled up the river for 122 miles to Fort Yuma. The cost was high—seventy-five dollars a ton. Heintzelman was "damned" if he was going to stand for it, and he appealed to the War Department to make a reconnaisance of the lower river, that it might be determined whether or not it was navigable by small steamboats.

Saving the government money was such a refreshing request that Washington acted on it at once, and late in 1850 Lieutenant D. H. Derby and his party of U.S. Engineers arrived in the Gulf in the schooner *Invincible.*

By the Treaty of Guadalupe Hidalgo, the two thousand square miles of the Colorado Delta remained under the Mexican flag. It extended from the international boundary to the Gulf and from the Sonoran mesa on the east to the mountainous peninsula of Baja California in the west. In 1850 it was a wild terra incognita, inhabited by bands of nomadic Cocopah Indians, who were even then on their way to disappearance. It was an ugly, almost treeless land of mud flats, plastered with red silt and salt slime in seasons of low water. When the water was high, it became a maze of lakes and lagoons, with a thousand blind channels that led nowhere.

When Derby sailed up the Gulf of California in the schooner *Invincible,* his only knowledge of the Gulf and the river he was

to ascend had been gained from reading the journal of Lieutenant R. H. W. Hardy, Royal Navy, published in London, in
1828.[3] Hardy had made his way up the Colorado for some
twenty-five miles before grounding his vessel on a sandbar.
While he was in the Delta he had explored several of its false
channels and left his name to grace what was in time to become
its recognized main channel. But what interested Lieutenant
Derby more was what Hardy had to say about the great tidal
bore that occurred when the incoming tide met the outpouring
of the river. When those two opposing forces met, a wall of
water was sent roaring up the river, "sweeping all before it."

We know today that before the Hoover Dam and other barriers took the sting out of the Colorado its tidal bore was the
highest of all the world's rivers, varying from four feet for most
of the year to twenty-five to twenty-eight feet during the month
preceding the September full moon and the following thirty
days.

The contracting shores of the long, narrow Gulf of California,
as it neared its head, increased the pressure of the water and
was responsible for the bore. With a roar like thunder and at
express-train speed it raced up the river and was often felt as
far away as Yuma. Any vessel that met it head-on was reasonably
safe, once it had survived the initial shock. Caught unprepared
for its onslaught, it couldn't escape being rolled over.

Derby was at Tiburon Island, opposite the town of Hermo-
sillo, when he had his first experience with the bore. He brought
the *Invincible* through it without damage and reached the
mouth of the river. By way of Hardy's Channel, he sailed some
twenty-five miles up the Colorado. But the water was low, and
the *Invincible*, with draft, could go no farther. Leaving the
schooner, he continued up the river for another sixty miles,
where he encountered a detachment from the post coming
downstream to meet him.

Derby made a detailed topographic map of the Colorado,
with all its twists and turns, as of that moment, and submitted
it with a lengthy report on the navigability of the Colorado. It
was not encouraging. But the government was determined to do

something for Fort Yuma, and gave Captain George A. Johnson
a contract for transporting supplies from San Francisco to the
fort. Johnson brought his freight to the head of the Gulf in his
schooner, the *Sierra Nevada*, where he built flatboats, piled
cargo on them and dragged them up to Fort Yuma with ropes.

The following year, at Puerto Ysabel, Captain Trumbull reassembled a boat that had been brought down from San Francisco in the hold of a schooner, and named her the *Uncle Sam*.
She was only sixty-five feet long, with a draft of less than twenty-
four inches. She ran the lower river for two years, never getting
above Yuma. Her only claim on history is that she was the first
steamboat on the Colorado.[4] When she sank as she was tied up
at Pilot Knob, a short distance downriver from Yuma, on June
22, 1854, Captain Trumbull just left her there.

The next steamboat to test the Colorado was the side-wheeler
General Jessup. She was 108 feet long, with a beam of 28 feet,
and of very light draft. She was owned by Captain George A.
Johnson, the flatboatman. By schooner, he brought her down
from San Francisco in sections to the delta and put her back
together at Puerto Ysabel, where there was a machine shop of
sorts and a primitive drydock. The latter was a basin scooped
out of the sand and lined with planks. It had dock gates but no
pumps or the other equipment that is usually a part of such
enterprises.

At Puerto Ysabel (Port Isabel to Americans) the tidal range
was as much as twenty feet, and it did the work of filling or
emptying the basin as well as pumps could have done. The gates
were opened at low tide; on the next high tide a boat could be
brought into drydock. When the tide fell, the gates were closed,
and kept closed until the work being done was finished, after
which, at the low tide they were opened and kept open until the
tide built again and the imprisoned boat floated out, free to go
its way. If waiting on the not-to-be hurried turnings of the tide
slowed the work, no one fretted; all it cost was time, and time
was the cheapest of commodities. Port Isabel long ago became
only a memory.

The *General Jessup* was the first steamboat to go above

Yuma. In August of that year, 1854, she struck a rock below Picacho and sank. She was raised, and later that year she made it as far up the Colorado as Black Canyon (Hoover Dam). Much later, in 1859, she registered another first, giving the Colorado its only steamboat explosion, blowing her boiler as she lay moored at Yuma and killing one of her crew.

The blast opened her seams, and the *General Jessup* sank for the second time. She was raised at once, and after the damage to her superstructure was repaired, she went on about her business.

XIX

Desert Steamboating

JOHNSON QUICKLY PROVED that Colorado River steamboating was a profitable business. Although he kept the *General Jessup* on the go, he was receiving more cargo than she could handle. He had too much respect for the vagaries of the river to run at night. A cautious man, with a long memory for snags and sandbars, he made himself an excellent pilot, the best the Colorado was ever to know.

The *Uncle Sam* was running opposition to the *General Jessup,* but she was too small and too slow to take much trade away from Captain Johnson's boat. He announced a schedule of regular sailings for such upriver points as Castle Dome, Ehrenberg, Aubry, Camp Mohave and Hardyville, which he was seldom able to meet. But men with ore to ship to San Francisco didn't mind waiting a day or two if the *General Jessup* happened to be late.

An emissary from the large Mormon colony in southern Utah came to see Captain Johnson. They needed a market for what they were producing and a means of getting the supplies they needed. They would find a way of getting their wagons to Callville, up in Nevada, if he could reach that adobe settlement with his boat. Johnson believed he could in high water. At least, he was willing to try. On his next trip up the river he got through El Dorado Canyon and picked his way up the remaining twenty-six miles to Callville. The *General Jessup* was 380 miles from the Gulf.

She was an open-deck boat, as most of the Colorado River steamers were, which was a godsend to her passengers, giving them some relief from the stifling heat that lay like a blanket on the river. On her upper deck were the galley, dining room and cubbyholes that passed as staterooms.

In 1855, Johnson, Benjamin Hartshorne and a Captain Wilcox organized the Colorado Steam Navigation Company. In California they bought a steamer that was being built for the Sacramento River trade and had it shipped down in sections to Port Isabel, on the Delta, where it was reassembled and finished. She was 120 feet long, a stern-wheeler, with graceful lines, double engines, and easily the finest boat yet seen on the river. Appropriately, she was named *Colorado*. She was to serve the company well for years. When she was dismantled in 1862, her machinery went into the finer and larger *Colorado* (No. 2), which was built at Yuma.[1]

When the *General Jessup* was in Black Canyon in January, 1858, she met Lieutenant Beale's expedition, which was returning east over Beale's Road from California to test its usefulness as a winter route. In Beale's account of the meeting, dated January 23, he says:

We reached the Colorado early in the morning, having encamped in a rain storm the night previous a few miles from it. Shortly after leaving camp, my clerk, F. E. Kerlin, who with two of my party had been dispatched the day previous in order to have my boat ready for crossing, was seen returning. Various surmises were immediately started as to the cause, and as soon as he was within speaking distance he was questioned eagerly for the news. He gave us a joyful surprise by the information that the steamer *General Jessup,* Captain Johnson, was at the crossing waiting to convey us to the opposite side. It is difficult to conceive the varied emotions with which this news was received. Here, in a wild, almost unknown country, inhabited only by savages, the

great river of the West, hitherto declared unnavigable, had for
the first time borne upon its bosom that emblem of civilization,
a steamer.

In a few minutes after our arrival the steamer came alongside
the bank, and our party was transported at once, with all our
baggage, to the other side. . . . I brought the camels with me, and
as they stood on the bank, surrounded by hundreds of wild unclad
savages, and mixed with these the dragoons of my escort, and the
steamer slowly revolving her wheels preparatory to a start, it was
a curious and interesting picture.

Beale is in error when he says that the river "had for the
first time borne upon its bosom that emblem of civilization, a
steamer." The *General Jessup* had been running on the Colorado for almost four years. But the federal government was apparently as unaware of it as Beale, for in 1857 it decided to make
another survey of the river; and for that purpose they sent out
to Yuma in sections a strange, stub-nosed, iron-hulled contraption they called the *Explorer*. It was January 11, 1858, before
she was put in the water. Under command of Lieutenant Joseph
C. Ives, she headed up the river. Everything happened to her
that shouldn't happen to a steamboat. She located numerous
mudbanks by the simple expedient of getting hung up on them.
Before reaching Black Canyon, she hit a rock that bashed in her
nose. Somehow Ives got her repaired and proceeded on his way.

It was the middle of March before the *Explorer* passed
through Black Canyon, two months after Beale and his party
had crossed. To the amusement of several hundred Indians,
who followed her along the bank, she finally made her way up
to the mouth of the Virgin River, which was as far as any boat
was to go.

Ives' difficulties continued as he brought her downriver. Five
miles below Ehrenberg he hung her up on a mudbank that he
somehow had managed to miss on his way north. He was working her off, when the *Colorado,* with Captain Johnson at the
wheel, passed, giving her a mocking toot of the whistle, which
must have further shattered the lieutenant's composure.

The jaunt of the *Explorer* had accomplished nothing. She

was offered for sale as she lay moored below Yuma Crossing. But nobody wanted her. As though to close the page on another governmental mistake, a flash flood roared down the Colorado and deposited her out on the desert. Drifting sands eventually covered her. There she lay, entombed and forgotten for half a century and more, when a party of surveyors working southwest of Yuma, on one of the Colorado's long-abandoned courses, were attracted by a rusty iron plate protruding from the sand. A little excavating revealed that what they had found was the shattered hull of the little *Explorer*.

The few who had predicted that if the Colorado could be opened to steam navigation it would become the lifeline of the territory saw their prophecy fulfilled. From every landing, good roads took off for a score of distant camps and settlements. Business with the Mormons became one of the most lucrative developments of the trade. The Colorado Steam Navigation Company, to protect its monopoly, put more and better boats on the river, building or assembling at Port Isabel the *Cocopah* (No. 1), the *Cocopah* (No. 2), the *Mohave* (No. 1), the *Mohave* (No. 2), the *Gila*, along with a number of barges. When Captain Thomas Trueworthy and the Philadelphia Mining Company put the steamers *Esmeralda* and *Nina Tilden* on the river, Colorado Steam made the opposition's business so unprofitable that the two boats wound up as part of Colorado Steam's fleet.

After seven years of service on the river, the *Nina Tilden*'s lines parted as she was moored at Port Isabel. She drifted out into the channel, where the bore caught her, turning her over and carrying away all of her upper works. Subsequently during low tides, a hole was punched in her side, and her boilers and machinery were taken out and shipped to San Francisco for sale.

The *Mohave* (No. 2) was the finest and the largest steamer the Colorado was ever to see. She was a stern-wheeler, a handsome two-stacker, with an overall length of 149.5 feet. Her cabins and dining saloon were on the upper deck, and they were elegant enough to rate comparison with the best on the Mississippi. At last it was possible to travel on the Colorado for pleasure, rather than from necessity.

The *Mohave* (No. 2) had for master young Jack Mellen, who had survived the wrecking of the schooner *Victoria,* carrying half a million board feet of lumber, at Port Isabel, in 1864, and who had been on the river ever since, twelve years by the time the *Mohave* (No. 2) was launched. He stayed with her until she was sold to the Southern Pacific Railroad Company. And that was the beginning of the end for Colorado River steamboating.

Captain Johnson and his partners knew long in advance that the Southern Pacific was building eastward with the intention of eventually reaching New Orleans, and would cross the river at Fort Yuma. It didn't disturb them, for like their brethern of the Mississippi of an earlier date, they made the grave mistake of believing that the railroad would be a great feeder for the boats.

The railroad reached the west bank of the Colorado in the spring of 1877, and spent all summer building the bridge across the river. And now occurred one of the most unexplainable stupidities to be found in the history of American politics, for although the Southern Pacific had been given permission to build the bridge, when it was finished the government refused to allow trains to run over what it called "a federal river" or across the military reservation on the east bank.

One night, surreptitiously, while the garrison was asleep, a head of steam was built up in a locomotive and it trundled across the bridge. When it reached the little settlement on the eastern bank of the river that had begun its unincorporated life as Colorado City, and was now Yuma, the engineer tied down the whistle cord and used up all the steam he had to celebrate the arrival of the iron horse in Arizona Territory. The aroused garrison, with fixed bayonets, charged across the bridge and forced the invaders back into California. The attendant publicity was so damaging to the government that it changed its untenable position and granted the railroad company a charter to build across the territory.[2]

The Southern Pacific proved to be no boon to steamboating. Some freight arrived at Yuma for transshipment up the river, but it was not enough to keep the boats busy. The schooners, which had made a regular business of running down the coast and up the Gulf with cargo for the river, stopped coming. Port Isabel was abandoned. Colorado Steam began to feel the pinch. It had nine boats in its fleet. One by one it began selling them off.

In 1878, Colorado Steam sold what it had left of its fleet to the Southern Pacific as a sacrifice. The railroad company continued to run the boats for years, picking up what local business they could.

When the big *Mohave* began accepting charters for Sunday school picnics, it indicated how things were going. The end was in sight. It came with everlasting finality when the Laguna Dam was built on the Colorado in 1908. The railroads were in the saddle and riding hard, crisscrossing the territory with branch lines. Arizona no longer needed the steamboats.

XX

River of the Gold Boats

IN SAN FRANCISCO, not far from old Portsmouth Square, there is a narrow thoroughfare named Leidesdorff Street, and of the thousands who use it, it is safe to say that few, very few, can tell you whom it commemorates. He was William A. Leidesdorff, the city's leading merchant in the days before James Marshall found gold in John Sutter's millrace and, to use an old but apt cliché, became the father of steamboating on San Francisco Bay and the rivers that are a part of it.

Leidesdorff, a German, had been doing a profitable business with the Russian colony in Alaska, and when the Russian bark *Naslednich* dropped anchor off what had been Yerba Buena and was to be San Francisco, on an August day in 1847, the cargo she carried was consigned to Leidesdorff. It was a mixed cargo, and in addition to smoked fish, spirits, gunpowder and assorted trade goods calculated to appeal to the Spanish-speaking *Californios,* she had in her hold the knocked-down pieces of the tiny steamboat *Sitka,* which the Russians had been using in Alaskan waters for several years. Leidesdorff had bought her, a pig in a poke, in the belief that she would materially increase business with New Helvetia, Sutter's colony up the Sacramento at the mouth of the American River. Sutter was his best customer.

The parts of the *Sitka* were put ashore on Yerba Buena Island, and under the guidance of a Russian engineer she was reassembled. She was a side-wheeler, only thirty-seven feet long, with less than ten feet of beam. Small though she was, her wheezy little engine had so little power that it had to be coaxed to keep her moving.

After trying her out on the Bay for several weeks, Leidesdorff decided that it was safe to entrust her with a cargo. The three men he had hired to run her were rash enough to agree to get her up to New Helvetia. They set out on November 29, encountered high water, lost their bearings several times, and were six days in reaching Sutter's Fort, 120 miles upriver. It was not very encouraging; a man on foot could have got there sooner.

The *Sitka* did better on subsequent occasions, but she was not to be around long; in February, 1848, a howling norther caught her in the Bay and sent her to the bottom. She was raised, her engine removed to go into a sawmill, and ended her days as the schooner *Rainbow*. No matter how brief and inglorious her career, the *Sitka* was a steamboat—the first to ply the inland waters of California. From that humble beginning there was to come a great fleet of river packets, with the new boats, from year to year, always finer, faster and more luxurious than those they replaced.

Architecturally, many closely followed the traditional Mississippi River pattern; others had a style of their own, which, for want of a better term, can be called original California. In addition, there were boats with salt water in their veins—the steamers from the East Coast that had gone down the Atlantic with their decks boarded up so that every ton of fuel they were capable of carrying could be stowed away, and through the storm-tossed Straits of Magellan and up the Pacific to San Francisco Bay. With their deep draft and rounded hulls, they can be regarded as steamboats only because they too were paddle-wheelers.

With the cry of gold in California reverberating around the world and tales being told in every port of the fortunes to be made transporting men and supplies up the Sacramento River to the diggings, it is not surprising that by sail and steam the rush to get in on the bonanza began.

There are no records to tell how many of the ships that started for the Golden Gate never made it; of those that did, many found fortunes awaiting them. The Sacramento River was the principal thoroughfare to the Mother Lode country. It was a winding tortuous route of sloughs, false channels, and without a single aid to navigation. But it had one thing in those days, before hydraulic mining filled its tributaries, the Feather and the American, with untold tons of "slickens" that found their way into the big river, and before irrigation projects siphoned away its lifeblood—and that was water. In the spring of 1849, even the famous *Senator*, built in New York for the ocean run between Boston and St. John, New Brunswick, with her deep draft, made her way up the Sacramento without difficulty to the thriving settlement that was beginning to refer to itself as Sacramento City.

The thrilling and gaudy tapestry of California history is too well known to need recital here, other than to piece together the important part played by the Bay steamers and riverboats of the Delta and the San Joaquin and Sacramento rivers for more than half a century. It was here, in California, that the steamers were to make their last gallant stand against their great enemy, the railroads.

Although the *Senator* was the first steamer from the East Coast to reach San Francisco Bay under her own power and ready for service, preceding her by a few weeks the *Lady Washington*, a small, flat-bottomed stern-wheeler, had arrived in the hold of a schooner and been put together on the Bay, very likely at Benicia. On her first voyage she reached Sacramento City and continued up the American to Coloma, which was only a whoop and a holler from where James Marshall's discovery had touched off The Great Excitement. On her return trip the *Lady Washington* struck a snag that sent her to the bottom. She was raised, and after being repaired continued as the *Ohio*. Another similar craft, the *Pioneer*, was put together that year at Benicia.[1] A third boat of the same dimensions was hauled overland in sections to Washington, across the river from Sacramento, assembled there and named *Sacramento*. Captain Van Pelt, her owner, advertised a schedule of her sailings (which was a first) to the settlement at the mouth of the San Joaquin that was bearing up bravely under the unlikely name of "New York of the Pacific," and is today the thriving steel town of Pittsburg, California.

Close on the heels of the *Senator*, a small flotilla of invaders from the East Coast steamed into San Francisco Bay. Among them came the *California* and the *Sarah*, from Newburyport, Massachusetts, the *Commodore Preble*, late of the Boston Steam Packet Line, and the ill-fated *General Warren*, which was to take forty people to their death on Clatsop Spit at the mouth of the Columbia.[2]

They were all fine, sturdy boats, as they had to be to have survived the long voyage around the tip of South America. Far from being bound to the Sacramento, they could and did run coastwise, north to the Columbia and Portland, or south to San Diego and beyond, whenever it was profitable.

Culminating with the loss of the *Brother Jonathan*, in 1865, when in a driving gale she struck a ledge off Crescent City, California, carrying almost two hundred passengers and crew to the bottom, the rugged, often storm-lashed coast between the Golden Gate and the Columbia was the graveyard of many steamers. But if other steamers from the East Coast alternated between the river and running outside, the slim, graceful *Antelope*, a former Long Island Sound excursion boat, was never tempted to try it. When, with what must be regarded as the greatest good fortune, she reached the sheltered water of San Francisco Bay, she was content to remain there.

In her photographs she looks frail, with her open decks and her walking beam at rest. She was a single-stacker, 202.6 feet overall. And she was fast. In time, the Sacramento was to be served by finer boats, but none, not even the fabled *Chrysopolis*, was held in greater affection than the *Antelope*. To her fell the honor of racing to San Francisco on April 15, 1860, with the first mail to arrive at Sacramento by Pony Express. She was accident-free, which must have been one of the reasons why Wells Fargo entrusted her with bringing downriver to its San Francisco bank millions of dollars in gold dust and bullion.

More refugees from the East Coast continued to steam into San Francisco Bay. Biggest of the lot was the ornate 530-ton side-wheeler *New World*. Her stormy career began when, as other steamers had, she slipped out of New York harbor without clearance papers, after being attached for debt. A British frigate chased her into the harbor at Rio de Janeiro. Being without papers, she would have been a lawful prize. On his way ashore, Captain Edgar Wakeman, her master, managed to fall overboard from a small boat, and hoodwinked the American Consul into believing that he had thereby lost the boat's papers while in the water. Armed with proper clearance, the *New World* was coaled and proceeded on her way, leaving behind at Rio eighteen of her crew who had died with yellow fever.

At Valparaiso she was ordered into quarantine for twenty days. But Wakeman protested so violently that at the end of eight days the boat was released. On reaching Callao, he was informed that news of his flight from New York had reached the Pacific and that an effort would be made to arrest him when he reached Panama.

The *New World* took on enough fuel to get her to San Diego, but when Wakeman reached Panama, he anchored behind the Island of Tabago, and getting out of his uniform went ashore dressed in rough clothes to find out what the situation really was. He learned that two deputy marshals, armed with extradition papers, were waiting to take him into custody.

The town was filled with several hundred Americans who had tramped across the Isthmus and were desperate to get to California as quickly as possible. Wakeman told them he would give them transportation to San Francisco at three hundred dollars a head if they would take care of the two deputies and the guard of ten soldiers. The gold seekers assured him that they would tar and feather, lynch or otherwise dispose of the officers in any way he might suggest.

At sunrise, the *New World* anchored in sight of the city, with the canvas removed that had covered her gilt name on her wheelhouse. The two deputies realized their helplessness and tore up their papers. The *New World* was provisioned and, with two hundred passengers aboard, steamed into San Francisco Bay on July 11, 1850.

She went to work on the river at once, and for fourteen years she was a fixture on the Sacramento. When the California Steam Navigation Company came into existence in 1854, the *New World* became its flagship. When that corporation sold her to the Oregon Steam Navigation Company for $75,000 in 1864, she still had some history to make. On the Columbia she was profitable for several years, but when business fell off, she was sold again and went to Puget Sound. By then Jacob Kamm had bought a half interest in her for $20,000. As traffic at that time did not warrant her retention in the north, she was sent back to San Francisco for the Sacramento trade. She was promptly libeled by California Steam for breach of contract, as the agreement made when she was sold to Oregon Steam Navigation provided that she was to be kept out of California waters for ten years. After considerable litigation, she once again sported the house flag of California Steam.[3]

She ended her days as a Vallejo ferry and went to the wreckers in 1879.

The *New World* was 225 feet long, with a 27-foot beam and 9-foot hold. Her walking beam engine measured 46 by 121 inches. Her cabin contained 35 staterooms and 111 berths. In her early and best years her fixtures, appointments and the quality of the food she served were unequaled.

On Alviso and Petaluma creeks, on the San Joaquin and Sacramento, there were dozens of steamers of one sort or another. In fact, there were too many for their own profit. And yet it was not until 1853 that the first steamboat built on the Pacific Coast, the 120-ton *Shasta,* was launched at the Rincon Point yard of Littleton and Company in San Francisco. She was 110 feet long, with a beam of 23 feet and a draft of only 18 inches. Her two engines of 60 horsepower each and her boilers were from an Eastern foundry. But San Franciscans boasted that in another year local foundries would be producing complete power plants for California-built boats. The new state was coming along so fast that it didn't propose to be beholden to the East for anything.

With her shallow draft, the *Shasta* was well suited for the Feather, American and upper reaches of the Sacramento. In 1850, the little *Aetna* had reached up the American as far as Norristown; the *Jack Hayes* had got to Redding, on the Sacramento, with the help of high water, a record that was never bettered. In 1851, the *Orient* got almost that far. They were all stern-wheelers. No record of their dimensions is available. The somewhat larger *Shasta* was a side-wheeler, which prevented her from setting any records. But she could reach Marysville easily enough, and was doing a good business until Thomas Lyle put the *John Bragdon,* the *Urilda* and the *Camanche* (all importations from the East Coast) on the run and drove her off. Having done away with competition, Captain Lyle boosted the freight and passenger rates. Marysville businessmen howled and struck back by building a boat of their own, named the *Queen City,* and threw their trade to her. She could get to Marysville even in low water, which Lyle's steamers could not. Having drawn first blood, the Marysville Steam Navigation was ready to put a second boat, the *Young America,* on the river, when Lyle made peace with the town.

In a country that was as yet largely without roads, the prosperity of any budding river town was definitely tied to its having steamboat connection with Sacramento and San Francisco. An armada of small steamers attempted to answer the demand, only to find in many instances that they were operating at a deficit, which sent them scurrying off to find a more profitable run.

Down in the Delta country, including the Mokelumne River and the San Joaquin, a few had better luck. Stockton, one day to become California's most important inland deep-water port, was already establishing itself as the coming capital of the great and immensely fertile San Joaquin Valley, from which greater riches were to come than were washed out of the streams and hillsides of the Mother Lode.

Looking at the San Joaquin River as it is today, navigable only by launch or rowboat, its precious water drained away by numerous irrigation projects and the upriver Friant Dam, one finds it difficult to believe that when the little stern-wheeler *Georgiana* left Stockton, on May 1, 1850, on an exploratory voyage, she was able to get up as far as what was then known as Firebaugh's Ferry (present town of Firebaugh), 217 miles south of Stockton. Not being content to stop there, she turned off into the Tuolumne River and got as far as Tuolumne City, a long-abandoned dream of which only a few adobe bricks remain.

Returning to Stockton, the skipper of the *Georgiana* was so elated that he announced regular sailings up the San Joaquin to landings that few people had ever heard of—Dunham's Ferry, San Joaquin City, Graysonville, Ward's, South Merced, Temple's Landing, Firebaugh's Ferry. Presently he was running much farther upriver, to Watson's Ferry and Sycamore Point, a distance of 272 miles.

The *Georgiana* did a prosperous business from the start, carrying up the San Joaquin tools, farm machinery, staple groceries such as sugar, coffee and flour, and bringing down green hides, tallow, wheat and oats. Soon her limited deck space could not accommodate the freight she was being offered, and to supplement her carrying capacity she began hauling a barge up and down the river. Such prosperity could not be concealed from the owners of other boats. It soon followed that she had company on the river that wound away through the flatlands to the south.

The *Erastus Corning* switched from the San Francisco–Stockton run to the San Joaquin. But two years of extremely low water in succession so curtailed navigation that the boats were withdrawn and the river abandoned until two Stockton businessmen built the small stern-wheeler *Christiana* and put her on the San Joaquin to serve the upriver landings. In favorable water, she went as far as Sycamore Point, from where it was only a short haul by wagon to Fresno City (Fresno).

The *Christiana* changed hands after several years. Her new

owners, the California Pacific Railroad Company, later supplanted her with the steamers *Tulare* and *Empire City,* which
gave two opposition boats, the *Clara Crow* and *Harriet,* no
quarter.

The competition between steamboatmen to win the Stockton–San Francisco business became so intense that efforts to
woo it reached the ridiculous. Away back in November, 1849,
Captain Ike Warren's little side-wheeler, the *John A. Sutter,*
had brought steam navigation to Stockton and the San Joaquin.
It was a notable event, and when Warren announced that he
was inaugurating triweekly service to San Francisco, Stockton
went wild. Businessmen pledged him that whatever they had to
ship would be carried by the *John A. Sutter.*

They were as good as their word, and in a few months Warren
pocketed ten times what his boat had cost. Dipping down into
his profits, he delighted Stocktonites by putting a bigger and
better steamer, the *El Dorado,* on the run. Success invited competition, and it came with the arrival of the *William Robinson.*
Instead of slashing rates, Warren got together with the owners
of the *Robinson,* and freight charges and passenger fares remained pegged where they were. Stockton howled and accused
Warren of entering into a combine with the *Robinson* to keep
the rates up. Gone were all the promises of loyalty and goodwill
they had once given him. When Captain Farwell arrived with
the steamer *Mariposa* to buck the monopoly, he was welcomed
as the town's deliverer. And now the combine slashed rates with
a vengeance. Before long the *Mariposa* was carrying passengers
to San Francisco at twenty-five cents a head. The combine went
even further, announcing that anyone who wanted to go to the
Bay City had only to step aboard one of its boats and he would
be carried free.

Of course, the drinks sold at the bars were not free, but the
revenue derived from that source could not keep a boat out of
the red. Everybody was losing money. And then the unexpected
happened; the owners got together and decided there was business enough for three boats and that they would stop cutting
one another's throats and instead put the rates up high enough

to recoup their recent losses. Overnight the fare to San Francisco was advertised at twelve dollars for deck passage (eighteen dollars if you wanted a berth), and cargo would be carried at twenty dollars a ton. Stocktonites complained, but they could either stay home with their goods or pay the outrageous prices.

The steamboat tycoons learned that by pooling their boats they could control the river business, end the costly rate wars, as well as do something about holding down the steadily increasing number of boats on the rivers, of which there were already too many. Nothing was done until a March day in 1854, in San Francisco, when a dozen owner-captains and their bankers sat down together in secret meeting and brought forth the California Steam Navigation Company. It was promptly assailed as a monstrous monopoly that would crush all opposition and bleed the public with the high tariffs it would impose.

California Steam did nothing of the sort. It brought order out of chaos, stabilized rates at a reasonable figure and was, perhaps, the best thing that could have happened to river transportation. Certainly it set the pattern that the Oregon Steam Navigation Company was to follow on the Columbia, six years later.

Every day, ships, both steam and sail, from American and foreign ports were coming through the Golden Gate and dropping anchor in the Bay or berthing along the Embarcadero. They found a new San Francisco awaiting them.[4] The first great fire had leveled the tin and tarpaper shacks of 1849. The second fire had swept away the jerry-built town that had replaced it, and now on the "made" land below Montgomery Street, where old hulks had once formed the waterfront, substantial buildings were being erected. The old thoroughfares, which had been bottomless quagmires, were giving way to planked streets.

Among its thousands were men of every race, color and creed. With them had come criminals of every stripe. Many of them organized themselves into gangs and roamed certain sections of the town, robbing and killing almost at will. Nowhere was murder cheaper. Miners who had come down from the diggings with their gold were their favorite target. The lawless element was asking for "vigilante law," and they got it in 1856. It was hasty and drastic, perhaps not always just, but it gave the city law and order.

Oakland and other East Bay towns were growing. Small side-wheelers were converted for ferry service and found it a profitable business. Up the river at thriving Sacramento some apprehension was felt when a sandbar in front of the Embarcadero began growing at an alarming rate, preventing deep-draft steamers from landing. "It's the slickens the Little Giants are pouring into the river!" was heard right and left. There couldn't be any doubt of it. Hydraulic mining was going full blast. Sacramento was acquainted with the river damage farmers claimed the Little Giants were doing, but it had not paid much attention to it; after all, it was a "gold town." That growing bar down at the Embarcadero gave it some concern, however. If something wasn't done to keep the slickens out of the river, the pessimists predicted, the time was not far off when only flat-bottomed puddle jumpers would be able to get up to the town.

What no one could foretell was that the greatest mining war in California history was just getting under way and would last forty years before the hydraulics acknowledged defeat.

Captain Bill Corlett, substitute master of the *Goodman Castle,* made short work of the bar by tying half a dozen iron plows together, dropping them overboard, and dragging them up and down the waterfront on a hawser, chewing up the bar and leaving it to the current to carry the debris downriver to lodge somewhere else.

And then, in the spring, the great flood of 1861 occurred, tearing out the dikes the farmers down at Grand Island had built, drowning livestock, devastating orchards, gardens and grain fields. The murky waters spread out until the whole Delta country, with its uncounted sloughs and tiny islands, was under twenty feet of water. At its height, Stockton steamboats cut directly across country for Sacramento, guiding themselves by the chimneys of submerged farmhouses.

When the flood waters receded, farmers saw that they had lost everything; if they wanted to go on, it meant making a fresh start from scratch. That took courage, for they knew what they had just come through could happen again—and it did, again and again. Delta farmers built higher dikes, wider at the base and stronger. But every few years the Sacramento broke through them. The annual rainfall had not increased. Rain wasn't the culprit; Reuben Kercheval, the lowland's leading spokesman, put his finger on the truth when he said, "Where great steamers ran in the fifties with depth to spare, small fruit boats scrape their bottoms now." The great river was growing shallow with the debris the hydraulics were pouring into it. The truth could not be denied, but it was not until the federal government created the California Debris Commission Act in 1893 that the discharge of debris into the rivers was declared illegal forever.

Proof that the river bottom was changing came when the famous *Antelope,* her bell tolling, denoting tragedy, was speeding to Sacramento with the dead and wounded of the *Washoe,* which had exploded and burned off Rio Vista; the *Antelope* got hung up on a mud bar within sight of her berth at the foot of K Street at four thirty in the morning. She was able to back off, but being held up for four hours, as she was completing a mission of mercy, was acutely embarrassing to Captain Albert Foster, for it occurred in water with which he had been familiar for twelve years.

XXI

Last Days of the Steamboats

THE MOST EXCITING PLACE to be of an afternoon in San Francisco was at the Embarcadero. Several thousand people would be there; men, women and children and their friends who had come down to see them off, crowding aboard the steamers, which were due to leave at four o'clock. Half a dozen boats would be getting away for upriver points. Over at Long Wharf the *Defender's* calliope would be filling the air with its music in competition with the brass bands blaring forth aboard the *New World, Chrysopolis* and *Washoe,* berthed at the foot of Pacific Street, all intent on attracting passengers.

On the wharf a small army of "runners" for the different steamers would be crying out the superior accommodations of their respective boats and propelling the undecided in the proper direction. From the upper deck, in the vicinity of the wheelhouse, the various captains, resplendent in their brass buttons and gold-braided caps, were sure to be seen gazing down at the throng below.

Very likely the steamers would be carrying a number of Chinese, going up the Sacramento as contract laborers. If so, they would not be in evidence, for they would have been herded below decks into the so-called China hold in advance of the sailing hour, being regarded as no better than work animals. Many years were to come and go before Californians began to realize that John Chinaman was a good man to have around, faithful, loyal and honest.

Wafting shoreward from the galleys would come assorted appetizing odors, giving notice that dinner would be served as soon as the boats pulled away from the wharf. The moment of expectancy would arrive with a tinkling of bells in the engine room and a tooting of whistles. The big wheels would turn, lashing the water to foam as the steamers backed out from their berths. It would take them a few minutes to straighten out, and then they were off, trailing smoke behind them as they pointed for the upper Bay. Up forward, the clutter of male deck passengers would swing their hats in a noisy farewell.

For many, those afternoon sailings begun so happily were to end in tragedy, sometimes by drowning or fire, but oftener in scalding steam.

Of the accidents, in which a total of more than two hundred people, including Chinese, lost their lives, that occurred over the years, 90 percent were due to racing.[1] California Steam frowned on racing but could not stop it. Powerful though it was, it never had a complete monopoly of the river business. From time to time strong independents appeared and formed opposition companies. The one that gave the Old Line the most trouble was the California Navigation and Improvement Company, headed by Captain G. W. Kidd, the pestiferous owner of the big *Nevada* and *Washoe,* both of which were involved in a string of accidents. They were always on the prowl for trouble, and they often found it.

The speedy little *Antelope* was the *Nevada*'s favorite target. Several times as the two boats were coming out of Benicia, northbound, she bore down on the *Antelope* with the obvious intention of raking her from stem to stern. But the *Antelope* was too fast for her, and she got away with no greater damage than a few feet of battered railing. Also once at Benicia, the *Nevada* went after the *New World*. The *New World* caught her amidships and pushed her up on a mudbank.

Kidd was not one to suffer such ignominy without doing something about it. One night some time later, as the two boats were racing, the *Nevada* attempted to cut in front of the *New World*. Instead of making any effort to avoid her, the *New World* chased her into Steamboat Slough at full speed. Captain Kidd's pilot failed to see a swirl that indicated a snag. Instantly the air was filled with the sound of splintering timbers. The hold of the *Nevada* began to fill at once. Kidd managed to get her upon the bank at Cache Slough, but the bank was all quicksand. The *Nevada* began to settle and became a total loss. The crew did heroic work and no lives were lost. However, the sinking of the *Nevada* was one of the costliest accidents in river history.

Captain Kidd had no better luck with the *Washoe*, which came out in 1864. And again it was the *New World* that bested him. One evening, again at Benicia, the *New World*, her engines rung off, was drifting up to the wharf on her headway. When she got close enough to toss her lines ashore, the men on the wharf refused to take them. This failure to extend the usual courtesy was not only due to the fact that Benicia had a grievance against the "Big Line" and was strongly anti-California Steam, but because a short distance astern of the *New World*, the *Washoe*, with full steam ahead, was making for the wharf.

With her engine idling, the current carried the *New World* back downstream several hundred yards. The *Washoe* came on, all 530 tons of her, and cut across the *New World* with the obvious intention of being first to tie up and preempt the wharf. She reckoned without Captain Enos Fouratt, who as pilot and master carved his name deep in the history of Sacramento River steamboating. Bells jingled in the *New World*'s engine room. She shot ahead and rammed her bow into the portside of the *Washoe* like an angry bull, doing so much damage that her crew was lucky to get her ashore before she sank.

A piece of splintered timber struck one of the *Washoe*'s passengers and killed him. Fouratt was indicted by the Solano County grand jury, charged with manslaughter. Hearings were held, but the trial was postponed several times, and finally the case against Fouratt was dropped. No doubt California Steam had quietly expended some money where it would do the most good. The *Washoe* was raised and rebuilt, which was unfortunate, for she was to come to a gory end.

Shortly after four o'clock, the accepted hour of departure for the Sacramento River steamers, on the afternoon of September 5, the *Paul Pry,* the fleet *Antelope,* California Steam's big *Yosemite,* 1,319 tons, 283 feet long, and then only two years old, and Captain Kidd's *Washoe* got away within a few minutes of one another, the *Paul Pry* and the *Antelope* in the lead, followed by the *Yosemite.* The *Washoe* brought up the rear, but moved fast and passed the *Paul Pry,* which was quickly dropping back. A race appeared to be in the making. That racing was responsible for the disaster which occurred that evening was denied under oath by Captain Kidd and First Pilot Baldwin of the *Washoe* at the inquest to determine the cause, and they were sustained by the captain of the *Yosemite.*

Very likely that was true, but it does not take into account that the *Washoe* hung on to the *Yosemite* all the way up to Rio Vista and passed her there when the Big Line steamer stopped to discharge cargo and passengers. The *Antelope* had outdistanced both of the bigger boats and was so far ahead that she escaped the worst of the heavy tule fog that was settling over the river.

Five miles above Rio Vista, shortly after nine thirty that evening, with the terrifying unexpectedness that is always a part of such calamities, the starboard boiler of the *Washoe* exploded, reducing most of her superstructure to kindling and setting her afire. Below decks, her seams had opened and her hull began filling with water.

Far up the river, the lookout on the *Antelope* saw the red glow in the sky, magnified by the fog, and reported it to Captain Foster, who realized immediately that a boat, either the *Washoe* or the *Yosemite,* or possibly both, was afire. He turned back at once to go to her rescue.

At full speed she hurried down the river until she encountered the swirling, almost impenetrable blanket of fog that, with some regard for her own safety, slowed her down to the proverbial walk. As a result, almost an hour passed before she reached the stricken steamer. From abaft her shattered wheelhouse to her fantail the *Washoe* was a blazing inferno. Her foredeck was littered with her dead and dying. Many of the injured had leaped overboard, preferring death in the cold water of the river to the advancing flames. In all, sixteen of her passengers were dead, not including the score of Chinese who had perished like rats in the trap below decks. Thirty-six were so seriously injured that several died after being brought to Sacramento. Twice that number suffered burns. It was the worst accident ever recorded in the history of California steamboating.[2]

Captain Kidd did not give up easily. After examining the wreck of the *Washoe,* he had her raised. A few months later, repaired and repainted, she was back on the river. But the public put her down as a bad-luck boat and avoided her. It was a feeling that time was to justify, for after a series of minor misadventures she caught fire again in 1878, and this time she went to the bottom and stayed there.

Without question the boats of the California Steam Navigation Company received better care than their rivals. Several times a year each was sent to the Rincon Point Works for a general overhaul and tuning up. It was a hard-nosed organization that arrogated to itself the right to set rates and wage scales. Its captains knew that to be caught racing meant instant dismissal, and no excuses accepted. But no company edict could have any effect on a faulty boiler or a crystallized paddle-wheel crank. So there were accidents that "just happened," like the one that befell the big *Yosemite* as she was pulling away from Rio Vista, bound downriver, at six o'clock in the evening of October 12, 1865.

Her wheels had barely begun turning when her starboard boiler let go with a mighty roar, mingled with the crashing of splintered stanchions and flying sections of her forward superstructure, scalding steam and the screaming of her panic-stricken passengers.

Her forward deck gave way and crushed the twenty-nine Chinese caught in her China hold. Thirteen Americans died and half a hundred were injured. The *Chrysopolis,* on her way to Sacramento, picked up a number of bodies and all the wounded and hurried them to the capital, as the *Antelope* had done with the maimed of the *Washoe* the previous year. The inquiry that followed revealed that the boiler was made of inferior iron. That didn't head off the lawsuits that were filed. Before California Steam was finished with them, the *Yosemite* explosion became the most costly accident in its long history.

The *Yosemite* was towed to San Francisco, where extensive alterations were made. She was lengthened and new boilers— steel this time—were installed. When she was put back in service she was practically a new boat, her luxurious furnishings costing an estimated $30,000. As the "new" *Yosemite,* her luck was good; she was returned to the Sacramento run with the famous *Chrysopolis,* the two boats leaving San Francisco on alternate days, and for almost ten years she maintained that schedule. Before then, the railroads had arrived and taken command of California steamboating.

In 1869 the Central Pacific, the western half of the transcontinental Union Pacific, terminated at Sacramento. Travelers bound for San Francisco could proceed by the river steamers or transfer to the little California Pacific Railroad, sixty miles of indifferent rails that ended at South Vallejo, where there were twice-daily steamers to the metropolis. That the Big Four of the Central Pacific—Huntington, Stanford, Crocker and Hopkins— did not intend to stop at Sacramento became evident almost at once. They acquired control of the California Pacific and bought California Steam. It did not herald the demise of steamboating, as many predicted. Far from it. But the Big Four meant to serve their own ends, with their eyes all the time on the day when their rails would reach Oakland, across the Bay from San Francisco.

This called for some readjustments. The *Yosemite* was taken over to Oakland and laid up for four years. Commodore John Irving, of Victoria, B.C., the founder of the Canadian Pacific Navigation Company, saw her as she lay decaying with idleness.

He bought her for a fraction of what she was worth and sent her north. Refurbished, she ran for many years between Victoria and New Westminster until she finally stranded and was lost in Puget Sound.[3]

When the Central Pacific changed its corporate title to the Southern Pacific Railroad Company, with the four nabobs who had fathered the original enterprise still solidly in control, it gave to American business the most bitterly reviled and fervently hated name in its history, Standard Oil not excepted. It bought state officials, legislators, judges and lesser fry with shameless audacity. If what good it did is not remembered, it is perhaps because the good was always motivated by self-interest. However, there can be little question that, if it had thrown its support to the hydraulic mining industry, legislation to prohibit the befouling of California's rivers would not have been enacted. The railroad company had a vested interest in the Sacramento River, and it acted accordingly.

River improvements and aids to navigation were a long time coming. When they did, they were considerable. It is to be doubted, however, that the federal government would have cut the deep-water canal through to Stockton, shortening its distance from San Francisco by many miles or have improved the Sacramento if the Southern Pacific lobbyists in Washington had not brought their influence to bear.

The East Bay cities of Oakland, Berkeley and Alameda had been growing almost as fast as San Francisco. To the north, in Marin, Sonoma and Napa counties, little towns, some old and some new, like Napa, Sausalito, San Rafael, Petaluma and Santa Rose, were attracting hundreds of San Franciscans, many of whom enjoyed commuting by steamer to their work in the city. It was a short run to Sausalito. To San Rafael and the towns farther north, the commuting was a weekend business. The boats were all small one-enders. With nostalgia one recalls such names as the *Grace Barton*, the *Mary Garrett, Napa City* and, of course, *Petaluma* (No. 3), which outlasted all the others.

Before the Ferry Building was built in 1920 in San Francisco, most of the upper Bay boats used the old Hyde Street Wharf.

More often than not the captains of the little fleet did double duty as their own pilots. They were so well acquainted with San Pablo Bay that it was their boast that they could navigate it with their eyes closed, which, in effect, they sometimes had to do, for on a dark night, with a heavy fog rolling in, a pilot had to depend on memory and the echos from shore.

Petaluma Creek, which was more of a narrow salt water estuary than a creek, with a tide variance of ten feet when the moon was full, was the trickiest of all, filled with twists and turns. On a pitch-black night, his engines rung down to slow speed, a pilot literally had to feel his way, tooting his whistle every few seconds and measuring the distance from shore by the echo that came back to him. Many times boats "hit the mud," as the old saying had it, but the only serious accident occurred when the *Pilot* exploded two miles below Petaluma, killing seven, but doing little damage to herself. It was a different story across San Pablo Bay at South Vallejo.

A little after six on a dark and foggy morning, the little side-wheeler *Julia,* an oil burner, the only one on the Bay, nudged into the South Vallejo wharf. Her lines had scarcely been taken in when a terrific explosion occurred. In a few seconds she was aflame. Her storage tanks on the wharf caught fire, making it impossible for rescuers to reach her passengers and crew. When the fog lifted and the flames had burned themselves out, volunteer firemen and sailors from the Mare Island Navy Yard began counting the dead. Of the sixty-eight people aboard the *Julia* that morning, more than half perished.[4]

When California Steam sold out to the Central Pacific Railroad in 1869, few rivermen could doubt that the end of steamboating as a profitable business was in sight. They knew what had happened on the Mississippi and other rivers when the steamers came into competition with the railroads. No matter where the collision occurred, it was always the packets that had been forced to retire. There was little reason to believe that the decision would be reversed on the Sacramento and the San Joaquin.

That the ultimate goal of the Central Pacific was the elimina-

tion of the steamboats can be taken for granted. But it was in
no hurry to bring that about. With its purchase of California
Steam it had control of transportation by both land and water,
and instead of abandoning the steamboats, it made them part of
a very profitable dual operation; when freight could be handled
cheaper by water, the boats got the business; otherwise it went
by rail. If as cargo carriers the boats became less and less important during the succeeding years, passenger traffic on the
Sacramento, skillfully managed, mushroomed into a bonanza.

For more than half a century, as both the Central Pacific and
the Southern Pacific, the railroad company invested over
$2,000,000 in new and more luxurious steamers, exclusive of its
San Francisco–Oakland ferry fleet. The ultimate in Sacramento
River steamers was reached when it built the huge (and identi-
cal twins) *Delta Queen* and *Delta King,* in 1926. They were
registered at 1,837 gross tons, were 250 feet long and their boilers certified for 225 pounds pressure.

Breaking with tradition, they left Sacramento and San Francisco in the morning, on alternate days. But the innovation
proved to be unpopular and the daylight run was discontinued,
with the *Delta King* and *Delta Queen* shifted to the night schedule that the smaller *Apache, Navajo, Modoc* and *Seminole* had
maintained for years.

After a torrid day in Sacramento it was a relief to board a
steamer for the night ride down the river, shower in one's stateroom and then relax on deck and enjoy the breeze. Out in the
darkness the lanterns bobbed on the poles that the fishermen
kept burning to guard their nets. In the morning, when awakened, the passengers would be in San Francisco, with the whole
day before them.

There are some oldsters—and not too old, at that—who do not
believe that speeding over a concrete highway, fighting snarling
traffic, drinking gasoline fumes and then slipping across a
gaunt, gray toll bridge is any way to enter the city that sits beside the Golden Gate. Of course, they are outnumbered by the
rushing thousands who never had it any other way than they
have it today. Most of the latter never saw its waterfront when

it was thronged with shipping from foreign ports and the sparkling waters of the Bay were alive with small steamers, and the big black and white Southern Pacific and orange-colored Key Route ferries were scurrying back and forth between the Ferry Building and Oakland, to be joined by the Western Pacific and Santa Fe boats at a later date.

Always they were accompanied by flocks of sea gulls. The eerie screaming of the scavengers, as they fought for the scrapings from the kitchen that were tossed overboard to them, was one of the delights of crossing the Bay. The average running time between the Oakland Mole and the Ferry Building was forty-five minutes. But people were not in such a hurry in those days.

Everyone had his favorite boat. Perhaps it was the second *Alameda,* the largest of them all, not including the huge car ferries *Solano* and *Contra Costa* that the Southern Pacific used to get its trains across the strait at Carquinez, the *Berkeley, Claremont, Oakland* or *Piedmont.* They are all gone now, sold off or sent to the wreckers.

There was one, the *Oakland,* whose loyal fans were sorry to see go. For years she had carried thousands of commuters back and forth across the Bay. But sentiment was no substitute for progress. Now jammed into an electric train, commuters are whisked across the Bay on the great steel bridge in a few minutes. The leisurely mornings on the *Oakland,* the screaming of the gulls, the wind in one's face and the tang of salt air are all gone.

If a boat has a soul—and many who love them insist that they do—then, deep in her timbers, the *Oakland* must have felt something akin to the human misery that comes to the aged when they realize that they are only in the way and no longer wanted.

The few who came down to the wharf at odd times to commiserate with her were those who were familiar with her history. She was old—very old. She had first become waterborne in 1860. And this was 1940. The graceful lines of her youth were gone. She had been lengthened and broadened out. Three times she had undergone major surgery; first in 1875, when she became the ferryboat *Oakland,* then again in 1898, and a third time in 1920. In the course of her metamorphoses her old boilers had been removed from the guards and replaced by new ones that were put down in her hull beside her original engine. Her hull and engine were about all that remained to remind her of her days of glory when she was the recognized queen of the Sacramento, the fleet, incomparable *Chrysopolis.*

John North had built her for California Steam. Her timbers, personally selected by him, were hauled down from the forests of Mendocino County. Only the best was to be good enough for the *Chrysopolis.* The famous Allaire Works, in New York City, fabricated her boilers and vertical-beam engine, which rated 1,357 horsepower. She came down the ways at Steamboat Point on the evening of June 2, 1860, and as she rested on water for the first time, she was the last word in sumptuous Victorian elegance, painted white and gold inside and her hull a gleaming white outside. In her main cabin hung paintings by Bierstadt, Tom Hill and other already famous California artists. Her hull measured 245 feet at the waterline, with a depth of 10 feet and her beam an even 40 feet. With her twin stacks and slatted wheel-housings, she was a thing of beauty.

In the course of her long and popular career as the "Queen of the Sacramento," the *Chrysopolis* was regarded with such affection by Californians as no other boat had ever won. The little *Antelope,* with which for a time she ran on alternate days, was her closest rival. She had long been gone from the river when the huge and magnificent *Delta King* and *Delta Queen* came along. But in her time the *Chrysopolis* took second place to none. She never had occasion to demonstrate just how fast she was. On December 31, 1861, however, she ran down from Sacramento to San Francisco in five hours and ten minutes, a record that was never bettered.

Perhaps the spirit of the old *Chrysopolis* was still alive when the junkies got her in January, 1940, and began taking out her doors and window frames and attacking her ironwork with their acetylene torches. Perhaps she had something to do with the torch that was carelessly upset down in her oil-slick engine room. She was quickly afire.

She burned all day. When the flames were finally put out, there wasn't much left for the junkies to claim. That evening, homeward-bound commuters may have looked down from the bridge and seen spirals of smoke still rising from the blackened hulk. To a few it may have occurred that a gallant old lady had passed to her reward—that the last rites would be performed when she was towed away from the wharf and sunk in the cold waters of the Bay.

NOTES

Notes

1. The first steam calliope of which any record exists was on the *Unicorn*, a small Ohio River boat, as late as 1858. A few months later none of the bigger packets was considered complete without one.

2. Seventy-five percent of all Mississippi-Ohio River steamboats were built along the Ohio, from Jeffersonville, Indiana, to the Pittsburgh district. From the famous yard of James and Edward Howard, father and son, came several of the most famous, among them the *A. L. Shotwell* and the *Eclipse,* the latter considered by many to have been the fastest of all river steamboats, and the longest ever built, 365 feet. The great *J. M. White,* the third of that name, unequaled for her luxury, was built by the Howards. She burned at Bayou Sara, Louisiana, 1888.

3. Nicholas J. Roosevelt was the brother of President Theodore Roosevelt's grandfather.

4. Lydia Latrobe, the daughter of Benjamin Henry Latrobe, the famous architect who designed the Washington Capitol that was gutted by the British in the War of 1812, was only seventeen when she married Nicholas Roosevelt, in 1808. He was thirty-seven, only four years younger than her father. Latrobe and Roosevelt had been engaged in several business ventures, the most successful being the building of Philadelphia's water system, designed by Latrobe, and for which Roosevelt had built the pumps.

In 1814, after the British burned the White House and applied the torch to the Capitol, Latrobe found the work of years in ruins. With his finances at a low ebb, Roosevelt persuaded him to go to Pittsburgh to "superintend the construction of some of the boats" being built for the Fulton group. Latrobe left Washington for Pittsburgh in 1813. What he contributed to the building of the later Fulton boats is obscure. As he was an architect and designer, it would seem that his talents must have been employed in that direction; yet Fulton says "they were built after my design." There may have been alterations and improvements which, characteristically, he refused to acknowledge. (See the Latrobe Collection, Maryland Historical Society.)

5. In an address before the Maryland Historical Society in 1882, the famous architect's son, J. H. B. Latrobe, said: "There were two cabins. One after for ladies and a larger one forward for gentlemen. In the former there were four berths. Mr. and Mrs. Roosevelt took possession of the cabin, as they were the only passengers." However, Captain Gould in his monumental *History of River Navigation* says: "Mr. Latrobe . . . seems to have been a passenger on the *New Orleans* during this, her first trip."

6. On July 14, 1814, after carrying General Coffee and troops to aid Old Hickory in the defense of New Orleans, the *New Orleans* was caught by a fall of the river while tied up at Baton Rouge. The receding water left her impaled on a stump. The crew, in trying to get her off, ripped a wider hole, and her hull crumpled like paper as she went down, a total loss.

CHAPTER II

1. The *Enterprise* was for some time employed entirely in transporting troops. She made one trip to the Gulf of Mexico as a cartel ship, and one trip to the rapids of Red River. During the battle for New Orleans on January 8, Shreve served one of the fieldpieces which destroyed the advancing column of British General Keane.

2. Shreve was the first to put flues in his boilers, thereby dispensing with the heavy, bulky condenser, saving valuable deck space that could be more profitably used for cargo.

3. Steamboat hogging was usually concealed by the cabin construction, but not always. On San Francisco Bay and the West Coast it was called the "gallows frame." They are the same.

4. Feathering was developed into a fine art on the fast steamboats on the Sacramento River of California, adjustable buckets being timed to catch the full effect of the bow swell.

5. The *planter* and the *sawyer* were the twin nightmares of steamboating. Either, when met head-on, was capable of ripping a hole in the hull and sending a boat to the bottom. A planter was a waterlogged tree trunk floating completely submerged, or nearly so, on or just below the surface; a sawyer was also a wholly or partially submerged trunk whose roots had not yet torn loose from the bottom, permitting it to bob up and down with the current. In the riverman's lexicon, both were known as "snags."

Captain Shreve's snag boat was really two boats with double hulls, held together by heavy beams, the one at the bow plated with iron and projecting in front of it a plow (or cow-catcher similar to that employed on railroad locomotives). When a planter or sawyer was discovered, it was Shreve's practice to back off a few yards and charge it under a full head of steam, bucking it to bits.

6. Audubon *Journals*, Vol. 1, pp. 450–451. New York, 1897

CHAPTER III

1. The ox-drawn, two-wheeled Red River cart was admirably adapted for the rough terrain over which it had to pass. The high wheels were four to four-and-a-half feet in diameter. The body was usually just a slatted crate, over a tarpaulin that was lashed down.

2. In May, 1863, 1,856 Winnebago Indians were removed from Blue Earth County. On May 8, most of them were camped on the riverbank at Mankato, awaiting the boats that were to carry them away. They were sullen and defiant. In the center of the camp they raised a scalp pole on which were displayed two Sioux scalps that had been taken recently. To the beating of tom-toms, they danced around the pole all night, singing their war songs. In the morning, May 8, 405 of them were herded aboard the steamboat *Pomeroy*. They had their scalp pole with them and they erected it on the hurricane deck. They were without arms, but their demeanor was so warlike that the company of soldiers overseeing the removal did not attempt to stop the Indians' barbaric farewell to their homeland. In the list of forced governmental removals of other tribes, their leave-taking stands apart; they were a beaten people, but they had not been humbled.

They could have been marched three hundred miles across country from their fertile lands in the Minnesota Valley to the arid wastes in Dakota, on which they were to be confined, but with the typical fatheadedness that appears to have characterized most of our dealings with the Indians, they were taken down the Minnesota River to Fort Snelling, down the Mississippi to the Missouri and up that river to Crow Creek—nineteen hundred miles in all.

3. Publishing a so-called newspaper aboard a steamboat undoubtedly originated with Captain Rogers of the *James E. Ferguson,* but the *City of Memphis* was the first to do it successfully. The *New Era II* was also a claimant.

4. At the time of the accident the *Sultana's* railings and texas were still draped in black crepe, for she was the first steamboat to bring down the river news of President Lincoln's assassination.

CHAPTER IV

1. The *Effie Afton* passed under the bridge, then lost way and drifted back against it, caught fire and sank, damaging the bridge. It was charged by the railroad company that she had been sent upriver for the express purpose of destroying the bridge.

Fred Erving Dayton, in his *Steamboat Days,* credits F. J. Nevens, valuation engineer of the Rock Island System (1925), with uncovering the story of the war between the steamboat interests and a Rock Island subsidiary, the Mississippi and Missouri Bridge Company, precipitated by the building of the bridge. Speaking of the legal action that followed, he says: "The *Effie Afton's* owners sued for damages. The directors of the bridge company knew popular feeling was with the steamboat fraternity. Owing to the prevailing sentiment, a strong and popular man was needed to handle the case for the railroad's subsidiary. A young lawyer from Sangamon County, Illinois, was recommended as one of the best men to state a case forcibly and convincingly, with a personality to appeal to any judge or jury hereabouts. He was Abraham Lincoln. . . . The case was tried before Justice John McLean. The jury failed to agree and was discharged."

When retried, the bridge company won handily.

2. See *History of River Navigation*, by Captain E. W. Gould.

3. See *The Story of American Railroads*, by Stewart Holbrook.

4. See *The History of River Navigation*, by Captain E. W. Gould.

5. In the spring of 1871 Donald Smith went to London to secure what the Canadian directors of the Hudson's Bay Company considered their adequate share of the three hundred thousand pounds which the company had received for relinquishing its governing rights. He returned with one hundred and seven thousand pounds.

6. For an unprejudiced account of the Riel Rebellion, see J. S. Willison's *Sir Wilfrid Laurier;* also George Bryce's *History of the Hudson's Bay Company.*

7. Beyond question the annexation of Manitoba had considerable support in the United States, reaching even into Congress. Although O'Donoghue claimed to have the support of the Fenian Brotherhood, that organization had flatly rejected his overtures. An abortive invasion actually occurred on October 5, 1871. Instead of any army of several thousand, O'Donoghue's followers numbered only thirty-seven. They were quickly overcome and captured by troops from Fort Pembina. Some went to trial but eventually were given their liberty. See U.S. War Department File 3248 for a detailed account. Also Joseph Peter's *Fenians at Pembina* (New York, Westerners Brand Book, Vol. 10, No. 1, 1963).

8. Hill had been invited by Donald Smith and George Stephen to become a member of the syndicate buildnig the Canadian Pacific and had served as a director for years. He resigned when it became obvious that the Hill Lines were in competition with the C.P.R. Smith, Stephen and William Cornelius Van Horne, its general manager (installed at Hill's urging and his greatest gift to the Canadian Transcontinental), received either baronetcies or knighthood from a grateful Crown for their great accomplishment.

CHAPTER V

1. The pronunciation "Arkan-saw" was fixed legally in that state by an act of the Legislature in 1881.

2. *The Arkansas*, Clyde Brion Davis, New York, 1940.

3. *Great American Cattle Trails*, Harry Sinclair Drago, New York, 1965.

4. *Down the Texas Road*, Grant Foreman, Norman, 1936.

5. *A Guide to the Indian Tribes of Oklahoma*, Muriel H. Wright, Norman, 1951.

6. On October 31, 1837, the steamboat *Monmouth* left New Orleans for Creek Agency with 611 Creek Indians aboard. Going through Prophet Island Bend she met the *Trenton,* in tow of the steamer *Warren.* The boats

collided in the darkness. The *Monmouth's* cabin broke in two as she was sinking. Of the 611 Creeks, 300 were drowned. It was a major river disaster, but the New Orleans newspapers gave it very little space, no doubt reflecting the general opinion that a few hundred Indians were expendable. (See *Steamboat Days,* Fred Erving Dayton, New York, 1925).

7. *River Transportation in Arkansas,* Mattie Brown, *Arkansas Historical Quarterly,* Vol. I, 1942.

CHAPTER VI

1. Her name is often given as Talihina, which is an error. The marriage, of course, was a Cherokee marriage, consummated without ceremony and not recognized by white men as being within the bonds of matrimony.

2. *University of Texas Library Writings,* Vol. 5, pp. 4–5.

3. *Ibid.,* Vol. 1, pp. 185–186.

4. *Sam Houston,* an autobiography, edited by Donald Day and Herbert Ullom (New York, 1858, p. 64).

5. *Western Journals of Washington Irving,* edited by John Francis McDermott, Norman, 1944.

6. *A Tour of the Prairies,* Washington Irving, edited by John Francis McDermott, Norman, 1956.

7. *Adventures of Captain Bonneville* is not one of Irving's major works. He may have been induced to write it by John Jacob Astor, mutual friend of Bonneville and himself. Hubert Howe Bancroft, the noted historian, dismissed the book as "imaginative fiction."

8. It hardly could have been surmised, however, that in the not too distant future its officers were to become the very flower of the Army of the Confederacy. Never before or since has there been such a concentration of military genius in a single regiment. Colonel Albert Sidney Johnston was in command. Lieutenant Colonel Robert E. Lee was not with his regiment that morning, having been assigned temporarily to court-martial proceedings at Fort Leavenworth. But all the others were present: William J. Hardee, Earl Van Dorn, Edmund Kirby Smith, John B. Hood, Theodore O'Hara, Fitzhugh Lee—and that Union great, George H. Thomas, "the Rock of Chickamauga."

9. With the outcome of the great struggle between the states no longer in doubt, Stand Watie and fewer than a hundred members of the Indian Brigade captured the steamboat *J. R. Williams* as she was moving up the Arkansas from Fort Smith laden with supplies for Fort Gibson. On the night of June 15, as she was steaming past Pleasant Bluff, Stand Watie opened fire on her with three concealed pieces of light artillery and musketry. The *Williams'* smokestack and pilothouse were shot away, and a cannon ball crashed into her boiler. Her master beached her on a sandbar on the north side of the river, and he and most of his crew escaped, some to be captured later.

In a few minutes the Indians reached the stricken steamer and began plundering her. Half-starved, their scant clothing in tatters, the *Williams* proved to be a rich prize, but being without transport, all they could make off with was 16,000 pounds of bacon and several hundred Yankee uniforms. An estimated 150 assorted barrels of hominy, flour and salt pork were rolled into the river and sent bobbing downstream. Pushing the boat off the sandbar, they set her afire, and by the time she passed Fort Smith she was a blazing volcano, lighting up the river bottom for miles.

CHAPTER VII

1. Preston, Texas, was put underwater by the building of the great Denison Dam, in 1944, and the creation of Lake Texhoma.

2. The Creeks held slaves, but under tribal law, death was the penalty for any member of the tribe who married a Negro.

3. Greenwood Leflore, the venerable chief of the Choctaws, had bitterly opposed the ceding of tribal lands in Mississippi to the government; but when the Treaty of Dancing Rabbit Creek was offered to the Choctaw nation, he suddenly reversed himself, and because of his personal popularity, it was signed. It meant exile for 25,000 Choctaws. Not for him, however. He repaired to the Teoc country (Mississippi) with his third bride. His resources multiplied as the United States increased his original grant, and he became a great landed baron. His apologists claim that he acted for the best interests of his people, but that is questionable.

4. See *Red River Valley*, by Harry Sinclair Drago, Clarkson Poeter, Inc., New York, 1962.

CHAPTER VIII

1. From its founding by the French, in 1714, Natchitoches was on the main channel of Red River. In the bad flood of 1832, the river moved eastward, leaving the town behind but easily reached by Cane Lake River.

2. For a complete log of Red River steamboats see N. Philip Norman, "Red River to the South," *Louisiana Historical Quarterly*, April, 1942.

3. An unknown junior officer, Lieutenant Colonel Joseph Bailey, is credited with suggesting to Commodore Porter that the river be dammed.

4. See *Louisiana State Guide*, New York, 1941.

5. What the showboat meant to the poor whites and Negroes even its grubbiest years has been caught with amazing charm and color by Ben Lucien Berman in his novel *Blow for a Landing*, Houghton, Boston, 1938.

CHAPTER IX

1. At Christmas, 1842, a band of Texans had "invaded" Mexico at Mier, and were defeated. On their way south in chains to the prison fortress at Jalapa, they were forced to draw a bean from a hat. A white bean meant life; those who drew black beans were lined up against a wall and shot. Ewing Cameron, often called the first cowboy, was among the unfortunates.

2. Confederate General Richard (Dick) Taylor, who defeated General Nathaniel Banks in Louisiana during the Red River campaign, was his son. President Jefferson Davis was his son-in-law.

3. Santa Anna had ordered the massacre of the garrison at the Alamo

after the siege of February 23–March 6, 1836, in the Texan War of Independence, and on March 27 had permitted his troops to kill Captain Fannin's surrendered men, numbering 371. In an intrigue that must stand to the discredit of President Polk and his Secretary of State, Santa Anna was spirited into Mexico on the understanding that he would seize control of the government and make peace with the United States.

4. Of King's beginnings little is known other than that he was born of poor Irish parents, in New York, July 10, 1824, and possibly (there is no documentation for it) stowed away on the ship *Desdemona* when he was only eleven. Two years later he became a steamboat "cub" on an Alabama River steamboat. He had practically no education.

CHAPTER X

1. Rio Grande steamers made no attempt to offer the traveling public luxury accommodations. Passenger traffic was the minor part of their business. The best that could be said for the Kenedy boats was that they were clean and the food palatable.

2. Kenedy married Petra Vela de Vidal, the young and beautiful widow of a Mexican army officer, and the mother of several children. She had sons by Kenedy. One of them, James (Spike) Kenedy, when he was twenty-three, won everlasting notoriety as the slayer of Fannie Keenan (alias Dora Hand), the toast of Dodge City's night life, when that rambunctious Kansas town was truly *The Cowboy Capital*. (See this author's *Wild, Woolly and Wicked* Chapter 28.) Richard King married Henrietta Chamberlain, the daughter of the Reverend Hiram Chamberlain, a Presbyterian minister of Brownsville. She was his only wife and the mother of his five children.

3. Harbert Davenport, in his *Notes on Early Steamboating*, reporting an interview with Frank C. Pierce.

CHAPTER XI

1. The value of goods transported over the Santa Fe Trail in 1822 was only $15,000. By 1843 it had increased to $450,000. In 1855 it reached the fantastic figure of $5,000,000.

2. "It has been asserted," says Chittenden, see below, "that the *Far West* bore the first news of the Custer massacre to the world; but this is not so. General Terry's dispatch to General Sheridan (at his headquarters in Milwaukee), written in camp on the Little Big Horn June 27, was sent by courier to Fort Ellis, 240 miles distant, and there put on the wire."

3. "Kenneth McKenzie, the ablest trader the American Fur Company produced, was at this time in charge of Fort Union, at the mouth of the Yellowstone, and of all the company's operations in the tributary country along the upper rivers." (Chittenden, *History of Early Steamboating on the Missouri River*, p. 134.)

4. "This affords a glimpse of the crafty and oppressive methods of the company, which bore with intolerable hardship upon its employees. To pay wages in merchandize at an advance of three or four hundred per cent

upon their cost was a great saving to the company, but an unqualified fraud upon its servants." (*ibid.*)

5. With him as his guest, Chouteau brought George Catlin, the artist, who was to spend eight years living with the Indians, making hundreds of drawings and paintings, and collecting great quantities of Indian artifacts. Although never a great painter, he was to become world-famous for the accuracy of detail and faithfulness of his work. His paintings hang in many museums, including the Smithsonian Institution, in Washington. Pierre Chouteau, Jr., throughout his life, extended to artists, writers and men of science such courtesies as were at his command.

6. Maximilian was accompanied by his servant Driedoppel and Charles Bodmer, a Swiss artist of considerable ability, noted particularly for his coloring and draftsmanship. In the United States he is known principally for his drawings and paintings that were used to illustrate Maximilian's *Travels.*

CHAPTER XII

1. This is contrary to the widely held belief that General William Clark, out of his deep regard for Sacajawea, raised and educated her son.

2. Westport Landing merged with Westport and Independence to form the new town that was officially organized in 1847 and called Kansas Town and which was incorporated in 1853 as Kansas City.

3. La Barge was just beginning his storied career on the river. It was to be said of him that "he knew the Missouri better than any man who ever peered through a pilothouse window." He captained many boats, some of which he built as well as owned, and in his adventurous career he made and lost several fortunes.

4. Sarpy County, Nebraska, was named for Pierre Etienne Sarpy, the brother of John B. Sarpy. He was in charge of the post at Bellevue for many years.

5. John Durac was an English sailor who had come up the Mississippi from New Orleans and drifted into the Missouri River trade. He received his master's certificate in 1844. Later, as captain of the steamboat *El Paso,* he established the record for the run from St. Louis to Fort Benton. When Harris mentions "our black Pilot Desiree," he is referring to Jacques Desire, always known as Black Dave. He was a Creole, not a Negro. La Barge calls him an excellent pilot.

CHAPTER XIII

1. The island took its name of Bloody Island because it was a famous dueling ground. Senator Thomas Hart Benton and Charles Lucas fought there twice, on August 12 and September 27, 1817. In the second encounter Benton killed his antagonist. Joshua Barton, brother of the first U.S. Senator from Missouri, and Thomas C. Rector fought there on June 30, 1823. Barton was killed. The most famous of all duels fought there occurred on August 31, 1831, between Major Thomas Biddle, Paymaster U.S.A., and Congressman Spencer Pettis. Both men were killed.

2. Shortly after the fire, the City of St Louis passed an ordinance compelling all boats to use iron hawsers when tying up.

3. The bell of the *Saluda* was blown out on the bank while still ringing. It was purchased by a resident of Lexington, who sold it to the Christian Church in Savannah, Missouri, where, it is said, "It has done duty for the past fifty years."

4. When gold was discovered at Alder Gulch, the district was in Idaho Territory, and it was not until a year later that the part of Idaho Territory east of the Continental Divide was set up as a separate territory under the name of Montana Territory.

5. La Barge named the *Emilie* for one of his daughters. Pierre Chouteau, Jr., thinking it had been named for Mrs. Chouteau, offered appreciatively to supply the colors (flags) for the boat. On learning his mistake, he graciously agreed that Emilie La Barge had first claim on the honor. The *Emilie* was a side-wheeler, 225 feet long, with a beam of 32 feet. She should not be confused with the *Emilie La Barge,* an even finer boat, built on the Ohio, which the Captain put on the Missouri in 1869, only to discover that what remained of the declining business on the upper river was controlled by the Northwestern Transportation Company, a subsidiary of the Chicago and Northwestern Railroad, which had reached Council Bluffs in 1867. Realizing the futility of bucking the railroad, he disposed of the *Emilie La Barge* at a loss—one of the few mistakes of his long career.

CHAPTER XIV

1. Chittenden, *History of Steamboating on the Missouri River,* p. 235.

2. On June 16, 1866, the steamer *Peter Balen,* taking advantage of a sudden rise of the river, ascended the Missouri to within six miles of the Great Falls, which put her thirty-one miles above Fort Benton. Later, the *Tom Stevens* and the *Gallatin* are said to have equaled or bettered that record.

3. Barsness, Larry, *Gold Camp,* p. 266.

4. Concerning the incident at Fort Randall, a widely believed story, at the time, was that the eight Indians had been arrested by a detail of troops for stealing horses, and that they were shot down as they were being marched back to the fort, allegedly because they were trying to escape.

CHAPTER XV

1. Larpenteur and Boller, in their narratives, claim that the crew of the yawl were impressed and clung to the side of the steamer until Miller, the mate, brandished an ax and threatened to cut off their fingers if they did not let go. This can be dismissed as a bit of melodramatic invention, for it was vigorously repudiated by Stinger, a participant, and Alexander Culbertson, a reliable witness.

2. The smoke of the battle on the Little Big Horn had scarcely blown away when his detractors began a campaign to degrade him. Mistakenly, they believed they had accomplished their purpose in establishing that he

was not a war chief, merely a medicine man. Sitting Bull was much more than that. He was an Indian statesman and, by all the rules that apply to white men, a patriot.

3. The *Amanda* was on her way up the river to meet Colonel Reeve, who was returning from establishing a military post on the Judith River. Colonel Reeve came aboard at the mouth of Milk River and promptly took command of the boat and put the Indians ashore to walk home. "The anger of the Crows was fired to a desperate pitch by this action," says Chittenden. They tossed their presents into the river and tore up the treaties they had been offered.

4. The Union Pacific bridge across the Missouri, between Council Bluffs and Omaha, was opened on March 15, 1867. Omaha quickly supplanted St. Joseph as the leading river port between Sioux City and St. Louis.

CHAPTER XVI

1. "It is safe to say that no other vessel built afterwards attracted anywhere near as much attention as this pioneer of the Pacific; and from the day that her keel was laid until she went down the British Channel and disappeared from sight on the trackless ocean, she was watched with the closest interest. Over 150,000 people, including King William and a large number of the nobility of England, witnessed the launching, and cheers from thousands of throats answered the farewell salute of her guns as she sailed away for a new world." *The Marine History of the Northwest,* E. W. Wright, Portland, 1898.

2. *Ibid.*

3. "A good idea of the size of the *Hoosier* can be gained from a statement made by one of her crew, who says that when she broke her shaft one day, four miles below Salem, the engineer and a deckhand carried it back to the city to have it welded." *(Ibid.)*

4. As master of the *Colonel Wright,* White was paid $500 per month until she came under the control of the Oregon Steam Navigation Company, when Captain Ainsworth, the president of that organization, who dearly loved a dollar, told him that he considered a salary of $500 per month for a steamboat captain excessive. White refused to take less and was replaced by a Sacramento River man at $300 per month.

5. Alki Point was long ago incorporated into the city limits of Seattle. Alki is Chinook jargon for "maybe" or "by and by."

6. Royal Chinook salmon, varying greatly in size and weight, ten to forty pounds, could not be fed into the machines. But with smaller fish, of relatively uniform size, the "iron chinks" became indispensable.

CHAPTER XVII

1. W. H. Webb, the builder of the *Goliah* sold her to parties who intended her for the Sacramento River trade. They got into financial difficulties, the boat was attached and a deputy U.S. marshal placed aboard. He awakened one morning to find himself on the way to California. The

Goliah had slipped out of New York harbor without clearance papers and with very little coal aboard. Miraculously, she reached St. Thomas, in the Virgin Islands, where she secured fuel and provisions, and proceeded on her way.

2. John C. Ainsworth was born at Springborough, Warren County, Ohio, on June 6, 1882, and died at Oakland, California, December 30, 1893.

3. The first locomotive assembled at the Cascades became known far and wide as "the Oregon Pony."

4. Kamm had acquired vast holdings of land and timber, in addition to his steamboat interests. Apprehensive over the effect the arrival of the railroads would have on the river trade, he disposed of his stock in the O.S.N. prior to its sale to the Northern Pacific, thereby losing several hundred thousand dollars.

5. He expended more than $3,000,000 in transforming a stretch of barren oceanfront in southern California into the popular seaside resort of the nineties, Redondo Beach, building hotels, a narrow-gauge railroad and a harbor.

CHAPTER XVIII

1. It was at Beale's urging that Secretary of War Jefferson Davis imported camels and drivers from Tunis and Egypt for desert transportation. Thirty-three of the animals were landed at Indianola, Texas, in 1856. The following year, forty-seven more were brought over. It was Beale's dream that they could be used as a Camel Express for carrying mail and express between Tucson and Los Angeles. But the animals, accustomed to padding over the soft sands of Africa, soon went lame on the lava-strewn sands of Arizona, and the costly experiment was abandoned. The camels were turned loose to wander at will over the wastes of California and Nevada. A decade and more passed before the last of them were exterminated by irate ranchers whose stock they were stampeding.

2. Butterfield's Overland Mail Company represented the best in long-distance stagecoaching. At a much later date, its efficiency may have been equaled by Wells Fargo, but not surpassed. In its peak year the Butterfield line employed 100 Concord stages, 1,000 horses, 500 mules, and 750 drivers, shotgun guards, hostlers and station personnel.

3. Hardy's voyage to the Gulf of California, in 1826, in the schooner *Bruja,* was undertaken in behalf of the General Pearl and Coral Fishery Association of London to search for pearl oyster beds, which were believed to exist somewhere off the Mexican port of Guaymas. Any traveler along the western coast of Mexico is familiar with the small but delicious Guaymas oysters.

4. Frank Waters, in his *Colorado,* in the *Rivers of America Series,* credits the little stern wheeler *Yuma,* with being the first steamboat on the Colorado. There is a legend to that effect, but no proof that it was first.

CHAPTER XIX

1. The second *Colorado* was built under the guns of Fort Yuma, rather than down at Port Isabel, Mexico, to prevent her possible capture by

Southern partisans, who were numerous in Arizona during the Civil War.

2. The Southern Pacific received its charter from the Arizona Legislature on October 8, 1878, after sixteen months of windy haggling, the real purpose of which was to drive up the price of votes. Collis P. Huntington, the caustic president of the Southern Pacific, was reported to have said contemptuously that he could buy an Arizona Legislature for $4,800.

CHAPTER XX

1. The *Pioneer* is often listed among the steamboats that transferred from California rivers to the Columbia, which is an error. Two boats of that name are listed in Wright's *Marine History of the Northwest,* but neither was an importation from California.

2. The destruction of the *General Warren* is covered in Chapter XVII.

3. When the Oregon Steam Navigation Company disposed of the *New World* it was to a partnership of Captains Hale, Crosby and Winsor. It was from them that Kamm bought a half interest in the boat. In turn, they sold her to the California Pacific Railroad. The litigation which followed was between the railroad company and California Steam.

4. Although no photographic corroboration exists of the picture San Francisco Bay presented in 1849–1850, when several hundred deep-water ships lay idly bobbing with the tide, deserted by their officers and crews in a mad rush for the diggings, countless artists have used brush and pencil to portray it. In time many of the abandoned, and therefore under the rules of the sea ownerless, barks, schooners and brigantines, their rigging cut away, were pushed up against the shore and became a part of the waterfront, housing saloons, hotels and shops. At high tide, others were moved to the sand flats of San Pablo Bay and left to rot.

CHAPTER XXI

1. A checking of the records reveals that seventeen accidents in which loss of life occurred were registered prior to 1881. Many times, only one or two died. When it is stated that "a hundred lives" were lost in this or that accident, the writer is only making use of a handy figure.

2. When a Chinese died along the river, the protective association to which he belonged usually claimed the body and sent it back to China. In this instance, however, the Chinese who died in the *Washoe* disaster were buried at Rio Vista.

3. In addition to the *Yosemite,* Commodore Irving brought up from California at least three other steamers, including the famous *Wilson G. Hunt,* once the running mate of the *Senator.* The *Wilson G. Hunt* ran on the Columbia for a while as well as on Puget Sound.

4. This *Julia* should not be confused with the boat of the same name that the Oregon Steam Navigation Company put on the Columbia for the Portland-Cascades run. This boat was built in British Columbia and originally intended for the Fraser River trade.

BIBLIOGRAPHY

Bibliography

Arizona, the American Guide Series, New York, Hastings House, 1941.

Askew, Garret L., *The Pageant of the Packets,* New York, Holt, 1929.

Audubon, John James, *The Audubon Journals,* edited by Marie Audubon, and *The Life of John James Audubon,* edited by Lucy R. Audubon and Elliott Coues, New York, Scribner, 1871.

Barsness, Larry, *Gold Camp,* New York, Hastings House, 1962.

Bill, Fred A., "Early Steamboating on the Red River," *North Dakota Historical Quarterly,* Vol. IX, 1942.

Brown, Mattie "River Transportation on the Arkansas," 1819–1890, *Arkansas Historical Quarterly,* Vol. I, 1942.

Burman, Ben Lucien, *Blow for a Landing,* Boston, Houghton Mifflin, 1938.

Chittenden, Hiram Martin, *The American Fur Trade of the Far West,* 3 Vols., New York, Press of the Pioneers, 1902.

Chittenden, Hiram Martin, *History of Early Steamboating on the Missouri,* Minneapolis, Ross and Haines, 1903.

Chittenden, Hiram Martin, *Life and Adventures of Joseph La Barge,* Minneapolis, Ross and Haines, 1903.

Chittenden, Hiram Martin, "Report on Steamboat Wrecks on the Missouri River," *Nebraska Historical Magazine,* Vol. VIII, 1905.

Cunningham, Frank, *The Confederate Indians,* San Antonio, The Naylor Co., 1959.

Dana, Julian, *The Sacramento,* Rivers of America Series, New York, Farrar and Rinehart, 1939.

Davis, Clyde Brion, *The Arkansas,* Rivers of America Series, New York, Farrar and Rinehart, 1940.

Dayton, Frederick E., *Steamboat Days,* New York, Frederick K. A. Stokes, 1925.

De Voto, Bernard, *Across the Wide Missouri,* Boston, Houghton Mifflin, 1947.

Deatherage, Charles P., *Steamboating on the Missouri in the 'Sixties,* Kansas City, published by the author, 1924.

Donovan, Frank, *River Boats of America,* New York, Crowell, 1966.

Eifert, Virginia S., *Men, Birds and Adventure,* New York, Dodd, Mead, 1962.

Ewan, Joseph, *Rocky Mountain Naturalists,* Denver, University of Denver Press, 1950.

Foreman, Grant, *Down the Texas Road,* Norman, Okla., University of Oklahoma Press, 1936.

Gould, E. W., *Fifty Years on the Mississippi,* St. Louis, Nixon-Jones, 1889.

Haig-Brown, Roderick L., *Return to the River,* New York, William Morrow, 1941.

Hall, James, *The West,* Cincinnati, published by the author, 1848.

Harris, Edward, *Up the Missouri with Audobon,* edited by John McDermott, Norman, Okla., University of Oklahoma Press, 1951.

Herriot, Marion, "Steamboat Transportation on the Red River (north)," *Minnesota History,* Vol. XXI, September, 1940.

Holbrook, Stewart H., *The Columbia,* Rivers of America Series, New York, Farrar and Rinehart, 1956.

Hunter, Lewis C., *Steamboats on Western Rivers,* Cambridge, Mass., Harvard University Press, 1949.

Irving, Washington, *A Tour of the Prairies,* edited by John McDermott, Norman, Okla., University of Oklahoma Press, 1956.

Jennewein, J. Leonard, *Dakota Panorama,* edited by Jennewein and Jane Boorman, Mitchell, South Dakota; South Dakota Centennial Commission.

Larpenteur, Charles, *Forty Years a Fur Trader on the Upper Missouri,* edited by Elliot Coues, New York, Scribner, 1889.

Lea, Tom, *The King Ranch,* Boston, Little-Brown, 1960.

Leavitt, Francis H., "Steam Navigation on the Colorado," *California Historical Quarterly,* Vol. XXII, 1943.

Lesley, Lewis Burt, *Uncle Sam's Camels,* Cambridge, Mass., Harvard University Press, 1929.

Lucia, Ellis, *The Saga of Ben Holladay,* New York, Hastings House, 1959.

Macmullen, Jerry, *Paddle Wheel Days in California,* Palo Alto, Stanford University, 1944.

McFarling, Lloyd, *Exploring the Northern Plains,* Caldwell, Idaho, Caxton Printers, 1955.

Mills, Randall V., *Stern-Wheelers up the Columbia,* Palo Alto, Stanford University, 1847.

Niles' *Register for 1916–1924,* Baltimore.

Norman, N. Phillip, "The Red River to the South," *Louisiana Historical Quarterly,* Vol. XXV, 1942.

Nutthall, Thomas, *Manual of the Ornithology of the United States and Canada,* Cambridge, Mass., Hilliard and Brown, 1832.

Orcutt, Ada M., *Tallamook: Land of Many Waters*, Portland, Binnsford and Moss, 1951.

Oregon, End of the Trail, American Guide Series, Portland, 1940.

Petersen, William J., "Steamboating in the Upper Mississippi Trade," *Minnesota History*, Vol. XIII, 1932.

Petersen, William J., *Steamboating on the Upper Mississippi: the Water Way to Iowa*, Iowa City, University of Iowa, 1937.

Porter, May Reed and Odessa Davenport, *Scotsman in Buckskin*, New York, Hastings House, 1963.

Quick, Herbert and Edward, *Mississippi Steamboatin'*, New York, Henry Holt, 1926.

Robertson, Frank, *Fort Hall*, New York, Hastings House, 1963.

Ross, Marvin, *The West of Alfred Jacob Miller*, Norman, Okla., University of Oklahoma Press, 1951.

Sharf's *History of St. Louis*, published by the author.

Thwaites, R. G., ed., *Maximilian's Travels in the Interior of North America*, from the German, Cleveland, Arthur H. Clark Co., 1904.

Townsend, John Kirk, *Narrative of a Journey Across the Rocky Mountains*, Philadelphia, H. Perkins, 1839.

Twain, Mark, Life on the Mississippi, any edition.

Way, Frederick, Jr. *Way's Steamboat Directory*, published by the author, Sewickly, Pa., 1942.

Winther, Oscar O., *The Transportation Frontier*, New York, Holt, Rinehart & Winston, 1964.

Wright, E. W., *Marine History of the Pacific Northwest*, Portland, Lewis and Dryden, 1895.

Wright, Muriel, "Early Navigation and Commerce Along the Arkansas and Red Rivers in Oklahoma," *Chronicles of Oklahoma*, Oklahoma Historical Society, Vol. VIII, 1930.

INDEX

Index